MEMORIES AND COMMENTARIES

Memories
and Commentaries

IGOR STRAVINSKY

and

ROBERT CRAFT

faber and faber

First published in 2002
by Faber and Faber Limited
3 Queen Square London WC1N 3AU
Published in the United States by Faber and Faber Inc.,
an affiliate of Farrar, Straus and Giroux LLC, New York

Material included in this book was first printed in *Conversations with Igor
Stravinsky* (1958), *Memories and Commentaries* (1960), *Expositions and
Developments* (1962), *Dialogues* (1982) and *Themes and Conclusions* (1972)

Photoset by Agnesi Text, Hadleigh
Printed in England by Clays Ltd, St Ives plc

A CIP record for this book
is available from the British Library

ISBN 0-571-21242-5

2 4 6 8 10 9 7 5 3 1

Elliott and Helen Carter
cherished friends of Igor and Vera Stravinsky

Contents

Acknowledgements

The idea for this book occurred to my wife, Alva Celauro, while cataloguing unauthorized 'borrowings' from the individual volumes of 'Conversations with Stravinsky' for a copyright lawyer. She found the autobiographical material fascinating and rightly thought it should be made available to a new generation. She and I also recognized that the subject matter would have to be rearranged, and that the regrouping should be chronological, following the composer's emigrations.

In the reordering of the narrative, I was deeply indebted to Olivia Pittet, who kept the word count to the limits required by the publisher, typed several drafts of the manuscript, contributed countless corrections and suggestions, and proofread the printed text. I am unable adequately to express my full appreciation to this extraordinarily intelligent, cultivated, infinitely painstaking individual. I am also most grateful to my sister, Phyllis Crawford, for her readings of the text.

From the beginning, Belinda Matthews of Faber and Faber showed a keen and discerning interest in the prospective book and expeditiously brought the project to fruition. In producing and publishing it, she was ably assisted by Jill Burrows, Faber's copy-editor; by Ron Costley, the designer; and by Denise Oswald at Farrar, Straus and Giroux in New York. I also wish to thank the Oscard Agency in New York for their help.

R.C.

List of Illustrations

Preface

The *Conversations* were taken down by me in informal talks. I was able to do this because for twenty-one years I lived with the Stravinskys in their Hollywood home, or in a nearby apartment, and for two more years in a next-door hotel room in New York. In the early 1950s I accompanied the composer on his concert tours, and from the mid-1950s to the end of his life shared the conducting of his concerts.

The *Conversations* books, unlike the ghosted *Poétique musicale* and *Chroniques de ma vie*, the pamphlets on Pushkin and Diaghilev, are the only published writings attributed to Stravinsky that are actually 'by him', in the sense of fidelity to the substance of his thoughts. The language, unavoidably, is very largely mine. The late Paul Horgan, one of his biographers, attempted to orthographize the composer's pronunciation of English words. Even if this were possible on a large scale – to me, an entire book written in Stravinskyese is scarcely conceivable – the result would be laborious to read. Indeed, it is true that American writers have sometimes succeeded in spelling out the regional drawls, local accents, and native burrs of the people they write about, most recently William Buckley Jr's imitation of Elvis Presley ('Ah cayunt do it . . .'), but Stravinsky's polyglot English presented too many challenges.

Six *Conversations* books were published in America (1958–69), five in the UK (1958–72), but the British edition, the text used in this one-volume recension of the series, was more complete.[1]

1 One chapter, 'Some Observations on V.D.', in the Knopf *Themes and*

The titles and most of the contents of the first three volumes are the same in both the Faber and Faber and Doubleday/Knopf editions. Stravinsky signed the contracts for *Conversations* with Doubleday on 31 March 1958, and with Faber on 29 April 1958. Dr Donald Mitchell edited the Faber books. Herbert Weinstock edited the third and fourth Doubleday volumes as well as the Alfred A. Knopf *Themes and Episodes* and *Retrospectives and Conclusions*, books five and six, published in 1966 and 1969 respectively.[2] Faber consolidated books five and six into one volume, *Themes and Conclusions*.[3] In order to incorporate the interviews, reviews, open letters, and programme notes from Stravinsky's last years, the publication was delayed and appeared posthumously (1972).

Stravinsky's literary agent throughout the period was Miss Virginia Rice of New York.[4] My correspondence with her reveals that on 17 May 1961, in answer to her inquiry, 'When will I receive the chapter from Volume 4 about *Oedipus Rex*?', I wrote:

The *Oedipus* section has grown so large that we will need two more weeks . . . It is obvious that my 'questions' are *ex post facto,* and that they look ridiculous followed by such long answers; yet they should be retained.

Shortly after Stravinsky's death, when Knopf was preparing a selection of my diaries for publication,[5] I wrote to Weinstock, who had left Doubleday for Knopf, proposing that Knopf follow Faber's example and not include excerpts from my diaries in the later books, which we had done in the US simply as padding. I proposed this because the American editions were raising the cry that Stravinsky and I were an amalgamation.

Episodes, a scurrilous reply to an attack on Stravinsky by Vernon Duke [Vladimir Dukelsky] titled 'The Deification of Stravinsky', was omitted from the British edition of the book as 'too specifically American in interest', though the real reason was the greater stringency of British libel laws.

2 Knopf had wanted to publish the first book, but did not meet Stravinsky's financial terms.

3 The preceding four titles are *Conversations with Igor Stravinsky, Memories and Commentaries, Expositions and Developments*, and *Dialogues*.

4 In February 1979, shortly after Miss Rice's death, her executor, Judge Morris Lasker, released the files of her thirteen years of work for Stravinsky to me.

5 *Stravinsky: Chronicle of a Friendship, 1948–1971* (New York, 1972).

Both of us realized this for the first time at a dinner in New York in November 1963, when Luigi Barzini (author of *The Italians*) complimented Stravinsky on his description of returning to Russia, which had been published in *Encounter* under my name, and was written by me. But *Retrospectives and Conclusions*, with diaries, was selling too well. 'Herbert says that if this keeps up, they will go into a second printing,' Miss Rice wrote on 11 May 1970, and my suggestion was rejected.

The subject matter of Faber's *Themes and Conclusions* comprehends three centres of interest: Stravinsky's medical ordeals, his wide reading – his chief diversion after 1966, when he stopped composing – and the music he listened to and played. Not many days, including those spent in hospitals, were without recorded concerts, though he did not neglect his daily diet of Bach on the small muted upright piano that was installed in his bedroom at the Essex House, New York, where he lived from October 1969 to March 1971. Some of his comments about scientific developments, people, television, and life in New York City can be traced to entries in the logbooks of nurses at this time, when the composer was losing patience with his doctors.

The *Themes and Conclusions* interviews tend to follow a formula, noted in my reply to the following letter from Miss Rice:

I just had a phone call from Murray Fisher. [He] implores you to mention all of his questions, and if Mr Stravinsky does not want to answer some of them – as, for example, the question on rock 'n' roll – will he please say why. He can be as brusque as he wants to be, but it seems that the readers, and many of them are very young, will be eager to hear Mr Stravinsky's reaction to popular music . . .

I answered:

I can do nothing about Mr Fisher's questions . . . since they spark no interest in Mr Stravinsky, and do not fit in with the mood of the article. Perhaps this has become stereotyped: a 'sardonic' first part, a 'serious' middle, a 'personal' ending. But the ending, Stravinsky's old-age view of his childhood, is the justification of the whole, and I do not want to destroy its effectiveness.

These reminiscences, along with the comments on composing, provide whatever lasting interest the books may have, regardless of the slips of memory and other inaccuracies exposed by subsequent studies, the most important of which is the annotated omnibus of the *Conversations* published in the USSR shortly after Stravinsky's death. The *Conversations*, particularly the spontaneous early ones, capture some of Stravinsky's feelings about his past and the people in it, whatever their shortcomings in historical exactitude,[6] something that can be left to biographers.

In April 1956, Deborah Ishlon, Vice President of Columbia Records, wrote to Stravinsky from New York inviting him to read passages from his *Autobiography* for a documentary recording of his voice. He answered, from Hollywood, on 18 April:

A few days ago . . . I read through the possible material, a lecture I delivered at various American universities, and the *Poetics of Music*. My feeling is very strong that this material is inappropriate for recording. More than that, I no longer would say the same things in the same way . . . A further problem is that, when I wrote these lectures over a generation ago, I was entirely at the mercy of translators for my English style. I do not like reading myself in another person's style. And now for me to compose in English, which would be the only suitable thing to do, is too great a labour to undertake just at this time . . .

. . . I do not consider the project as definitely closed. I am indeed very interested in it and would like to do it at a later date when there is more time. It would certainly be of more interest to you to have a statement from me in my own style and from my present point of view. I will try to write this during the free time on our travels, and I can work on it with Bob Craft during our concert tours . . .

In New York, in late June 1956, at the start of a six-month tour, Stravinsky consented to an interview through Miss Ishlon

6 Here are some examples of corrections from the Soviet book: 'In *Dialogues* Stravinsky drew a plan of his father's apartment from memory. Bridge of Kisses is not shown correctly on the plan. In reality, this is Decembrist Bridge, which goes across Kryukov Canal by way of Decembrist Street. Bridge of Kisses is built across the Moyka River by way of Glinka Street.' 'The naval barracks were not located at the confluence of the Kryukov Canal and the Neva, as Stravinsky says later; they were located where the Kryukov Canal crosses the Moyka River . . .' 'By giving his preference to the artists of [Diaghilev's] *The World of Art*, Stravinsky ignores the master works of realistic art. These are primarily I. Repin's *The Duel* and *Counsel of State*, and V. Surikov's *Suvorov Crossing the Alps*, in whose creations the great traditions of Russian realism found their continuation.'

with Emily Coleman, a friend of hers (and famously of Djuna Barnes), as well as the music and dance editor of *Newsweek*. He spoke at length, but only a fraction of his comments was transcribed, and he did not allow these to be published:

To be a good listener, you must acquire a musical culture . . . you must be familiar with the history and development of music, you must listen. The person with the subscription ticket for concerts is not necessarily a musically cultured person. He is musical only because the music is performed in front of him. To receive music you have to open your ears and wait for the music; you must feel that it is something you need . . . To listen is an effort, and just to hear is no merit. A duck hears also.

The larger the audience, the worse. I have never attached much importance to the collective mind and collective opinion . . . Music never was for the masses. I am not against the masses, but please do not confuse the value of music addressed from one ear to a million ears . . . Do not make the mistake of merely multiplying.

No audiences are good anywhere, but . . . the best musical level is that of the Germans. They have a higher level of listeners because of their musical history and musical culture . . . In the seventeenth and eighteenth centuries, the people who listened to music were much more learned; music for them was a language which they knew well. They knew not only by passive listening but by active playing. Everybody played – harpsichords, organs, flutes, violins. They had the habit of music played with their own hands.

. . . Now we hear music by the gramophone. This gives maybe more people a connection with music, but the result is not the same because the passive is not the active . . .

We think that very difficult works, like all the last works of Beethoven, are better understood now. No, people are simply more accustomed to them. It isn't that they understand better . . . A composer thinks about the audience, but not primarily. If you think about audiences, you do not think about your work, but about a reaction . . . If the audience is yourself, that is quite different, but to be the audience yourself is difficult [for] it is difficult to multiply yourself.

Clearly Stravinsky's conversational partner would have to be someone who was almost constantly in his company.

The next development occurred on 3 December 1956, in the Ritz Hotel, Paris, where I met with Pierre Souvtchinsky, Pierre Boulez, and Gerard Worms of the Editions du Rocher, Monaco, who commissioned me to write a book, *Avec Stravinsky,* and tried to persuade me to obtain a preface by its subject. When I mentioned the matter to Stravinsky, who had been visiting Pavel Tchelichev in another part of the hotel, he proposed instead to contribute a dialogue touching on a variety of subjects. Much of the result, 'Answers to Thirty-Six Questions', was written during Boulez's visit to Los Angeles three months later, and under his influence.[7] He promised to translate the text into French and to check the French version of the remainder of the book (which was published in German as well). 'Answers to Thirty-Six Questions' appeared in several languages at the time of Stravinsky's seventy-fifth birthday (June 1957) and became the cornerstone of the *Conversations*. A televised 'conversation' between Stravinsky and myself in NBC's *Wisdom* series, filmed at the same time, was the incentive to continue. The questions for the NBC chat came from Robert Graff, who directed it. Here are some of them with Stravinsky's written but unused answers:

Q. Where do musical ideas occur to you?
A. Well, sometimes in the bathroom.
Q. Do you write them down?
A. Sometimes.
Q. Does chance or accident play a role in musical ideas?
A. Of course.
Q. How do you know when a work is finished?
A. Because *I* finished it.
Q. Of all your music . . . which [piece] do you like best?
A. All of them, when composing them.
Q. Do music critics perform a useful function?
A. They could if they were competent.
Q. How does a composer of serious music survive economically in our time?
A. The same as in any time, very badly.

7 Stravinsky wrote to Miss Ishlon, 14 March 1957: 'May I ask you to note a change in the last frase [*sic*] of the questionnaire? Here is the new text: "Webern is for me just before Music (as man can be 'just before God') and I do not hesitate . . .", etc. until the end. I made this change because the French ['*juste*'] was not clear enough for the reader and the sentence is so important to understand . . .' A letter to Boulez from Miss Ishlon, 8 April 1957, establishes that Stravinsky had entrusted her with the preliminary editing of his manuscript. On 21 March, she telegraphed to Stravinsky: 'Weinstock interested in republishing *Chroniques* [*de ma vie*] with questions [and] new updating chapter . . .' Stravinsky answered the same day that further 'answers' would not be forthcoming until he had finished *Agon*.

Q. How would you define music?
A. An organization of tones.

Soon besieged with requests for more 'interviews', Stravinsky realized that he had found both a way of controlling their contents, and a gainful enterprise. His acumen in discerning what should be published is evident from the deletions, rephrasings, underlinings, marginal comments (*'ridicule'*, *'non'*) in his hand – superseding the agreement signed by me – on the contract with Editions du Rocher for the 'Thirty-Six Questions'.

By December, Stravinsky had completed additional sets of answers. On the second of that month, Miss Ishlon wrote to him:

I find each set even more interesting than the previous one and I especially admired your answer about false 'limitations' on music and the stagnation of one-time explorers. I have, in fact, placed this answer at the end of the manuscript . . .

A 'book of dialogues of mine', as Stravinsky described the *Conversations* in a letter to T. S. Eliot, was offered to Faber and Faber in January 1958. Two months later, after Doubleday had purchased the American rights, the question of the title and accreditation of authorship arose. On 25 March, Stravinsky wrote to Doubleday's Ken McCormick, 'Columbia wants to record me reading excerpts from the book . . . we can't have "Conversations with Igor Stravinsky by Igor Stravinsky" but really should call the book "Conversations with Igor Stravinsky by Robert Craft".'

McCormick counter-proposed 'Afternoons with Igor Stravinsky', or 'almost anything but "Conversations", since we already have another title with this word on our fall list'. On 18 April, he suggested 'Dialogues with Igor Stravinsky, edited by Robert Craft', which 'does away with the cumbersome repetition of your name and gives Mr Craft proper credit'. Stravinsky objected, giving as his reason that 'a dialogue must involve two people'. But the word 'edited' had been anathema to him ever since the Russian Revolution had rendered him a stateless person, and the publishers of his music had added the names of prominent American musicians – Albert Spalding, the violinist, and Julia Burt – who were US citizens, hoping for the protection of US copyright law through the editors. This was not only humiliating for Stravinsky, but proved ineffective.

On 6 June, Richard de la Mare of Faber and Faber wrote to me, 'Our suggestion is that the main title should be given as: "Conversations with Igor Stravinsky", and that we should then put as a sort of subtitle "Igor Stravinsky and Robert Craft", with a short rule, perhaps, between the two, but not, we think, "by".'

Mr de la Mare wrote in the same letter, 'I spoke to Mr Eliot, who is now home again from America, about those queries you raise in the Satie letters, and his opinion was that the original words could be quoted without undue offence. His opinion was that to omit them and insert dots would be a mistake, but he suggested that the words immediately preceding the offending words in those letters in the French originals should be substituted for the English translation.'

Stravinsky wrote to McCormick that the book should appear at the time of 'the first performance of a new work of mine, *Threni*' (on 23 September 1958), but since a letter dated 10 June directs the publisher to send the proofs to Venice, the impossibility of this conjunction should have been apparent to the composer. On 27 August, Stravinsky wrote to Miss Ishlon from Venice, 'As Bob has already gone to Hamburg and instructed me to open his mail, I answer you in his place about the photos. It seems to me ridiculous not to use photographs of the people discussed in the text . . . and silly to use photographs of Prokofiev, Gide, Cocteau, who do not figure in this book but only in the one we are now preparing.'

As was the case with the 1935 *Chroniques de ma vie*, the first book of *Conversations* was too slender and failed to embrace any subject in sufficient depth. It nevertheless received worldwide attention and favourable notices. Stravinsky's endorsement of the Schoenberg school came as a surprise to most readers, and was an irritant to some, among them the composer William Schuman, who criticized the apparent reversal. When Doubleday began to solicit pre-publication blurbs for the second book, Stravinsky suggested that it be directed to the attention of general reviewers rather than music critics. 'The second volume is even less specifically musical than the first,' he wrote, and, 'The reactions of New York music critics to my works are as automatic as the Soviet veto at the UN.'

Stravinsky's outspokenness about his contemporaries and

collaborators, particularly in the original text of *Memories and Commentaries*, led to some unfortunate bowdlerizing of the autobiographical portions of this and the later books. Without consulting Stravinsky, McCormick sent a transcript of the composer's remarks about Nijinsky to the dancer's widow, provoking a letter from her San Francisco attorneys, Erskine, Erskine and Tulley (28 July 1959) withholding permission for the publication of any of her husband's correspondence with Stravinsky unless he deleted the comment 'although it is true that Nijinsky's brother became insane . . .' along with allusions to stories of intimacies with Diaghilev. Stravinsky complied, and his excisions, now irreparable, included valuable information about such matters as Nijinsky's hereditary syphilis, something about which few or no others would have known.[8] Stravinsky wrote to McCormick on 2 August:

I regret Mrs Nijinsky did not see the entire chapter of my book . . . for she would there see that the Nijinsky portion of it is, or so I think, very fair and very friendly. In fact, I had expected her to regard my discussion of Nijinsky here as something of a retribution for my remarks about him in my Autobiography – which offended her . . . I even hesitated to include Nijinsky's letter because of the damage it might do to Diaghilev. But it seemed to me such an extraordinary document, and so entirely favourable to Nijinsky's reputation, that I decided to publish it.

In retrospect, I regard the *Conversations* as a monument to a million missed opportunities. But at the time the books were compiled, Stravinsky resisted attempts to explore his past, which was my main interest in them. He wanted to air his critical views, and to castigate the bosses – conductors, composers, critics – of the current musical scene. The books provided an ideal rostrum for this, and the question–answer form accommodated his natural tendency for abrupt changes of subject. It must also be admitted that he was not indifferent to the pecuniary potential:

8 On 4 May 1934, Stravinsky had received a letter from Romola Nijinsky asking him to conduct *Petrushka* as part of a charity gala at Covent Garden on 3 July to raise money for her husband. In the same letter, Mme Nijinsky says that she is requesting the composer's support because she knows he was 'a friend and comrade to my poor husband'. Evidently Stravinsky did not reply, which may in part explain his widow's hostility twenty-three years later.

his correspondence concerning this aspect of the publications, especially those in *The New Yorker*, is nearly as long as the dialogues themselves.

This newly edited one-volume version of the *Conversations* brings together entries from all five books and presents them in chronological order according to the stages of Stravinsky's life: Russian, Swiss, French and American. This compartmentalization is admittedly unsatisfactory in some cases. Diaghilev and Stravinsky scarcely knew each other in St Petersburg before 1910, and *The Firebird* is Stravinsky's only major work composed entirely in Russia. The great creations of the Stravinsky–Diaghilev collaboration were presented to the world in Paris. Yet the connection between them was established in the Russian capital, which both of them continued to regard as home during the nineteen years of their working relationship. The new country-by-country linear structure brings Stravinsky's reflections on his family life, professional associates and personal friendships into sharper focus and places the major compositions in their cultural milieux.

I have omitted most of the commentaries on the musical scene, which has changed beyond recognition in the nearly half-century since the books appeared, and which now seem irrelevant. Gone, too, are most of the 'programme notes', and the testaments to Stravinsky's kerfuffles with critics. Only his thoughts about some of the music to which he was so deeply devoted in his late years have been retained, albeit in condensed form. Updating has been kept to a minimum, as well as corrections of proven errors of fact, Stravinsky's own recollections being the basis of the book.

THE RUSSIAN BACKGROUND

1882–1913

The Russian Background
1882–1913
The Firebird, Petrushka, Zvezdolikiy,
The Rite of Spring, The Nightingale

My most persistent memory images return to me without chronology. Recently, for instance, I have been picturing the Mariyinsky Theatre with its front entrance draped in black as it was at the time of Tchaikovsky's death. I remember how the curtains billowed in the winter wind and how moved I was by the sight of them. Tchaikovsky was the hero of my childhood.

I have also been recalling the first music I ever heard, a bristling fife-and-drum band from the marine barracks not far from our apartment. This music, and that of the full band which penetrated my nursery every day, and especially the sound of the tubas and the piccolos and drums, was the tickling pleasure of my cradlehood. I know that the wish to imitate this music led to my first efforts at composition, for as soon as I could reach the piano I tried to pick out the intervals I had heard, and in the process found other intervals that I liked better, which already made me a composer.

Other recent memories are of the appearances of Tsar Alexander III in the streets of St Petersburg when I was a child and, in consequence, I began to reflect on the political world into which I was born. The Tsar himself was a colourless figure, but his horses were a beautiful sight, one ahead of the Imperial sleigh, with a blue net behind to catch the snow, and a second galloping at the side. Even at that time, the Tsar was accompanied by grey-coated policemen who ordered all bystanders to 'Circulate, circulate.' When the Tsar's private train passed the country home of my wife, Vera de Bosset, she and her family were ordered to remain indoors behind tightly shuttered windows, and armed guards were posted along the track. The Tsar's own railroad car was painted blue, but three other cars in this particular train were painted the same blue, to foil still further a would-be assassin.

I saw the Tsar many times while walking with my brothers and governess along the quays of St Petersburg's Moyka River or by the adjacent canals. The Tsar was a very large man. He occupied the entire seat of a droshky driven by a troika coachman as big and obese as himself. The coachman wore a dark blue uniform, with medals decorating his chest. He was seated in front of the Tsar, but at an elevation from which his enormous behind, like a gigantic pumpkin, was only a few inches from the Tsar's face. The Tsar responded to greetings from people in the street by raising his right hand towards his temple. Since everybody recognized him, he was obliged to do this almost without interruption. His appearances gave me great pleasure and I eagerly anticipated them. We removed our hats and received the Tsar's acknowledging gesture, feeling very important indeed.

At an earlier age I had seen the Tsar in an unforgettable pageant, a parade that passed our street on its way to the Imperial Mariyinsky Theatre. It honoured the Shah of Persia and was the climax of an important state visit. We were given places in the first-floor window of our hairdresser's. The most brilliant procession of all kinds of cavalry passed by, Imperial guards, coaches with grand dukes, ministers, generals. I remember a long, forest-like noise, the 'hurrah' of the crowds in the streets, coming in crescendo waves closer and closer with the approaching isolated carriage of the Tsar and the Shah.

But other memories crowd upon me as I recount these. I think of my first visit to the circus, the 'Cirque Cinisselli', as it was called, where ladies in pink corsets rode horseback standing up, as in Seurat or Toulouse-Lautrec. And my first visit to Nizhni-Novgorod, a city of green cupolas and white walls, a city full of Tartars and horses, and redolent of leather, furs and dung. And my first view of the sea, in my seventeenth year, which is surprisingly late for I was born near it and lived close by all my life. I saw the sea for the first time from a hill in Hungerburg on the south shore of the Gulf of Finland, and I remember my astonishment that this narrow ribbon between earth and sky was, as it would be from a hill, so vertical.

*

R.C. How did it happen that you were born in Oranienbaum – that is, why did your family move there from St Petersburg?

I.S. Oranienbaum was a pleasant seaside village facing Kronstadt, built around an eighteenth-century palace. My parents had gone there a month before I was born to enjoy the early summer air. It was fashionable, Tolstoy, Nekrasov and Ilya Repin having lived and worked there, as well as Musorgsky, who spent the last summer of his life there (1880). We returned two years after my birth, when my brother Guriy was born there, and in 1885, but I have never seen it since[1] – if I saw it then. My Swiss friend Charles-Albert Cingria, a critic of 'the Stravinsky of the international style', used to call me 'le maître d'Oranienbaum'.

I was baptized by a prelate of the Russian Orthodox Church only a few hours after my birth, which occurred at noon. My parents summoned a priest to say prayers for me, sprinkle me with consecrated water, and draw a cross on my forehead in anointed oil – which was also done on Ash Wednesday. Frail babies were sometimes baptized summarily, in this fashion. Because I was a small baby, my frailty drew a great deal of attention throughout my youth, until it became my way of thinking about myself; and even today, as an octogenarian leading an active, not to say strenuous, life, I sometimes remind myself that I am, in fact, much too frail and had better stop.

I was more ceremoniously joined to the Russian Church on 29 June (Old Style), in the Nikolsky Sobor in St Petersburg, on the same canal as our apartment. Carried there in a bureau drawer – I did not yet have a cradle – I was stripped, covered by a chrism, like a peasant woman at her wedding, and, while the priest held my nose and mouth with one hand, immersed. These sacramental ablutions frightened me and produced an intestinal reaction, an omen, as it happened, of a complaint that has been lifelong. The rite of confirmation does not exist in the Orthodox

1 Stravinsky visited it on 5 October 1962, by which time its German name had been changed to Lomonosov, in honour of the great poet. [R.C.]

Church, incidentally, which means that Communion may be administered to the youngest and least reasonable of infants. I remember the taste of the tiny pellets of *prosphora*, Communion bread soaked in sweet Greek wine, that the officiating priest spooned into my mouth.

R.C. What is the origin of your name?

I.S. 'Stravinsky' comes from 'Strava', a small river in the region of Minsk. We were originally called Soulima-Stravinsky, but when Russia annexed this part of Poland, the Soulima was dropped. The Soulima–Stravinskys were landowners in eastern Poland as far back as can be traced. They moved from Poland to Russia[2] in the reign of Catherine the Great.

A Dr Grydzewski, editor of a Polish *émigré* weekly published in London, has kindly pointed out to me that Soulima is the name of a Polish crest of arms used by Zawisza Czerny, the hero of the Grünwald battle, as well as by a branch of the Stravinsky family. Dr Grydzewski also informed me that a certain Ignaty Stravinsky, quite possibly an ancestor of mine, was mentioned by Niesiecki in 1778 as *'podkomorzy litewski'* ('Lithuanian Chamberlain'), and that another Stravinsky, Stanislaus, was famous in the eighteenth century as one of the Bar Confederates who organized the unsuccessful kidnapping of Stanislaus Augustus. This Stanislaus Stravinsky then fled to Rome, joined a religious order, returned to the Duchy of Warsaw as a priest in the Augustov district, and wrote his memoirs. But I do not know whether we are actually related.

R.C. What else do you know about your ancestry?

I.S. The only great-grandparent about whom I had heard anything at all was Roman Fyodorovich Furman,[3] my mother's maternal grandfather, a Privy Counsellor to Nicholas I. His mother, Yelizaveta Engel, was born to another family of Privy Counsellors, and his aunt, Anna Engel, married into the aristocratic Littke family. One of her sons was the great-grandfather

2 One Stravinsky (Strawinsky) was Governor of Minsk province in the sixteenth century, and another was Castellan of Minsk and Vitebsk. The Stravinsky name is Polish.

3 1784–1851.

6

of Sergey Diaghilev, which made him my distant cousin. On my father's side I know only that his father, Ignaty Ignatyevich Stravinsky, moved to Poltava in the Ukraine. My father's maternal grandfather, Ivan Ivanovich Skorokhodov, was an agronomist but is renowned simply for having lived to the age of a hundred and twelve (1767–1879). Alexandra Ivanovna Skorokhodova was a Pole, therefore a Catholic, and Skorokhodov was Orthodox, and according to Russian law the children of a mixed marriage had to be Orthodox. My father was baptized in the Russian Church. Rimsky-Korsakov used to tease me, saying, 'So your grandfather's name was Ignaty? I smell a Catholic there.' Kirill Grigorevich Kholodovsky, my mother's father, was born in Kiev, a 'little Russian', as Kievlani are called. He was a Minister of Agriculture, served on the Tsar's 'Council of Thirty', and died in Tiflis of tuberculosis, a disease that has attacked our family ever since. My wife, Yekaterina Gavrilovna Nosenko, her mother (my aunt), and our elder daughter died of it; my younger daughter and grand-daughter spent years in sanatoriums with it, and I myself have suffered from it at various times, but most severely in 1939, when I spent five months in the sanatorium at Sancellemoz, France. This is all I have to say about my ancestry, though it is far more complex and even more boring than this résumé of it.

R.C. Perhaps, but please tell us something about your parents.
I.S. They met in my mother's city of Kiev, where my father was the first basso of the Opera, and were married there. My father[4] had been a law student in the Niéjinsky Lyceum when he discovered his good bass voice and good musical ear. He went from the Lyceum to the St Petersburg Conservatory and became a pupil of Professor Evarardi, whose school for the voice was as celebrated as Leopold Auer's school for the violin. At graduation he accepted a position in the Kiev Opera, which he held for a few years until he was ready for the Opera in St Petersburg.

R.C. What do you remember of your father?
I.S. He was not very *commode*. I lived in constant fear of him, in fact, which, I suppose, has deeply harmed my own character.

---

4 Fyodor Ignatyevich Stravinsky (1843–1902).

He had an uncontrollable, explosive temper, and life with him could be very difficult. He would lose himself in his anger, suddenly and unexpectedly, and without regard to where he might happen to be. I remember being humiliated in a street in Bad Homburg,[5] when he suddenly ordered me – I was in my thirteenth year – to return to our hotel room. I sulked instead of immediately obeying him, and the result was an open scandal in the street. He was affectionate to me only when I was ill, an excellent excuse for any hypochondriac tendencies I might have. Whether or not to gain his affection, I caught pleurisy when I was thirteen and was left with tuberculosis for a time afterwards. During this illness he behaved differently to me and I forgave him everything that had happened before. But he was a distant parent, distant not only to his children but also to others. He impressed me in his death more than he had ever done in his life. He had fallen on the stage of the Mariyinsky Theatre and soon after began to complain of pain in his back, where he had been struck by the fall. He went to Berlin for Röntgen treatment, but the carcinoma, which is what it proved to be, had developed beyond hope of cure. He died a year and a half later, on the couch in his study, saying, 'I feel so good, so very good.'

For me, my father's death was his most poignant moment of reality, and that moment is all that remains with me now. We anticipate our parents' deaths many times, but the event itself is always unlike what we have imagined, and always a shock. I realized that my father would die when an official, Teliakovsky, the Director of Imperial Theatres, visited him on his deathbed. When he appeared, I saw him as an emissary of death, and began to accept it. My father died on 21 November (Old Style; 4 December, New Style) 1902. The corpse was frozen like a piece of meat, dressed in evening clothes, and photographed. This was done at night. I was profoundly disturbed by the thought of this dummy of the beloved one in the next room. What are we to think about corpses? (Musil's description of this same feeling in Ulrich at the death of *his* father is one of the most brilliant things in *The Man Without Qualities*.) The funeral procession started from our house on an unseasonably

5 In 1895.

humid day. The grave was in the Volkov Cemetery.[6] The artists
and directors of the Mariyinsky Theatre were present, and
Nikolay Rimsky-Korsakov stood by my mother. A short litany
took place, after which holy water and dirt were sprinkled on
the grave. Mournings were solemn and strict in Russia, and
Gaelic-type wakes were unknown. We went home, each of us to
his own room, to cry alone.

After the death of my father, a new life began for me. I lived
more in accordance with my own wishes, though I once left
home, composing the traditional note for my mother to the
effect that life at 66 Kryukov Canal had become impossible. I
sought refuge with a recently married Yelachich cousin,[7] a man
devoted to any form of revolution or protestation, but after a
few days my mother managed to fall ill enough to force me to
come back. I should add that she did behave slightly less egotis-
tically after that, and her delight in torturing me seemed slightly
less intense. I continued to live at home during the first two
years of my marriage, but after the birth of my first son and
daughter, in 1908 and 1909, we moved to an apartment on the
English Prospect, where we lived until May 1910, when I left for
Paris and the première of *Firebird*.

*

R.C. And your mother and brothers?
I.S. I was close to no one in my family except my younger
brother Guriy. For my mother I felt only 'duties'. My deepest
attachment was to Bertha, my nurse, an East Prussian who knew
almost no Russian. German became the language of my nursery.
Bertha lived on to nurse my own children and had been forty
years in our family when she died – in Morges, in 1917. I mourned
her more than I would my mother, twenty-two years later.

When I remember my older brothers at all, it is to remind
myself how exceedingly they used to annoy me. Roman was a
law student. At eleven he caught diphtheria, which weakened
his heart and killed him nine years later. I thought him a very
handsome brother, and was proud of him, but I could not confide

6 The body was later exhumed and reburied in the Alexander Nevsky
Cemetery.
7 In fact, Stravinsky fled to the home of his elder brother Yuriy. [R.C.]

in him, for he was untouched by music. Yuriy – George – was an architectural engineer, and he continued to work as one in Leningrad until his death there in June 1941. He was not close to me as a child, or later, and he never wrote to me after I left Russia. I last saw him in 1908. His wife wrote to me once in Paris, and in 1925 their elder daughter, Tatyana, visited me there and in Nice. Yuriy died shortly before the Nazi invasion, as I learned from a friend of Rimsky's eldest son Michael, a Mr Borodin, who sent letters to me during World War II from somewhere on Long Island with news of friends in Russia. Borodin told me of Andrey Rimsky-Korsakov's death, though I had already had this news from Rakhmaninov – and of Maximilian Steinberg's death also.

Guriy began his career, like Roman and myself, as a law student, but he had inherited our father's voice and musical ear and was determined to become a singer. Rather than enter the Conservatory, he studied with Tartakov, a famous St Petersburg bass, and performed professionally in a private St Petersburg theatre from 1912 to 1914. To my regret, I did not hear him there, but Diaghilev did, and reported that I would have been very proud. Guriy was a baritone with a voice like our father's in timbre, but higher in tessitura. I composed my Verlaine songs for him and always grieved that he did not live to sing them professionally. He was conscripted in the 1914–18 war and sent to the southern front in a Red Cross unit. He died of scarlet fever in Iasi, Romania, in April 1917. He is buried next to my father in St Petersburg's Alexander Nevsky Cemetery, which the Bolsheviks later turned into a national artists' cemetery. Guriy and my father were both respected by the Bolsheviks.

Though I had not seen Guriy since 1910, his death made me very lonely. We had been together constantly as children, and we felt that as long as we were together, all was well with the world. We found in each other the love and understanding denied us by our parents, who favoured neither of us, though Guriy was in some respects the Benjamin of the family.

*

R.C. What do you recall of your childhood, your family life, your earliest friends, impressions of relatives, and first experiences in school?

I.S. Our apartment was in a large old building on the Kryukov Canal. A German bomb destroyed the house, but Ernest Ansermet, who visited my brother Yuriy there in 1928, could give you a more recent description than my own. It was a four-storey house, and we lived on the third floor; at one time, Tamara Karsavina and her husband occupied the floor above us. On the other side of the canal stood a very handsome Empire-style building, the ochre of the Villa Medici in Rome, but a prison, unfortunately. The building next to us was also an apart-ment house, the home of the conductor Nápravník.[8]

Our flat was furnished in the usual Victorian manner, with the usual bad paintings and mauve upholstery, but with an unusual library and two grand pianos. To recall it gives me no pleasure. I do not like to remember my childhood, apart from the four walls of my and Guriy's room, even though this was like Petrushka's cell. I spent most of my home time there. I was allowed out of doors only after my parents had subjected me to a medical examination, and I was considered too frail to participate in sports or games when I was out. I suspect even now that my hatred of sports is my jealousy at having been deprived of them.

The world of a child of that age is 'safe' in the morning, and my day began at seven o'clock. Classes in the St Petersburg Second Gymnasium did not start until two hours later, but the building was a long walk from our house. I was awakened by Bertha, the 'safest' person in my world, and her voice was the most loving I would hear in my childhood. Often, but not every day, Bertha's reveilles mingled with the rattle and torrential tumble of bathwater being drawn for me in the ancient zinc-plated bathtub (two steps up from the floor) at the end of the corridor. Culinary odours reached the bathroom, and they, too, indicated the presence of another 'safety', Caroline, our Finnish cook, a family fixture for thirty years.

---

8 A plaque marks the building, as it did when Stravinsky saw it in 1962, but nothing distinguished the entrance to his home of many years. When I remarked on this to our Soviet hosts, the reply was: 'But Stravinsky left us and went to the United States.' Even now, in 2002, the long-forgotten conductor's plaque is the only one in the doorway, though now the concert hall in the Conservatory of Music, around the corner, has been renamed Rakhmaninov Hall – for another fugitive to Hollywood. [R.C.]

Breakfast was served by the maids, or by Simon Ivanovich. I do not remember the maids, for the reason that they were often changed; as I grew older, my mother made certain that they were older, too. Simon Ivanovich was a small man with a neat, military-style moustache; he had been a subaltern to my Uncle Vanya at one time. He was remarkable chiefly for a bald head that reminded me of a bull. His room was a tiny antechamber under the front stairs; or, rather, he shared this cubbyhole with stacks of my father's books.

I loved Simon Ivanovich, and, in return, I think he supported me in most questions of family allegiance. I was probably saved from family disgrace by him on more than one occasion, but I have a clear recollection of only one of his rescues, that of my first inebriation. I had gone to a party with Yuriy and some of his engineering-student classmates. We were all in our mid-teens and all determined to exhibit our maturity – all except Yuriy, who had gone home early. At one point a fellow drinker asked me my sex, and it was then that I realized we were all drunk. I kept saying, 'I can't go home . . . If my parents see me . . .' And, in fact, I did spend part of the night in his room, which is where, with my brother's help, Simon Ivanovich found me, and then somehow managed to transfer me, undetected, to my room.

Simon Ivanovich lived with our family for thirty years and died just before the Revolution. One more island of 'safety' stood between him and school. This was Zackar, the doorman, a kindly old gentleman in an absurd Swiss beadle's uniform. He also seems to have been there all my life.

Uncles are 'safe', too, ordinarily, although I experienced my first deception in the arms of one of them. But, to be truthful, this 'uncle' wasn't quite a real one, which may have been the trouble. These other 'uncles' were my mother's cousins, an artist and two generals. The artist, Dadya (Uncle) Misha, was a mephistophelean character, but too shrewd to be 'safe'. Uncle Misha's 'Peredvishniky' school of realists was strongly opposed to the Diaghilev movement, and later in life I was embarrassed by the contradictory points of view of my uncle's school and those of my friends, especially since Uncle Misha's scenes of Ukrainian wheatfields and cows on riverbanks covered the walls of our apartment. The two generals were Dadya Vanya, a divisional general, and Dadya Kolya, the Commandant of Kronstadt, well known as the inventor of a new type of gun.

The deception occurred during a brief perambulation in Dadya Vanya's unmotherly arms, when he promised me that I would see a bird and no bird appeared. (This time-honoured tactic of the photographer is a serious evil, I think, and should be discouraged.) What I most vividly remember from that first photography session is the smell of Dadya Vanya's epaulettes and the cold, metallic braids on his uniform, which I sucked like candy.

Dr Dushinkin, our family physician, was another 'safety'. An elderly man, a general in charge of a military hospital, he called at our house once a week. I seem to remember him in uniform only, and only in winter as he came in from the street, his beard glistening with snow. Dr Dushinkin made me stick out my tongue, expose my chest to his icy stethoscope, report on my matutinal movements, and swallow a little black pill if I had none to report. I recall our family dentist, too, though dentists are never 'safe', and this one, to begin with, was a German. I do not recollect his name but am sure I could still find his office near the Isakievsky Cathedral.

*

The 'safety' of friends is mixed, and probably only those old enough to be non-competitors can qualify. One of my dearest old friends was Vladimir Stasov, the disciple of Mikhail Glinka – indeed, he had played piano duets with Glinka and was therefore a sacred cow – as well as the advocate and associate of the Russian 'Five'. Stasov was a giant of a man, with a long, white (when clean) Father Time beard, a tiny toque, and a dark, dirty *surtout*. His gestures were commensurately large as well as loud, and he was always shouting. When he had a confidence to tell you, he would cup a huge hand to your ear and shout it there; we called this 'a Stasov secret'. It was Stasov's habit to say only the good about everything, and to leave the bad to take care of itself. In fact, we used to say, 'Stasov won't speak badly, even about the weather.' Sometimes his energy and enthusiasm reminded me of a panting dog; one wanted to pet it but was afraid of being knocked over by its response. Stasov had known

Tolstoy intimately and had many delightful Tolstoy stories to tell. He said that once, when Tolstoy was speaking to a group of people on non-violence and non-resistance, someone asked him what to do if attacked by a tiger in a forest. Tolstoy answered, 'Do the best you can; it happens rarely.'

I remember Stasov best at his funeral and am unable to recall his apartment without seeing a coffin in it and Stasov in the coffin. What struck me most about this was that Stasov seemed so unnatural in his coffin because his arms were folded; he was the most open-armed man in the world. The room also seemed grotesquely narrow for such a huge man, though this was partly because of the rainy day, and because of our coats and umbrellas. I remember that when the coffin was carried through the door, the conductor Nápravník turned to me and said, 'They are taking out a piece of history.'

R.C. What other friends besides Stasov, 'safe' or 'unsafe', do you consider to have been the most influential in your life in the St Petersburg years?

I.S. My life from 1897 to 1899 was dominated by a man eight years my senior, Ivan Vasilyevich Pokrovsky. I was still in the gymnasium when we met, and he was already graduating from the university, i.e. far enough ahead of me to rate as an authority. My life at home was unbearable at that time, and Pokrovsky appeared to me as a kind of Baudelaire in contrast to the *'esprit belge'* of my family. I was soon spending all of my time with him, at the expense of my schoolwork. I stopped seeing him because I was jealous of his brother, who had a beautiful girl-friend with whom I myself was secretly in love. Pokrovsky shamed me in all my old ideals and loves, while cultivating a taste in me for everything French. He was the type of the pro-European himself, the counterpart to Turgenev's Bazarov. He was no mere amateur in music, having been a pupil of Anatoly Lyadov, if I remember correctly. I learned *Coppélia, Lakmé, The Tales of Hoffmann,* and much other music of the sort by playing it four-hands with Pokrovsky. He was thin and phthisical, and he died of his disease at an early age. His outstanding feature was his untamed hair – *'cheveux ébouriffés'*, as the French say.

Valentin Serov was also 'safe', but then, of course, he too belonged to an older generation. Serov and Mikhail Alexandrovich Vrubel were the best Russian painters of the day; I once owned a portrait of the former by the latter, a picture I especially valued because Serov, like Henry Green, declined to be photographed. Serov was the conscience of the *Mir iskustva* circle, but when Diaghilev referred to him as '*la justice elle-même*', he did so with regret; Diaghilev wanted to introduce his own rules. I knew Serov from the beginning of my association with Rimsky, and he was one of the first people to believe in and encourage me in my vocation.

*

R.C. What schools did you attend in St Petersburg?

I.S. I went to a government school, the Second St Petersburg Gymnasium, until I was fourteen. From there, in 1896 or 1897, I attended Y. G. Gurevich's Gymnasium, a private school where my brother Yuriy had been before me. The Gurevich Gymnasium was about six kilometres from our house, at the corner of Ligorsky Prospect and [what is now] Nekrasov Street. I was always late in the mornings for the tram, and would have to take a fiacre and pay forty or fifty kopecks. But the fiacre rides were what I enjoyed most about school, especially in winter. On the way home, it was a pleasure to drive through the Nevsky Prospekt in a sleigh, protected by a net from the dirty snow kicked up by the horse, and then, at home, to warm myself in front of our big white porcelain stove.

The Gurevich Gymnasium was divided into a 'classical' and a *Realschule*. My own curriculum belonged to the former: history, Latin, Greek, Russian and French literatures, and mathematics. I was of course a very bad pupil, and I hated this school as I did all my schools, profoundly and for ever.

R.C. Did you have any sympathetic teachers?

I.S. My mathematics professor – a man called Woolf – did understand me, I think. He was an ex-Hussar officer with a real talent for mathematics, but he had been, and still was, a drunkard. (Another of my professors was a drunkard, too, a man in perpetual disgrace who would walk to the window, turn his back to us, and steal a nip from a little bottle in his coat pocket; the other boys mocked him cruelly.) Professor Woolf was also an amateur musician. He knew that I composed – I had already been reproached for it by the school director – and he helped, protected and encouraged me.

Even though school was not quite 'safe', I came to love some people. In the Second Gymnasium, I was especially fond of two boys, both of them, though unrelated, with the name Smirnov: they were identified simply as 'Smirnov One' and 'Smirnov Two'. But the 'safest' person in this school was the priest who pronounced the 'nuisance' prayers – it was a nuisance to say them – with which classes began. He taught a course in catechism and biblical history called 'God's Law'. This Father Rozhdestvensky was very popular with the boys, but they baited him, nevertheless, and his class was inattentive and even chaotic. (I cannot imagine what tergiversation he tried to teach – 'God's Law', indeed.) I do not think I could have shown more interest than anyone else, and Father Rozhdestvensky must have known that I knew nothing. All the same, I was a favourite in his class.

Bible studies in Tsarist schools were as much concerned with language as with religion, because our Bible was Slavonic rather than Russian. The sound and study of Slavonic delighted me and sustained me through these classes. Now, in retrospect, most of my school time seems to have been consumed by language studies, Latin and Greek from my eleventh to nineteenth years, French, German, Russian and Slavonic – which resembles modern Bulgar – from my very first days in the gymnasium. Friends sometimes complain that I sound like an etymologist, with my habit of comparing languages. But language problems have beset me all my life; after all, I once composed a cantata entitled *Babel*. Even now, a half-century since I left the Russian-speaking world, I still think in Russian and speak other languages in translation. In spite of the 'safety' of Father Rozhdestvensky and a few comrades, I abominated the gymnasium and longed to be free of it.

The school meal was inedible, and the student strikes organized in protest were unsuccessful. I was always hungry, therefore, especially so because tea was not served in the late afternoon in our house, but only after dinner; in fact, not until bedtime did Simon Ivanovich bring in the samovar with the tray of bread and *confiture*. And our household routine was suspended only when my father sang at the Mariyinsky. On performance days, too, the whole house trembled, for my father was caustic and irritable when nervous, as he always was before a performance. (I am the same now, on my own concert days, and my irritation with an unwilling shirt stud or recalcitrant collar is no doubt exaggerated.) On performance days my father dined apart from the family, though we all sometimes ate together after the performance. I remember sitting on the stove in my room on these exceptional occasions and listening, hungrily, for the return of his carriage. After these late dinners, Mama or Bertha came to see us in bed and hear our prayers: 'Our Father who art in Heaven . . .' – '*Otchey nasch eezshey yehsee na nehbehskh . . .*' This is Slavonic; I do not remember it in Russian.

Were my parents believers? I do not really know. They were not practising churchgoers, in any case, and judging from the absence of relevant discussion at home, they could not have entertained strong religious feelings. But their attitude must have been more one of indifference than of opposition. The least hint of impiety horrified them. I remember someone giving my father a copy of Pushkin's blasphemous poem about the Annunciation and my father consigning it, with equally blasphemous imprecations, to the fireplace. It is true that my parents were to some extent anti-clerical, but that was no more than a badge of their class at the time and one having little to do with religion. I will add, though, that in their case it had even less to do with the new tide of liberalism. My parents were never liberals in any sense of the word.

Despite these parental attitudes, the fasts and feasts of the Church calendar were strictly observed in our household, and I was required to attend holy services and to read the Bible. The church of my parents' choice was the chapel of a military school not far from our house. I repaired there for all regular devotions, and to the Kazansky Cathedral for important holidays. In all my years of obeisance, which lasted until I was fourteen or fifteen, I remember only a single experience I would call religious. One day in my eleventh or twelfth year, while waiting my turn before the confessional screen, I began to fumble impatiently with my belt buckle; I was wearing my school uniform, the black boots and black caftan with the silver buckle initialled 's.p.2.g.' – 'St Petersburg Second Gymnasium'. Suddenly the priest came from behind the screen, took my arms, and pushed them to my sides. His action was not reproving; indeed, he was so gentle and full of grace that I was for a moment overcome with a sense of what Henry Vaughan called 'the deep, but dazzling darkness'. Why has this one instance survived, complete in its frame, the hour of the day, the light in the room, the hushed sound of the confessor, the sudden extraordinary awareness of myself?

But at fifteen I began to criticize and rebel against the Church, and before leaving the gymnasium I had abandoned it completely, a rupture that was left unrepaired for almost three decades. I cannot now evaluate the events that, at the end of those thirty years, made me discover the necessity of religious belief. I was not reasoned into my disposition.

*

R.C. Do you remember any adolescent love affair?

I.S. What else does one remember so well? The most serious of them was cruelly one-sided. Her name was Lidia Valter, and she was the daughter of a doctor, a professor in a clinic located near our house. Guriy, as a schoolfriend of her brother, knew her first. I was soon visiting the Valters every day, and before long was madly in love with Lidia. When I could contain my passion no longer, I sent her a letter, declaring the fact. I did not sleep that night, waiting for her answer, and when, in the morning, her rosy-coloured envelope came, I trembled to open it. Her answer was kindly expressed, but it was not rosy. I was too young, and, as I myself thought, too insignificant. I did not see her again after that. Two years later (I was sixteen when Lidia rejected me) I fell in love with a schoolmate of Yekaterina Nosenko's, who came with her to Ustilug. Kuksina was her name. I thought her pretty, but it was a summer romance, forgotten in the first wind of autumn and with disillusioning rapidity. The object of my final adolescent affair was the Princess Putiatina, the half-sister of my closest friend, Stepan Stepanovich Mitusov. (Mitusov's mother had remarried; her second husband was

Prince Putiatin.) I was twenty-one then and, of course, vastly more sophisticated. There were no ecstatic declarations.

Stepan Mitusov was my closest friend during my first years as a composer. He, too, was several years older, but we were friends, rather than master and disciple, and he was an amateur of the arts. I had met him as far back as my sixteenth year, since he was an intimate of the Rimsky-Korsakov family, but our friendship developed only in the year after my father's death. (My father was semi-paralysed in his last year, and the whole family remained at home most of the time.) Mitusov became a kind of literary and theatrical tutor to me at one of the greatest moments of the Russian theatre. We saw the plays of Chekhov together (Olga Knipper in *The Cherry Orchard*, *Three Sisters*, *Uncle Vanya*) when these plays were enjoying their first great success, and we saw plays by Ostrovsky, Molière (in Russian), Shakespeare (Komisarjevsky as Ophelia and Desdemona, the latter spoken in Russian opposite Salvini, whose Othello was in Italian), Alexei Tolstoy (*Fyodor Ivanich*), Gorky (*The Lower Depths*), [Leo] Tolstoy (*The Power of Darkness*), Fonvizin Griboyedov (*The Misfortune of Being Clever*, which I saw again the other day in Hollywood, acted by Russian *émigrés*, two of whom were my gardeners). We frequented the permanent French theatre (Théâtre Michel), too, where Racine was performed rarely and bad modern plays often: Scribe, Mounet-Sully, Edmond Rostand, and worse. I remember seeing Lucien Guitry there.

Mitusov was also an amateur of 'modern' painting, but the only significant painting in Russia at that time was connected with Diaghilev's *Mir iskustva*. I saw pictures by Cézanne and Matisse in a show on loan from Moscow, but little other modern art until my first trip to Paris in 1910, at which time I acquired two Picassos, lost during World War II in my Ustilug home.[9]

9 A painter who much interested me was the Lithuanian M. K. Ciurlionis. I purchased a handsome picture by him in 1908, partly at the prompting of Alexander Benois. It depicted an assortment of pyramids, of a pale, nacreous tint, in flight towards a horizon, but in crescendo, not in the diminuendo of orthodox perspective. The picture was, in fact, part of my life, and I remember it very distinctly still, though it too was lost in Ustilug. Romain Rolland was interested in this artist's work, and I recall talking to him about it in Switzerland.

Mitusov was an amusing as well as a cultivated companion. He had a special talent for inventing new, but unprintable, words to old and respectable songs. I still remember some of these for *Die schöne Müllerin*.[10]

It was through Mitusov, incidentally, that I first met Nicolay Roerich, a blond-bearded, Kalmuck-eyed, pug-nosed man. I think that this was in 1904. His wife was a relative of Mitusov's, and I often saw them at Mitusov's St Petersburg house. Roerich claimed descent from Rurik, the Russo-Scandinavian *Ur*-Prince. Whether or not this was true (he looked Scandinavian, but one can't say such things any more), he was certainly a *grand seigneur*. I became quite fond of him in those early years, though not of his painting, which was a kind of advanced Puvis de Chavannes.

*

R.C. What are your memories of St Petersburg itself, the sights, sounds, smells of the city?

I.S. The sounds of St Petersburg still resonate in my memory. Whereas visual images are recalled, in my case, mainly by unexpected shifts and combinations of pressures, sounds, once registered, appear to remain in a state of immediacy; and, while my accounts of things seen are subject to exaggeration, mistaken observation, and the creations and distortions of memory itself (a memory being a whole cartel of invested interests), my recollections of sound must be faithful: I am proving as much, after all, whenever I compose.

St Petersburg street noises are especially vivid to me, perhaps for the reason that, to my confining indoor life, any sound of the outside world was memorable and attractive. The first such sounds to record themselves on my awareness were those of droshkies on cobblestone, or blockwood parquetry, pavements. Only a few horse carriages had rubber tyres, and these few were doubly expensive; the whole city crackled with the iron-hooped wheels of the others. I also remember the sound of horse-drawn streetcars and, in particular, the rail-scraping noise they made as they turned the corner near our house and whipped up speed to cross the Kryukov Canal bridge. The noises of wheels and horses and the shouts and

10 'A kangaroo is naked but has a pocket.'

whipcracks of coachmen must have penetrated my earliest dreams; they are, at any rate, my first memory of the streets of childhood.

The cries of vendors resound in my memory, especially those of the Tartars – although they did not so much cry as cluck. '*Halaat, halaat,*' they used to say, '*halaat*' being their word for a kind of dressing-gown. Only rarely did they speak Russian, and the low, froglike noises of their own language were an irresistible invitation to mockery. The Tartars, with their glabrous skins, in that heavily bewhiskered epoch, and their rigid Mohammedan mores – they never drank alcohol – were always objects of mystery and fascination to me. They carried their wares on head trays, which required them to wobble their shoulders and caracole their bodies in perfect balance; they were more interesting to watch than to hear. In contrast, the Russians would bawl every syllable too distinctly and with annoying deliberation. They sold *prianiki,* cookies of the kind the Germans call *Pfefferkuchen,* and *marozhennoyeh* (ice-cream) in the streets. '*Nye pozhelayet'l marozhennoyeh*' ('Would you like some ice-cream?') was a familiar fair-weather cry in our street. (It is still a cry, or rather a 'musical jingle', in my street in Hollywood, and every afternoon I await with dread the sound of the Good Humor man's truck.) Other edibles hawked in this way were cranberries, or *klyookva,* the chief produce of the tundra (I still remember the old peasant *baba* who sold them), as well as apples, pears, peaches and even oranges. Grapefruit and bananas were unknown in St Petersburg then, and I did not taste them until many years later, in Paris. But the most memorable street cry of all was that of the knife-grinder.

The loudest diurnal noises of the city were the cannonade of bells from the Nikolsky Cathedral, near our house, and the noon signal from the Peter and Paul Fortress – a timepiece for the whole city – but I recall with more nostalgia the sound of an accordion in a suburban street on a lonely Sunday afternoon, or the trilling wires of a balalaika orchestra in a restaurant or café. A final, *ad absurdum,* example of memorable *musique concrète* was the St Petersburg telephone. It produced an even ruder tintinnabulation than the one we suffer today. In fact, it inspired the opening bars of Act II of *The Nightingale.* The first telephone call I ever made was to Rimsky-Korsakov; the Stravinsky and Rimsky households were among the first in the city to install the nuisance.

A city is also remembered by its odours. In the case of St Petersburg, the predominant ones emanated from droshkies. They smelled agreeably of tar, of leather, and of their horses, but usually the strongest odour was that of the driver himself. ('*Que hombre*,' we would say of a particularly redolent coachman when the savours of unwash had perfused layers of clothing as thick as a mummy's and as infrequently changed.) My own olfactory bearings were conditioned by the felt *bashlyk,* or hood, I was obliged to wear during the winter months, and my palate still retains a strong residual reek of wet felt. The general odour of the city returned in the spring, with the re-liquefaction of the rivers and canals, but I am unable to describe it.

One other aroma that permeated St Petersburg, and, indeed, all Russia, was of the tobacco called Mahorka (from '*mejor*', 'the best'); it was originally imported, probably from Spain through Holland, by Peter the Great. I loved its smell, and I continued to smoke it in Switzerland during the war and for as long thereafter as I could buy it. When I moved to France in 1920 a large stock of it went with me. Perhaps this is the place to mention the tastes of the city, its typical degustations, the crayfish, the sterlets, the *zakousky* that never had quite the same taste anywhere else. Incidentally, my favourite St Petersburg restaurant was the Dominique. It was there that Diaghilev first met with me for a serious talk about my future.

While I do not claim reliability for my memory of colour, I remember St Petersburg as an ochre and blue city, in spite of such prominent red buildings as Rastrelli's baroque Winter Palace and the Anichkov Palace, built by Tsarina Elizabeth for her lover Razumovsky – yes, of the same family that produced Count Andrey of Beethoven fame and a personal friend of Mozart – later presented to Potemkin by Catherine the Great. Though I am unable to describe colours, I can say that when in Rome I am often reminded of my native city. The architecture, as well as the colour, of St Petersburg, was Italian, and not merely by imitation but by the direct work of such architects as Quarenghi and Trezzini; the latter designed the Summer Palace near where the Fontanka Canal joins the Neva. In the Kunstkammer adjoining the university, Lomonosov reformed the Russian language and conducted his experiments in physics and chemistry. The great chemist Mendeleyev worked in a nearby laboratory.[11]

I have often considered that the fact of my birth and upbringing in a neo-Italian, rather than a Slavic or Oriental, city must have some connection with the cultural direction of my later life. Italian stylization and craftsmanship can be found in any work of the Catherine-the-Great period, whether in a building, a statue, or an *objet d'art*. And the principal palaces were Italian not only in design but in material (marble). In the case of the original St Petersburg building stone, which was a local granite or a local brick, the outer surfaces were plastered, and painted Italian colours. My favourite buildings were the Bourse; Rastrelli's Smolny Cloister (Lenin's headquarters during the Revolution); the Alexandrinsky Drama Theatre (now the Pushkin Theatre); the Admiralty, with its handsome spire (by Trezzini); and, above all, the Mariyinsky Theatre. The latter was a delight to me, no matter how often I saw it, and to walk from my home through the Offitserskaya to the Ulitsa Glinka, where I could see its dome, was to be consumed with Petersburger pride. To enter the blue-and-gold interior of that heavily perfumed hall was, for me, like entering the most sacred of temples.

My first experience of a public musical performance was at the Mariyinsky Theatre. My impressions of it are mixed with what I have been told, of course, but as a child of seven or eight I was taken to see *A Life for the Tsar*. The spectacle of the theatre itself and of the audience bewildered me, and my mother said later that as I watched the stage, carried away by the sound of the orchestra – perhaps the greatest thrill of my life was the sound of that first orchestra – I asked her, as in Tolstoy, 'Which one is the theatre?'

St Petersburg was also a city of large, open piazzas. One of these was the Champs de Mars. The Mardi Gras festivities took place there, and puppet shows were part of the carnival entertainment. 'Russian Mountains', roller-coasters for sleighs, were fixtures in the Champs de Mars, and the whole populace came

11 Curiously, Stravinsky does not mention the Yusupov Palace, which was close to his home. Two Yusupov sons who lived there were his friends. [R.C.]

there to sleigh. A more beautiful spectacle was that of sleighs drawn by elks. These elegant creatures were brought to the city in carnival season by Finnish peasants, who sold rides on them. The elks were part of a realistic fairy-tale world whose lost beauty I tried to rediscover later in life in Hans Christian Andersen (*The Nightingale*, *The Fairy's Kiss*). I might also mention that I learned to bicycle in the Champs de Mars, though, of course, that was in a warmer season.

Another attractive piazza was the Haymarket, where hundreds of wains were stored to supply the city's huge horse population; to walk there was to be reminded of the countryside. But my most animated promenades in St Petersburg were on the Nevsky Prospekt, a wide avenue three miles long, and full of life and movement all the way. Here was the beautiful Stroganov Palace (by Rastrelli); the Lutheran Church (which Miliy Alexandrovich Balakirev, the composer, a devout Orthodoxist, used to call the upside-down trousers); the Kazansky Cathedral, with its semi-circle of columns in imitation of St Peter's in Rome; the Duma (City Hall); the Gastinny Dvor (Merchants' Court); the Public Library; the Drama Theatre; and the Anichkov Palace, Tsar Alexander III's residence. The Nevsky Prospekt was the avenue for military parades and assorted Imperial convocations. I remember being taken there in my early childhood to see the Tsar, sometimes with visiting heads of state. I saw Sadi Carnot of France in one such procession; later he became famous because of his assassination. Incidentally, Debussy once told me that he had composed a part of *Pelléas* in a room wallpapered with a pattern that included oval portraits of Sadi Carnot.

The Nevsky Prospekt was also the principal arena for amorous assignations. At night it was patrolled by '*grues*' whose chief customers were officers and students. Lev Bakst wrote to me to me in Morges in 1915: '. . . you will remember how in the Nevsky Prospekt, on a beautiful, white, Russian night, the purple-painted whores yelled after you, "Men, give us cigarettes."' The '*Puffmutters*' in the brothels were from Riga.

When I try to recall St Petersburg, two different cities come to mind, the one gas-lighted, the other electric; the smell of gas and kerosene lamps pervades all memories of my first eight years. But I shall talk about my memories of St Petersburg interiors on another occasion, for life there, more than in any other city, was indoors. I remember how I used to blow on a five-kopeck piece to warm it, then hold it to the frost-covered window of my room, where it melted through to a view of the world. Electric lights – or, rather, oscillating carbon arcs – first appeared in the Nevsky Prospekt. They were pale, but St Petersburg was too far north to require much lighting: the winters glared with snow and the springs were bright with the aurora borealis. On one May night, while preparing for my university examinations, I was able to work until 4 A.M. with no other illumination than these 'northern lights'.

St Petersburg was also a city of islands and rivers. Most of the latter were called Neva – Great Neva, Small Neva, Great Small Neva, Middle Neva, and so on – but the other names escape my memory. The movements of boats and the life of the harbour are less significant in my recollections than one would expect, because of the long, icebound winters. I remember the reappearance of boats in the canals in our sudden Russian spring, but the picture of them is less vivid than that of the waterways used as thoroughfares for sleighs.

The most striking change of décor came at Easter. The week before Holy Week was known as Willow Week, when brightly beribboned bunches of willows were sold all over the city. The willow replaced the palm on Palm Sunday.

St Petersburg is so much a part of my life that I am almost afraid to look further into myself, lest I discover how much of me is still joined to it. But even these few reminiscences must show that it is dearer to my heart than any other city in the world.

R.C. What did you love most in Russia?
I.S. The violent Russian spring that seemed to begin in an hour and was like the whole earth cracking. That was the most wonderful event of every year of my childhood.

To ice-skate on the Neva was one of the greatest childhood pleasures, but to sleigh-ride across the frozen river in the tow of Finnish peasants who came to St Petersburg to earn a few winter kopecks was an even greater joy. The ice was several feet thick – a fact that will help you imagine the crash it made in that first hour of the spring thaw, when the noise was so great we could hardly talk.

I was always profoundly moved, too, by one observance of the church year, the Epiphany ceremony during which a cross was baptized in the Neva by Tsar Alexander III. Unlike most official church holidays, which had degenerated into something like national bank holidays, the Epiphany was an occasion of real solemnity. In this season the river was a road of ice, but a hole was cut, and through it the Tsar fished a large silver cross on a large silver chain. Prayers were said, and all present knelt in the snow or on the ice. This spectacle was so impressive that I think even the most agnostic spectator must have been moved. The Tsar and his officers in their grey uniforms and fur caps – the Tsar's cap had a red band with a gold cross on it – the Metropolitan, the archimandrites and attendant sacerdotes, and the crowds of people, all were strikingly colourful, in contrast to the winter sky and the white surface of the river. The whole scene is as alive to me now as it was then.

I remember also how I loved to watch the gulls, especially when the water rose in the rivers and canals; when the city stood up to its nose in water, the fish swam closer to the surface and the birds gyrated lower. A child does not wonder why the sight of gulls should move him so deeply, but an old man knows that they are reminders of death and were such even when I watched them by the Neva one November afternoon when I was seven or eight.

I don't know why I am old, if I must be (I don't want to be), or if 'I' am the same person. All my life I have thought of myself as 'the youngest one', and now, suddenly, I read and hear about myself as 'the oldest one'. And then I wonder at these distant images of myself. I wonder if memory is true, and I know it cannot be, but that one lives by memory, nevertheless, and not by truth. Memories are 'safeties', of course, far safer than the 'originals', and growing more so all the time. Moreover, the wrong ones can usually be chased away when they turn up, and the right ones again rummaged for in the favoured reliquaries. But through the crack of light in my bedroom door, time dissolves and I see again the images of my lost world. Mama has gone to her room, my brother is asleep in the other bed, and all is still in the house. The lamp from the street reflects in the room, and by it I recognize the image as myself.

Even now I am able to sleep at night only when a ray of light enters my room from a closet or adjacent chamber. I do not know the origin of this need, though it must extend from earliest infancy. I fail to remember any night lamp in the corridor beyond the room I shared with my brother, and I am certain the traditional oil-wick was not burned in front of the only icon in our house, which was in my mother's room. The light I still seek to be reminded of must have come from either the porcelain stove – incalescent at bedtime – in the corner of the room or from the street lamp outside my window on the Kryukov Canal. As the air-holes of the stove sometimes formed menacing faces, I think the street light must have been the reassuring one. Whatever it was, and whatever bogies it kept at bay, this umbilical cord of illumination still enables me, at seventy-eight, to re-enter the world of safety and enclosure I knew at seven or eight.

R.C. Do you remember your first attendance at a concert?

I.S. The first concert of which I have any recollection was the occasion of the première of a symphony by Glazunov. I was eleven at the time, and Glazunov was the heralded new composer. He had extraordinary powers of ear and memory, but it was going too far to assume from this that he must be a new Mozart: the sixteen-year-old prodigy was already a cut-and-dried academician. I was not inspired by the concert.

R.C. Do you remember your first ballet performance?

I.S. At the age of seven or eight, I was taken to see *The Sleeping Beauty*. (I realize now that I was older than this when I saw the opera *A Life for the Tsar*.) I was enchanted by the ballet, but had been prepared for what I saw, ballet being of the utmost importance in our culture and a familiar subject to me from my earliest childhood. I was able to identify the dance positions and steps, and I knew the plot and the music long in advance. Moreover, Marius Petipa, the choreographer, was a friend of my father, and I had seen him several times myself. Of the performance, I remember only my musical impressions, and perhaps those are really my parents' impressions, repeated to me afterward. But I do know that I was excited by the dance, and that I applauded it with all my strength. If I could transport myself back to that night seventy years ago, I would do so primarily to satisfy my curiosity about the musical tempi, for I am always interested in tempos in other periods.

R.C. What were your personal ties with the Tchaikovsky family?
I.S. Tchaikovsky had given an inscribed photograph to my father for his performance of the dramatic role of the monk in *The Sorceress*; the photograph became the most treasured object in my father's studio. Tchaikovsky has left an account of one of my father's performances, incidentally, in a letter to Mme von Meck (18 October 1887): 'The best of the singers were Slavina and Stravinsky. A unique burst of applause and unanimous approval from the whole audience was evoked by Stravinsky in the second act monologue; his performance should be a pattern for all future productions.' Slavina was the leading contralto of the Mariyinsky, and a good friend of my father. I remember her visits to our house, accompanied by a mysterious masculine lady friend, Kotchubei, a name of such high aristocracy that to pronounce a title before it was unthinkable. I should also mention that when Tchaikovsky died, two cousins of my mother, the Counts Littke, were by his bedside to keep the death vigil with him, and that my father was one of the composer's pallbearers, the one chosen to place the wreath on the sarcophagus.

Modest Tchaikovsky, Pyotr Ilyich's brother, bore a striking resemblance to the composer, and I, of course, saw the composer in him. I was introduced to Modest about fifteen years after Pyotr Ilyich's death, at an exhibition of Diaghilev's *Mir iskustva*. In the years following, especially in Rome during the completion of *Petrushka,* I came to know him well. I also knew Anatol, another of Tchaikovsky's brothers, whose physical resemblance to the composer, however, was slight. My father and Anatol were schoolfriends, and when I met Anatol in Vienna in January 1913, after many years, he talked to me about my father. Incidentally, I remember seeing the Archduke Ferdinand in Vienna then, at a performance of *Petrushka*. His assassination at Sarajevo a year and a half later ignited World War I. I came to Vienna by way of Budapest, where I saw the whole royal family in colourful Hungarian uniform, at a performance of *Firebird*.[12]

R.C. On 29 September 1893, you attended a performance of Glinka's opera *Ruslan and Lyudmila*, in which your father performed. It was less than a month before Tchaikovsky's death. Was this the occasion when you saw him in the foyer during the intermission?

I.S. Yes. It was the most exciting night of my life, and completely unexpected because I had no hopes of attending the opera at all; eleven-year-olds were rarely seen at grand, late-night social events. The *Ruslan* semi-centennial had been declared a national holiday,[13] and my father must have considered the occasion important for my education. Just before theatre time Bertha burst into my room saying, 'Hurry, hurry, we are going, too.' I dressed quickly and climbed into the carriage by the side of my mother. I remember that the Mariyinsky was lavishly decorated that night, and pleasantly perfumed, and I could find my seat even now – indeed, the eye of my memory leaps to it like filings to a magnet. A ceremony and a parade had preceded the performance. Poor Glinka, who was only a kind of Russian Rossini, had been Beethovenized and nationally monumented. I watched the performance through my mother's mother-of-pearl lorgnette binoculars. In the first interval we stepped from our loge into a small foyer behind. A few people were already walking there. Suddenly my mother said to me, 'Igor, look, there is Tchaikovsky.' I looked and saw a man with white hair, large shoulders, a corpulent back, and this image has remained in the retina of my memory all my life.

A party was given in our house after the performance, with the bust of Glinka that stood on a pedestal in my father's music

12 Stravinsky does not say that he criticized Pierre Monteux so harshly for the way he performed the piece that the conductor resigned and Diaghilev had to plead with him to complete the tour. The *Petrushka* in Vienna provoked another scandal when Stravinsky shouted at the orchestra during the rehearsal for its execrable playing and the orchestra walked out, saying '*schmutzige musik*' ('dirty music'). Again, Diaghilev prevailed and the show went on, but during it Stravinsky took a train back to Clarens. [R.C.]

13 Stravinsky is mistaken: the semi-centennial actually took place a year later, but he was present then as well. [R.C.]

room wreathed for the occasion and ringed around with candles. I remember also that toasts were downed in vodka, and that a large dinner was consumed. What I cannot explain is how I happened to be present, for the hour must have been late indeed; *Ruslan* is a five-act opera, and the intervals at the Mariyinsky were long enough for the consumption of successive courses of dinner between acts. The performance began at eight o'clock, and could not have ended before twelve.

Tchaikovsky's death two weeks later was a terrible blow to me. The composer's fame was so great that as soon as he was known to have caught cholera, the Government issued bulletins about the progress of his illness. Not everyone was aware of him, though. When I went to school and awesomely announced to my classmates that Tchaikovsky was dead, one of them wanted to know what grade he was in. I remember two memorial concerts. The first, on 6 November, was conducted by Nápravník in the Réunion des Nobles. Besides the *Pathétique* Symphony, the programme included the *Romeo and Juliet* Overture and the Violin Concerto played by Leopold Auer. The second, on 30 November, in the Conservatory, was partly conducted by Rimsky-Korsakov, partly by Blumenfeld. (I still have my ticket for this.) The programme included *Francesca da Rimini* and the Fourth Symphony. Tchaikovsky's portrait was on the cover of the latter programme, framed in black.

*

R.C. When did you first become aware of your vocation as a composer?

I.S. All I remember is that these thoughts started very early in my childhood, long before any serious musical study.

R.C. Did your parents recognize your musical talent?

I.S. No. The only member of the family who believed I had any was my uncle Alexander Yelachich. I think my father judged my possibilities as a musician from his own experience and decided that the musical life would be too difficult for me. I can hardly blame him. After all, I had written nothing before his death and though I was progressing in my piano technique, it was clear that I would not become a virtuoso performer on the instrument.

Alexander Yelachich had married my mother's sister Sophie five years before my father's marriage. His five children were therefore just enough older than I was to ensure that I suffered an ample amount of taunting and misery. I still resent the way they despised me because of their superior age, and I am even now a little triumphant that I have outlived them all. But Uncle Yelachich himself was kind to me. He owned vast farms and forests in the Samara Government, east of the Volga, where he invited us to spend our summers with him. I composed my first large-scale work there, the lost – fortunately lost – Piano Sonata.[14]

The four-day trips on the Volga to Pavlovka, as the Yelachich Samara estate was called, were among the happiest days of my life. I made the first two trips with my parents in 1883 and 1886, but of that I remember only a portrait of the Tsar on the wall of our state-room, which was supposed to have made me cry 'conductor', for his cap and uniform were like those of a railway conductor. My next and last excursions came in 1903 and 1904, and my companion on the first of these was Vladimir Rimsky-Korsakov. We heralded his father with postcards from each of the boat's stopping places: Rybinsk (literally, 'fish-town'), a white and gold city with monasteries and glittering churches, which looked like a set of *Tsar Saltan,* as one came upon it round a sudden bend in the river; Jaroslav, with its blue and gold churches and its yellow, Italian-style office buildings. I saw coloured slides of Jaroslav recently in Manila, at the home of United States Ambassador Charles Bohlen. At Nizhni-Novgorod, surrounded by mendicant monks, we walked to little booths where we bought and drank kumiss, mare's milk.

Uncle Yelachich idolized Beethoven and was, I think, a good guide in my early understanding of the composer. There were two portraits on the wall of my uncle's study, Renan – Uncle Yelachich was a liberal – and Beethoven. The latter was a copy of the Waldmüller portrait. It seemed to contradict the prevalent hero-worshipping notion of Beethoven. In fact, as a small child, I did not know it was Beethoven until one day, while playing in the sand dunes of the Alexander Park, I saw an old woman whose face was exactly the face on my uncle's wall, which

14 This Sonata is now published by Faber Music. [R.C.]

prompted me to ask my uncle who the woman was. In any case, I did not hero-worship Beethoven, nor have I ever done so, and the nature of Beethoven's talent and work are more 'human' and more comprehensible to me than are, say, the talents and works of more 'perfect' composers like Bach and Mozart; I think I know something of how Beethoven composed. I have little enough of Beethoven in me, alas, but people have found that I have some.

R.C. Did anyone in your family beside your father possess musical ability?

I.S. I think not. At least I never heard my father or mother claim any musical talent for their parents or grandparents, and I know that my father considered his own musical ear and memory as a kind of supra-Mendelian phenomenon. I should add, however, that my mother was an accomplished pianist and a good sight-reader, and that she was keenly interested in music all her life.

R.C. Who were your earliest music teachers?

I.S. My first piano mistress was a certain Alexandra Snetkova, from the St Petersburg Conservatory. She had been recommended to my father by Professor Soloviev, also of the Conservatory, the composer of *Cordelia*, an opera in which my father had sung a leading role. I was nine then, and I must have remained with her for two years. I remember her telling me about the preparations at the Conservatory for Tchaikovsky's funeral, but I do not remember having learned anything about music from her.

My first harmony teacher was Fyodor Stepanovich Akimenko, himself a pupil of Balakirev and Rimsky. A composer of some originality, Akimenko was regarded as a promising talent; I remember that when I arrived in Paris for *Firebird*, French musicians surprised me by enquiring about his compositions. I found him unsympathetic, and I did not remain with him long.

My next teacher, Vasily Pavlovich Kalafati, was a small, black-faced Greek with huge black moustaches. Kalafati was also a composer, though his gifts for teaching were stronger and more pronounced. I did the usual exercises with him, the species of counterpoint, invention and fugue, the harmonization of chorale melodies. He was a most exacting reviewer of these exercises, particularly about part-writing, and scornful of the 'interesting new chords' young composers cared about most. He was also a silent man who rarely said more than 'yes', 'no', 'good', 'bad'. When pressed beyond these monosyllables, he would answer, 'But you should hear why yourself.' Kalafati taught me to appeal to my ear as the first and last test, and for that I am grateful. I worked with him for more than two years.

Much of my free time during the period of preliminary study with Akimenko and Kalafati was spent at rehearsals and performances of operas. My father had obtained a pass for me that allowed me to attend almost all rehearsals at the Mariyinsky, and by the time I was sixteen I would spend as many as five or six nights a week at the opera. Rimsky was often to be seen there, though I did not yet speak to him. I did come to know many of the principal singers and orchestra players, and of the latter I became especially friendly with the two first violinists, Victor Valter and Volf-Israel. The latter conspired to help me obtain cigarettes. I began to smoke at the age of fourteen, but my parents discovered this only two years later. One day Volf-Israel boldly borrowed a cigarette from Rimsky-Korsakov himself and gave it to me, saying, 'Here is a composer's cigarette.' I smoked it anyway – there are no souvenirs pressed between the covers of my books.

R.C. Would you describe your piano lessons with Leokadiya Kashperova?

I.S. She was an excellent pianist and a blockhead, a not unusual combination. By which I mean that her aesthetics and her bad taste were impregnable, but her technique was of a high order. She was well known in St Petersburg, and Rimsky had praised her; though her name would not appear in *Grove* or *Riemann*, I think she might have been listed in a Russian dictionary of the time. She talked endlessly about her teacher, Anton Rubinstein; I was attentive to this because I had seen Rubinstein in his coffin and could not forget this memory. I was somewhat prepared for this experience because at an even earlier age I had seen the dead Tsar Alexander III – a yellow, waxen, uniformed doll – lying in state in the SS Peter and Paul Cathedral. Rubinstein was white, but with a thick black mane. The body was in full dress, as though for a concert, and the hands were folded over a cross. I did not see Tchaikovsky in his coffin, incidentally, because my parents thought the weather dangerously bad for me to risk going out.

I learned to play the Mendelssohn G minor Concerto with Kashperova, and many sonatas by Clementi and Mozart, as well as sonatas and other pieces by Haydn, Beethoven, Schubert, and Schumann. Chopin was forbidden, and she tried to discourage my interest in Wagner. Nevertheless, I knew all of Wagner's works from the piano scores, and when I was sixteen or seventeen, with the money to buy them, from the orchestra scores. She and I played Rimsky's operas together four-hands, and I remember deriving much pleasure this way from his opera *Christmas Eve.*

Kashperova's only idiosyncrasy as a teacher was in forbidding the use of pedals; I had to sustain with my fingers, like an organist – an omen, perhaps, as I have never been a pedal composer. I am most in Kashperova's debt for something she would not have appreciated. Her narrowness and her formulas greatly increased the supply of bitterness that accumulated in my soul until, in my mid-twenties, I broke loose and revolted from her and from every stultification in my studies, my schools and my family. The real answer to your questions about my childhood and youth is that it was a period of waiting for the moment when I could send everyone and everything connected with it to hell.

*

R.C. Do you remember anything of your early childhood in L'zy?
I.S. The name L'zy actually designated two villages facing each other across a river, Greater and Lesser L'zy. The L'zys were about a hundred and seventy kilometres from St Petersburg, in the Pskov District, and about forty kilometres from Ustilug. The L'zys were surrounded by birch forests and the cool breezes from the nearby Valdye Hills made them popular summer resorts; an outflux of Petersburgers retired there for the hot months, my parents among them. Rimsky-Korsakov's favourite summer home, in Vechasa, was only six kilometres from L'zy; Lyubensk, where he died, 8 July 1908, was not far from Vechasa.

A suspicion that I might possess musical talent was first kindled in L'zy. The peasant women of L'zy sang an attractive and restful song on their way home in the evening from the fields, a song I have recalled in the early hours of evening at odd times throughout my life. They sang it in octaves – unharmonized, of course – and their high, shrill voices sounded like a billion bees. I was never a precocious child, and I have never enjoyed extraordinary powers of memory, but this song was branded in my ear the first time I heard it. My nurse brought me home from the village, where we had been perambulating one afternoon, and my parents, who were then trying to coax me to talk, asked me what I had seen there. I said I had seen the peasants and heard them sing, then sang what they had sung. Everyone was astonished and impressed, and my father remarked that I had a wonderful ear. I was happy about this, of course, and must have purred with pride. Whether my career should be attributed entirely to the early realization that love and praise can be won through a display of musical talent is another matter.

Though I spent only one summer there, that of 1884, my memory of the L'zys is not mere hearsay. I returned in 1904 on my way home from Samara, where Vladimir, Rimsky's son, who had been with me, urged me to accompany him to the house of his father, who came to Vechasa because of his asthma. It was at this time that Rimsky encouraged me to take music lessons. He gave me pages from *Pan Voyevoda* to orchestrate, the opera he was then composing, and his criticisms of my efforts constituted my first lessons with him. He could hardly have been kinder or more helpful to me than he was during that week, both in and out of music. Only rarely ever again would I see him in such a happy mood. I told him about the summer of my infancy in L'zy, and we went together to look for my father's house, even though, of course, I would not have recognized it if we had found it. But we did come upon a deserted cottage with a piano in it, which Rimsky struck and declared to be 'a piano in A'.

You may imagine how I remembered Rimsky from those happy summer days of 1904 when four years later I journeyed to L'zy to meet his coffin and accompany it back to St Petersburg. I had received the news of his death in Ustilug and telegraphed his sons to meet me in Balagoyeh, the railway terminal.[15] From

15 Stravinsky's account of his route to meet the composer's sons and escort the body to St Petersburg for the funeral and burial is still controversial. The

there we drove together by droshky to L'zy, where I saw the face I had kissed only a short time before in St Petersburg, and the mute lips that had blessed me as I undertook the composition of *Fireworks*.

*

R.C. What do you recall of your childhood summers in Pechisky?

I.S. My memories of it are, in the main, *triste*, and I revive them with little pleasure. Pechisky is nevertheless important in the landscapes of my past.

My mother's sister Yekaterina owned a large estate there, where I spent the summers of 1891 and 1892. I remember it as a dull place, especially as compared to Yarmolintsi, thirty miles away, which was lively, picturesque, and renowned for its fairs. Indeed, the great fair at Nizhni-Novgorod, which I saw later, did not impress me more than the exhibitions of peasant handicrafts and the competitions of livestock and especially grains, for Yarmolintsi was in the mid-ocean of Ukrainian wheat. At fair time, too, the peasant costumes were brightly bedizened, and the people wearing them were equally gay and attractive. The dancing contests were my chief delight at these fairs. I first saw the *presyatka* (heel dance) there, which I later used in the coachmen scene of *Petrushka*. The *kazachok* (kicking dance) and the *trepak* were also incorporated in *Petrushka*. I heard much peasant music in Pechisky, too, though most of it was produced by accordions. Gypsy camps existed in the neighbourhood, but I did not hear any gypsy music. My parents had so frightened me of gypsies that I am still afraid.

Pechisky was not a happy home for me. My parents openly showed their favouritism for my oldest brother, Roman. I was starved for affection, but none of the adults around me noticed, which may be why, all my life, I have been quicker to give my own love to children and animals than to adults. Aunt Yekaterina was an orgulous and despotic woman who never

---

closest and most convenient itinerary from Ustilug would have been via Brest-Litovsk and the Warsaw railroad. The Balagoyeh station was some two hundred and fifty kilometres away, a long distance to have travelled in a horse-drawn carriage, as Stravinsky claimed. [R.C.]

managed to show me any kindness; though, to be just, her supply was too alarmingly small to allow of any partition. In fact her energies were entirely occupied at the time with the task of ruining the life of her daughter-in-law, a charming lady, born Lyudmilla Lyadov, the niece of the composer Anatoly Konstantinovich Lyadov.[16] Aunt Yekaterina had confiscated Lyudmilla's child, Alexei, after the death of her own son, Lyudmilla's husband, a situation that could be compared to that of Beethoven and his nephew, except for the fact that Aunt Yekaterina was totally without musical talent. Even so, she was not the most terrible of the perils of Pechisky. That distinction goes to a Miss Pavla Vasilievna Vinogradova, my governess and Guriy's, the most persequent pest of my early years.

We never had much success with governesses. The first one I can remember was French and good-looking, for which reason, I suppose, she did not last. The second was English, but I recall nothing else about her. England was succeeded by Switzerland, in the person of an aggressively ugly spinster who was rather too interested to see us boys into the bathtub. When my parents discovered this and others of her inclinations, she was replaced by Vinogradova, a bluestocking who tortured us with studies.

The least feminine woman I had ever seen, Vinogradova wore her hair in a *bubikopf*. Her hands were damp and red, her nails nibbled. She was in a perpetual state of agitation, and if Aunt Yekaterina or a visitor happened to ask me a question about my studies, she would stand by, glare at me, and nervously midwife the answer. One incident from the time of Vinogradova's tutelage still fills me with humiliation, and I recall it with discomfort even now, through the far end of the telescope of memory. One evening at dinner, my father, who rarely spoke to me, suddenly asked me what new French word I had learned. I blushed, hesitated, blurted out 'parqwa' (*pourquoi*), and then started to cry. Everyone laughed and made fun of me, my parents, my brothers, Bertha, the virago Vinogradova, and even Simon Ivanovich, who was serving the meal. Three-quarters of a century have

16 The Stravinsky family archives in St Petersburg seem to indicate that Stravinsky has confused Lyadov's niece with Lyudmila Konstantinova Romazansky, the widow of Kirill Nicolayevich Yelachich. [R.C.]

passed since then, and the laughers are all dead, but I cannot forget, and to forgive has no meaning now. (Is this incident a contributing cause of the headaches I still sometimes suffer at dinnertime – an example of Freud's *Entfremdungs* effect?)

I did not return to Pechisky in the summers after 1892. My parents allowed me to accompany them to Germany instead, and I was quite content to leave Aunt Yekaterina's hospitalities to my brothers. The last time I saw Pechisky was in 1897. I was with my parents in Bad Homburg when news was received from Pechisky of the death of my elder brother, Roman [on 10 June]. We took the first train there. I remember translating for my father, who spoke Polish, but no German, in the Vienna railway station. We were met at Proskurov by droshkies, and we drove the fifteen versts to Aunt Yekaterina's house in silence. Roman is buried in Pechisky.

R.C. Didn't you also meet your future wife, Yekaterina Nosenko, in Pechisky?

I.S. Yes.[17] She was my first cousin and came into my life as a kind of long-wanted sister. I was a deeply lonely child, in my tenth year, and I always wanted a sister of my own. Yekaterina was my dearest friend and playmate in Pechisky, and from then until we grew into our marriage.

Yekaterina was born in Kiev in 1881 and spent her childhood there. From 1903 to 1906, the three years before our marriage, she lived in Paris and studied singing. She had a light but pleasing soprano voice, and music was of the greatest importance in her life. She was gifted also as a calligrapher of music notation, and in later years she became my best copyist; I still possess an elegant score of *Renard* in her hand. Her sister Lyudmila was said to be 'musical' – preposterous expression – but it took her and the rest of her so-called 'musical' family long enough to recognize any of my music as such.

Our engagement was announced in Ustilug in October 1905. Since an Imperial statute forbade marriage between first cousins, we had to find a kind of Graham Greene bootleg priest – one who would marry us without asking for the documents that

---

17 Actually they had 'met' as babies in August 1883 in Kiev. [R.C.]

would have exposed the true relationship between us. The corruptible cleric was discovered in the village of Novaya Derevnya (New Village), near St Petersburg. We drove there in two droshkies on 24 January (11, Old Style) 1906, and were married at noon. No relatives were present, and our only attendants were my best men, Andrey and Vladimir Rimsky-Korsakov, who knelt with us and held the gold and velvet wedding crown over our heads. When we reached home after the ceremony, Rimsky was waiting at the door. He blessed me, holding an icon over my head that he then gave me as a wedding present. Another of his wedding presents was the gift of his teaching – though he had also never accepted money from me before my marriage. We left for the Finland Station, where we took the train to Imatra, a small Finnish Niagara Falls, dreamily populated by newlyweds. Imatra was frosty and white, and though the larger cascades still poured over the cliffs, the smallest were hibernating as icicles. We stayed at Imatra for two weeks, photographing the falls and sleigh-riding. The music of the *Faune et bergère* was growing in my head, and when we returned to St Petersburg I began to write it down.

*

R.C. Would you describe the village and people of Ustilug, and the journey to Ustilug from St Petersburg? Also, what music did you compose there?

I.S. *'Usti'* means 'mouth', and Ustilug is the name of a village at the confluence of a small river, the Luga, and a larger river, the Bug. But 'village' is too grand, Ustilug being no more than a *mistyechko*, 'a little place', just large enough to warrant a postal clerk and a policeman. In the 1890s, Dr Gabriel Nosenko, my mother's brother-in-law (and from 1906 my father-in-law) purchased a distillery there and several thousand hectares of land. This Nosenko estate was surrounded by forests, rivers and wheatfields, and its climate was salubrious, for which reason I was sent there with my brother Guriy during the summers of 1896–1900. I say 'sent' because my brother and I lived there alone with my Nosenko cousins, Yekaterina and Lyudmila, while my parents went to Pechisky. We were looked after by our cousins' aunt, Sofia Velsovsky, a harsh woman, and by two prurient

Polish housemaids. Yekaterina's mother had died of tuberculosis.

After my marriage I built a house directly on the Luga, about one kilometre from Ustilug proper. The features of this house, which was constructed after my own plans, were two large fireplaces with two chimneys, and a riverside balcony. From 1907, when it was completed, until 1914, when I was cut off from Russia by the war, I lived in it for at least part of every summer. Ustilug was a haven for composing, and I had my Bechstein grand piano moved there from St Petersburg. Indeed, little else was to be done there, for though I became a boating buff and went rowing every day on the river, I did not learn to swim. My illness-fearing parents did not want me to swim because I had suffered severely from pleurisy as a child.

Ustilug was two-and-a-half days from St Petersburg by train, but the carriages were wide, the pace slow, and the trip was quite comfortable. The terminus in St Petersburg was the Warsaw Station, an Italian-style building that was also the point of departure for Berlin and Paris. The more luxurious trains had private rooms, but compartments could be reserved even in coaches. The buffet meals served at appointed places along the route were the most enjoyable part of the journey. The waiters, most of them Tartars, wore long white aprons and, from the first puff of the approaching locomotive, scurried about like attendants in an emergency hospital. The food was excellent, too, and in Russia to compare an ordinary restaurant to a railway station restaurant was a compliment indeed. Crimean wines and champagnes were available at these buffets, as was an abundance of good things to eat. The principal stops were Brest-Litovsk and, another 140 versts farther south, Kovel. At Kovel, the passenger had to change to a smaller line for Vladimir-Volynsk. From Vladimir-Volynsk to Ustilug, a distance of 12 versts, the only transportation was a horse-drawn carriage and, after 1912, an automobile. I myself remember this as a treacherous ride because of the sandy road; I was once stuck there in an automobile.

The Ustilug population – about four thousand souls – was entirely Jewish, a rabbinical community out of Isaac Babel and Chagall, and the cosiest, most affectionate community imaginable. The men wore beards, *peysy* ringlets, and long *lapserdak* coats. It could not have been a strictly Orthodox community, since I remember a wedding at which the guests danced with kerosene lamps in their hands instead of candelabra. I was popular with the villagers because the Nosenkos had given them land for a cemetery and because my wife founded a village clinic and appointed a doctor to direct it. The local Inspector of Forests and the doctor, a Polish intellectual named Stanislaw Bachnitzky, a friend and correspondent of Lenin's theorist, G. V. Plekhanov, were our only society. I was especially fond of one man in Ustilug, a Mr Bernstein, who had emigrated to America, made money, and returned to become the proudest resident of the *mistyechko* and the owner of its most prosperous business, a brick factory. Mr Bernstein was better known as 'Zolatiyeh Zuby' – 'Golden Teeth' – but though much gold work was visible in his mouth, the reference was more than dental. I purchased the bricks and other materials for my new house from him, and I remember the day he came to complete the agreement. I began rather rudely to discuss his prices with my cousin-in-law, in French, and in front of him, when suddenly he said, 'Gospodin Stravinsky, you can speak French and I won't understand, but I must warn you not to speak English', which I thought a clever rebuke. I fail to remember whether it was he or another of the villagers who gave me a violin, but, in any case, I learned to play the violin a little in Ustilug.

My Symphony in E♭ and two of my piano études were composed in the old Nosenko house in Ustilug. The *Fireworks*, the *Chant funèbre* for Rimsky-Korsakov, the first act of *The Nightingale*, and the *Zvezdolikiy* were written in the new house, the last piece immediately before, and, briefly, during the composition of *The Rite of Spring*. I cannot say exactly how much of *The Rite* itself dates from Ustilug, as I no longer possess any of my sketches, but I do know that I discovered the opening bassoon melody shortly before leaving there for Clarens.

*

R.C. Do you remember your first meeting with Rimsky-Korsakov?

I.S. I met him formally during a stage rehearsal of *Sadko*, though, of course, I had seen him publicly and privately countless times in the decade before that.[18] I was fifteen at the time of the *Sadko* meeting, but I cannot remember the particulars of it – perhaps because the then avatar of Russian music was a familiar figure to me, or perhaps because I would have regarded the meeting as inevitable anyway. But at *Sadko,* the atmosphere of the theatre and the excitement and thrill of watching a new opera in rehearsal were engaging all my emotions, and even the composer could not impress me as much as his opera. Rimsky may have deigned to notice me because of my father, whose performance in the drunken scene in Borodin's *Prince Igor* was one of the most successful characterizations in that opera; a similar scene in *Sadko* had perhaps been composed expressly for him.

Nor can I say exactly when I first saw Rimsky-Korsakov. I have tried to sort my earliest images of him but cannot fix them in any certain order. When a relationship is as close as mine was with him, chronological threads are difficult to establish – besides which, I am able to enter my memory only piecemeal and unexpectedly. I dimly remember Rimsky coming to our house to ask my father to sing Varlaam in his version of *Boris Godunov,* and I have another vague picture of him, from about the same time, as he entered the Conservatory in winter wearing a *boyar* hat and *shuba* (fur coat). I was five or six when the Conservatory was built, and this must have been only shortly after that.

My close ties with Rimsky were established in the summer of 1900, in Neckargemünd, near Heidelberg, where Andrey Rimsky-Korsakov was a student. I was vacationing with my parents at nearby Bad Wildungen, when Andrey's brother, Vladimir, a classmate of mine at St Petersburg University, invited me to stay with him. During this visit I showed Rimsky my first compositions, short piano pieces, 'andantes', 'melodies', and so forth. I was ashamed of myself for wasting his time, but I was also extremely eager to become his pupil. He looked at these tender efforts of mine with great patience, and then said that if

18 Stravinsky first saw Rimsky-Korsakov in 1886 at the opening of the new Conservatory with the production of his version of *Boris Godunov.* The première of *Sadko* was in Moscow, and the St Petersburg première took place in the Great Hall of the Conservatory, produced by Saava Mamantov's Russian Private Opera. [R.C.]

42

I would continue my work with Kalafati, I might also come to him twice a week for lessons. I was overjoyed, so much so that not only did I apply myself to Kalafati's exercises, but I even filled several notebooks with them by the end of the summer. Rimsky was careful, then and later, not to compliment me or encourage me with a loose use of the word 'talent'. In fact, the only composer I ever heard him refer to as talented was his son-in-law, Maximilian Steinberg, one of those ephemeral, prize-winning, front-page types, in whose eyes conceit forever burns, like an electric light in daytime.

R.C. What are your present feelings, personal or otherwise, towards Rimsky-Korsakov?

I.S. After fifty years, it is impossible to discriminate between memories personal and impersonal. All memories are personal, yet mine are so far removed from the person that they cannot be told otherwise than impersonally. Few people can have been as close to Rimsky as I was. After the death of my father, he was like an adopted parent. We try not to judge our parents, but judge them, nonetheless, and often unjustly. I hope I am not unjust to Rimsky.

A great difference existed between the Rimsky of the *Autobiography,* which is the one most people know, and the Rimsky who was my teacher. Readers of that well-written but matter-of-fact book think of him as someone not very easy with his sympathy and not abundantly generous or kind. Moreover, the artist in the *Autobiography* was sometimes shockingly shallow in his artistic aims. The shallow I cannot counter, for obviously there was nothing profound either in Rimsky's nature or in his music, but my Rimsky was deeply sympathetic, deeply and unshowingly generous, and unkind only to admirers of Tchaikovsky. Rimsky himself could not conceive of Tchaikovsky otherwise than as a rival. Tchaikovsky had been more influential in Germany than Rimsky, and Rimsky was jealous. (It seems to me that Tchaikovsky had a distinct influence on Mahler; listen to figs. 16 to 21 in the fourth movement of Mahler's First Symphony, and from fig. 21 in the fifth movement of his Second Symphony.) Rimsky would say, and never tire of saying, 'Tchaikovsky's music is in abominable taste', and, indeed, though much of it is, Rimsky might have realized that his own music could share honours with Tchaikovsky's on this count. Nevertheless, Rimsky was proud to exhibit in his workroom a large silver crown Tchaikovsky had given him for the première of the *Capriccio espagnol*. Tchaikovsky had attended the dress rehearsal and had so admired the brilliance of the music that he presented Rimsky with this token of homage the next day.

R.C. How would you describe Rimsky as a teacher?

I.S. A professor at the St Petersburg Conservatory himself, he nevertheless advised me not to enter it, and instead made me the precious gift of his unforgettable lessons (1904–6). These usually lasted a little more than an hour and took place twice a week. Training in orchestration was their main subject. He gave me Beethoven piano sonatas and Schubert marches to orchestrate, and sometimes his own music, the orchestration of which was not yet published. Then, as I brought him the work I did, he showed me his own orchestra score, which he compared with mine, explaining his reasons for doing it differently.

In addition to these lessons, I continued my contrapuntal exercises, but by myself, as I could not stand the boring lessons in harmony and counterpoint I had had with a former Rimsky pupil.

R.C. When you were Rimsky's pupil, did you esteem Tchaikovsky as much as you did later, in the 1920s and 1930s?

I.S. Then, as later in my life, I was annoyed by the too frequent vulgarity of Rimsky's music – annoyed in the same measure as I enjoyed the real freshness of Tchaikovsky's talent (and his instrumental inventiveness), especially when I compared it with the stale naturalism and amateurism of the 'Five': Borodin, Cui, Balakirev, Musorgsky and Rimsky himself.

R.C. What was Rimsky-Korsakov's attitude to Brahms, and when did you yourself first encounter Brahms's music?

I.S. I remember reading the notice of Brahms's death in *New Time* (the St Petersburg conservative newspaper; I subscribed to it for Vladimir Rozanov's articles) and the impression it made on me. I know that at least three years prior to it I had played quartets and symphonies by the Hamburg master.

Brahms was the discovery of my 'uncle' Alexander Yelachich,

husband of my mother's sister, Sophie. This gentleman, as I have said, had an important role in my early development. He was a passionate musical amateur who would spend days at a time playing the piano. Two of his five sons were musical, too, and one of them was always playing four-hand music with him. I remember going through a Brahms quartet with him in this way in my fourteenth year. Uncle Alexander was an admirer of Musorgsky, and as such had little use for Rimsky-Korsakov. Since his house was just around the corner from Rimsky's, I would often go from one to the other, finding it difficult to keep a balance between them.

Rimsky did not like Brahms. He was no Wagnerite either, but his admiration for Liszt kept him on the Wagner–Liszt side of the partisanship.

I adored Rimsky but did not like his 'mentality', by which I mean his almost bourgeois atheism (he would call it his 'rationalism'). His mind was closed to any religious or metaphysical idea. If conversation happened to touch on some point of religion or philosophy, he would simply refuse to allow that point to be considered in the light of 'revealed religion'. I was accustomed to dine with the Rimsky-Korsakov family after my lessons. We drank vodka and ate *zakousky* together before dinner. I would sit next to Rimsky and often continue to discuss some problem from my lesson. Rimsky's sons and daughters occupied the rest of the table. His second son, Andrey, had studied philosophy in Heidelberg, and he often came to dinner with one Mironov, a university friend. But in spite of these young people's interest in philosophy, Rimsky would permit no discussion of it in his presence. I remember someone introducing 'Resurrection' as a table topic, and Rimsky drawing a zero on the tablecloth as he said, 'There is nothing after death; death is the end.' I then had the temerity to suggest that this was also merely one point of view, but was made to feel for some time thereafter that I should have held my peace.

Rimsky was a strict man, and a strict, though at the same time very patient, teacher. (He would say *'ponimýete, ponimýete'*, 'you understand', again and again throughout my lessons.) His knowledge was precise, and he was able to impart what he knew with great clarity. His teaching was all technical.

But whereas he knew valuable details about harmony and practical orchestral writing, what he knew about composition itself was not all it should have been. He was for me, when I first came to him, *sans reproche* musically, but before very long I began to wish for someone even less reproachable, and for music that would satisfy the ideals of my growing mind, as Rimsky's was failing to do. The revival of polyphony and the renewal of form that had begun in Vienna in the very year of Rimsky's death were developments entirely unknown to the Rimsky school. I am grateful to Rimsky for many things, and I do not wish to blame him for what he did not know. Nevertheless, I had to discover for myself the most important tools of my art. I should mention, too, that by the time I became his pupil he was a musical reactionary who would oppose on principle anything new that came from France or Germany. I never ceased to be surprised by this attitude, since outside the arts he was a radical, anti-Tsarist progressive.

I thought I had found friends in Rimsky's younger sons, two gentlemen who, at least in provincial St Petersburg, were beacons of enlightenment. Andrey, a man three years my senior and a cellist of some ability, was especially kind to me, though this kindness lasted only while his father was alive; after the success of *Firebird* in 1910, he, and in fact the entire Rimsky-Korsakov family, turned against me. I thought this was musical, rather than personal. My music was too 'advanced' for them, and Glazunov was their darling. Andrey even reviewed *Petrushka* for a Russian paper, dismissing it as 'Russian vodka with French perfumes'. Vladimir, his brother, was a competent violinist, and I owe to him my first knowledge of violin fingerings. I was not as close to Soph'ya and Nadezhda, Rimsky's daughters, but my *Pastorale* was written with Nadezhda's voice in mind, and dedicated to her. (I later arranged the piece for violin and four woodwinds, for the reason that vocalises were no longer performed.) My last contact with the Rimsky-Korsakov family was through Nadezhda's husband, Maximilian Steinberg, who had come to Paris in 1924 and heard me play my Piano Concerto there. But you may imagine his response to that work when I tell you that the best he could do even for my *Fireworks* was to shrug his shoulders. After hearing the Concerto, he wanted to lecture me about the whole of my mistaken career. He returned to Russia thoroughly annoyed when I refused to see him.

*

Rimsky did not mention me in his *Autobiography* for the reason that he did not wish to show me any mark of deference; he had many pupils and was always careful to avoid favouritism. My brother Guriy *is* mentioned, because he had sung in the cantata that I composed for Rimsky and which was performed in his house, 6 March 1904. After this event, Rimsky wrote a charming letter to my mother in appreciation of her sons' talents.

R.C. What music of yours did Rimsky-Korskov know? What were his relations with new music: Debussy, Strauss, Skryabin? I.S. He knew my Symphony in E♭ in detail and also my vocal suite, *Le Faune et la bergère*. Both were performed in concerts arranged with his help and supervision. He had seen the manuscript of my *Scherzo fantastique*, but his death prevented him from hearing it. He never complimented me, but he was always very close-mouthed and stingy in praising his pupils. I was told by his friends after his death that he spoke with praise of the *Scherzo* score.

When asked to go to a concert to hear Debussy's music, he said, 'I have already heard it. I had better not go: I will start to get accustomed to it and finally like it.' He hated Richard Strauss, but probably for the wrong reasons. His attitude towards Skryabin was different. He didn't like Skryabin's music at all, but to those people who were indignant about it, his answer was: 'I like Skryabin's music very much.'

Rimsky attended my first two premières with me. The first of these, the Symphony, is dedicated to him (the manuscript is still with his family).[19] It was performed in St Petersburg on 27 April 1907. I remember the date because Uncle Yelachich presented me with a medal to commemorate the occasion. Rimsky sat next to me and, from time to time, made critical remarks: 'This is too heavy; be more careful when you use trombones in their middle

19 The family eventually gave the manuscript to the Saltykov-Schedrin Public Library, with some other manuscripts, perhaps including the *Chant funèbre* for Rimsky-Korsakov. [R.C.]

register.' Since the concert took place at noon, and the audience was not a paying one, I cannot say whether the applause I heard signified a success. The only bad omen was Glazunov, who came to me afterwards saying, 'Very nice, very nice.' The Imperial Kapellmeister Varlich, a general in uniform, conducted the performance. My second première, *Le Faune et la bergère*, conducted by Felix Blumenfeld later in the same year in one of Mitrofan Belyayev's Russian Symphony Concerts, must have irritated Rimsky's conservatism, incredible as that now seems. He found the first song 'strange', and my use of whole-tone progressions suspiciously 'Debussy-ist'. 'There, you see,' he said to me after the performance, 'I have heard it, but if I were to hear it again in a half-hour, I would have to make the same effort of adjustment all over again.' At this time, Rimsky's own 'modernism' was based on a few flimsy enharmonic devices.

Rimsky was a tall man, like Alban Berg, and he suffered from poor eyesight. He wore blue-tinted spectacles, sometimes keeping an extra pair on his forehead, a habit of his that I have acquired. When conducting an orchestra, he would bend over the score, and, hardly ever looking up, wave the baton in the direction of his knees. His difficulty in seeing the score was so great, and he was so absorbed in listening, that he gave almost no directions to the orchestra. Like Berg, too, he suffered from asthma. In the last year of his life, he suddenly began to fail from the disease, and, though he was only sixty-four years old, we were aware that he would not live long. He had a series of severe attacks in January 1908. Telephone calls came every morning from his house to ours, and I waited every morning, not knowing whether he was still alive.

R.C. Your autobiography does not mention whether or not you attended Rimsky-Korsakov's funeral.

I.S. I did not mention it because it was one of the unhappiest days of my life. But I was there and will remember Rimsky in his coffin as long as memory is. He looked so very beautiful, I could not help crying. His widow, seeing me, came up to me and said, 'Why so unhappy? We still have Glazunov.' It was the cruellest remark I have ever heard and I never hated again as I did in that moment.

The *Chant funèbre* that I composed in Rimsky's memory was performed in a concert conducted by Felix Blumenfeld in St Petersburg shortly after Rimsky's death. I remember the piece as the best of my works before *Firebird*, and the most harmonically advanced. The orchestral parts must have been preserved in one of the St Petersburg orchestra libraries; I wish someone in Leningrad would look for the parts, being curious myself to see what I was composing just before *Firebird*. Alas, the only homage I have paid Rimsky since then was by conducting his tone poem *Sadko* for a broadcast with the New York Philharmonic, 17 January 1937, a work I thought worth resurrecting.

*

R.C. Do you remember your first public appearance as a pianist?
I.S. As a soloist, no; I did play my Four Etudes somewhere, in 1908, I think, but do not recall the occasion. My first public performance as an accompanist took place on 2 December 1901, at a private concert by pupils of E. P. Tomulovsky's school in the V. N. von Derviz Hall, on Vasiliensky Island. At least four years before this solo appearance, I appeared in public for the first time, as accompanist to an English-horn [cor anglais] player. The concert was one of the 'Evenings of Contemporary Music' series, and the composer was a new Russian whose name I forget. Although I had acquired substantial accompanying experience before this concert, I was nervous, nevertheless. I do not know whether I played well or badly, but Nicolai Tcherepnin said afterwards that my slow tempo 'almost choked the English hornist to death', a remark that greatly offended me.

My activity as accompanist was motivated purely by economic reasons. Rehearsal pianists could earn as much as five roubles an hour, a sum that compared very favourably with my family allowance. I accompanied several singers, and in my nineteenth year became an accompanist of the well-known cellist Eugene Malmgreen. My material fortunes increased by ten roubles for every sugared hour of Malmgreen's salon repertoire. (Thirty-five years later, one of Malmgreen's nieces, Vera de Bosset, became my wife, at which time I learned that another uncle of hers, a Dr Ivan Petrov, had also been a cellist who had played duos with an amateur of the instrument, Anton Chekhov.)

Ability apart, I could not have made a career as a pianist because of the lack of what I call 'the performer's memory'. I believe that composers and painters memorize selectively, whereas performers must be able to take in 'the whole thing as it is', like a camera; I believe, in fact, that a composer's first memory impression is already a composition. But whether or not other composer–performers complain of this difficulty, I cannot say. I should admit, too, that my attitude to the performer's type of 'learning by heart' is psychologically wrong. To commit to memory a concerto or a symphony is a proposition of no interest to me, nor can I sympathize with the mentality of those whom it does interest.

As for the composer's memory, I will cite the story of Schoenberg, who, after having interrupted the composition of *Moses und Aron* for a long interval, complained of his inability to recall what he had already written. I experienced something similar to this while composing the second movement of my Piano Concerto. Some pages of the manuscript disappeared mysteriously one day, and when I tried to rewrite them, I found I could remember nothing of what I had written. I do not know to what extent the published movement differs from the lost one, but I am sure the two are very unalike. My memory as a performer is something else, but it is also, in its way, unreliable. My *Autobiography* describes how, at the first performance of this same Piano Concerto, I was obliged to ask the conductor, Koussevitzky, to remind me of the theme of the second movement. Another time, while playing the same Concerto, I suffered a lapse of memory because I was suddenly obsessed by the idea that the audience was a collection of dolls in a huge panopticon. Still another time, my memory froze because I suddenly noticed the reflection of my fingers in the glossy wood at the edge of the keyboard. A large psychological problem is involved with this movement, evidently. Alcohol affects my performing memory, too – I was moderately inebriated at least twice while playing the Piano Concerto – distracting me with the problem of my consciousness, and thus breaking down the automatic part of the memory machinery.

But whether or not I am a pianist, the instrument itself is the centre of my musical life and the fulcrum of all my musical

discoveries. Each note that I write is tried on it, and every relationship of notes is taken apart and heard on it again and again.
The process is like slow motion, or those greatly reduced-in-
speed recordings of birdcalls.

*

R.C. What do you remember of St Petersburg University?
I.S. As attendance at lectures was optional, I opted not to
attend, and in all my four years there I probably did not hear
more than fifty of them. I have only a vague and uninterested
memory of the subjects. I studied criminal law and legal philosophy, and I was interested in the theoretical and abstract questions of both, but when I entered the university, so much of my
time was spent with Rimsky-Korsakov I could hardly do justice
to any other work. I can recall only two incidents connected
with my life there. I was walking through the Kazansky Place
one afternoon in the politically tense months following the
Russo-Japanese War, when a group of students began to stage a
protest. The police were prepared, and the protestors were
arrested, myself with them.[20] I was detained for seven hours, but
seventy years will not erase the memory of my fears. The other
incident occurred during the last spring cramming session,
when, realizing that I would never pass one of my examinations,
I proposed to exchange names with Nicolai Yusupov,[21] that he
might take my examination and I one of his: we were better in
each other's subject. Our ruse was never detected because our
faces were quite unknown to the professors, but poor Nicolai
died shortly after passing my paper, in a duel in Tashkent.

R.C. What did you read in your university years?

20 Stravinsky was arrested at the time of the dispersal of the student gathering in the days following the signing of the Portsmouth Agreement, 23 August
1905 (not at the time of the decree of 6 August 1905, on the convocation of
the Duma). At this time, P. A. Stolypin was still a provincial governor, but in
July 1906 he became Prime Minister. During Stravinsky's last years in Russia,
Stolypin led a campaign of brutal repression, but later became a reformer, and
hence a target for Rightist extremists. President Putin has revived his reputation and made him a cult figure. [R.C.]
21 Brother of Prince Felix Yusupov, who originated and participated in the
plot to assassinate Rasputin.

I.S. Russian literature mostly, and the literature of other countries in Russian translation. Dostoyevsky was always my hero. Of
the new writers, I liked Gorky most and disliked most Andreyev.
The Scandinavians then so popular, Lagerlöf and Knut Hamsun,
did not appeal to me at all, but I admired Strindberg and, of
course, Ibsen. Ibsen's plays were as popular in Russia in those
years as Tchaikovsky's music. Hermann Südermann and Gerhardt
Hauptmann were also in vogue then, as well as Dickens and
Mark Twain – I later knew Twain's daughter in Hollywood –
and Walter Scott, whose *Ivanhoe* (pronounced in Russian as a
four-syllable paroxytone – *Ivanhoé*) was as popular a children's
book as it ever was in the English-speaking countries.

R.C. Did you inherit your bibliophilia from your father? What
kinds of books did he collect?

I.S. My father's library contained seven to eight thousand volumes of, mostly, history and Russian literature. It was a valuable
and famous library because of first editions of Gogol, Pushkin and
Tolstoy, as well as of the minor Russian poets. It was considered
important enough to be declared a National Library after the
Revolution.[22] At least the books were not confiscated or removed,
and I have the Lenin Government to thank for this, as well as
for allowing my mother to emigrate, in 1922. Shortly after
Lenin's death, I, 'Tovarich Stravinsky', was invited by Tovarich
Lunacharsky's Ministry of Public Education to conduct concerts
in Leningrad. My music was performed in Russia throughout
the period of the New Economic Policy.

I read omnivorously as a child, but I think the first book to
impress me was Tolstoy's *Childhood and Youth*. I discovered
Shakespeare, Dante and the Greeks in my father's library, all in
Russian, but these were discoveries of my late teens. I remember
being furiously excited by *Oedipus Rex*, in Pyotr Gnedich's
translation, I think.[23] The translator of Dante, Pyotr Isaiah

22 By a resolution of the Ispolkom of the Union of Communes of the
Northern Territory, the Stravinsky apartment was declared under guard. The
library's importance was sufficient to have it declared a national library after
the Revolution, and in 1919 Stravinsky's mother acquired the title National
Librarian, 'Bibliotekarsha Stravinskaya'. [R.C.]
23 Dmitri Merezhkovsky's 1896 translation was probably the one that
Stravinsky read. [R.C.]

Weinberg, I knew personally later, as he was a friend of Polonsky and an *habitué* of Les Vendredis. Weinberg's two daughters were also neighbours and friends of ours later, in Nice. Weinberg told fascinating stories about Tolstoy, and, according to him, every child in the village of Yasnaya Polyana looked like Tolstoy. Weinberg said that this was because Tolstoy was not handsome as a young man and therefore wanted to make love often as an old one, 'out of vengeance'.

R.C. Your father and Dostoyevsky were friends. I suppose that as a child you heard a great deal about him?

I.S. Yes, Dostoyevsky liked music, often went to concerts with my father, and even gave half-and-half song and poetry recitals with him. But he became in my mind the symbol of the artist continually in need of money. My mother talked about him in this way, saying that he was always grubbing. My parents complained that his readings from his own works were intolerably boring. I still consider Dostoyevsky to be the greatest Russian after Pushkin. Today, when one is supposed to reveal much of oneself by one's choice of Freud or Jung, Dostoyevsky or Tolstoy, I am a Dostoyevskian.

*

R.C. Would you explain your family relationship to the poet Jacov Petrovich Polonsky?[24]

I.S. Nicolai Yelachich, my cousin and the oldest of the five Yelachich brothers, married Natalie Polonsky, the daughter of the famous poet. I recall the wedding only because my parents had ordered a full uniform for me in which to attend the ceremony, a stiff suit with silver-bordered collar and shirt, and a boutonnière. I was eighteen at the time and immensely proud of this new suit. Nicolai was a fair pianist, and I remember the New Year's Eve of 1899–1900, which we spent with the Yelachiches in their house, and at which Nicolai accompanied my father in Schumann *Lieder*. What a happy night that was, and how momentous the dawn of 1900 seemed to us! I remember that we talked anti-English politics at the party, because of the Boer War.

24 Polonsky is best known today for having recognized Isaac Babel as the greatest Soviet creative writer. [R.C.]

Nicolai must have been twice my age, or old enough, one would think, to stop baiting me, though this was not the case. I remember that when he invited us to see his new apartment after the wedding, his manner was intended to provoke jealousy and to remind me of his natural superiority. I also remember a mocking remark of his when the Yelachich family came to see our family off at the railway station. Leave-takings in those days were sometimes very elaborate affairs. Hampers of food and wine were brought along, and friends and relatives settled down for intensive visits. When the train finally departed, everyone lined up on the platform or in the train and waved handkerchiefs. Just as we were ready to say goodbye, Nicolai, hoping to catch me in a gaffe, tried out one of those complicated questions of which he was so fond: 'Igor, is the limitation of your mental horizon increasing or decreasing?' I answered, 'Increasing', of course, and, of course, the Yelachich monsters split the air with their cachinnations.

I saw Polonsky often until my seventeenth year, when he died. He was a poet of the Jemchushnikov period, a contemporary and associate of Leskov, Dostoyevsky, Fet, Maykov. Though grey and stooped when I knew him, Polonsky was still a handsome man. I remember him wearing plaids, and the only time I saw him in evening clothes was when he was in his coffin. After his death, Josephine, his wife, organized literary teas in his memory, soon famous everywhere as Les Vendredis Polonsky. Russians are fond of this sort of thing – tea and rhyming resonance – but the grimaces and exalted voices of the poets were too much for me. Anyway, I suspect Mme Polonsky of subtly spiking the tea with sodium, to make it dark like a tea of high quality.

*

R.C. Would you tell the story of you and Guriy in Oslo, in June 1905?

I.S. Shortly after the separation of Norway and Sweden, Guriy and I went on a holiday through Scandinavia. My uncle was the civil governor of Finland, so of course we went there, then to Stockholm, where we stopped long enough to hear a performance of *The Marriage of Figaro*. We then sailed through the beautiful Swedish lake canals to Göteborg, where we changed boats for Copenhagen and Oslo. It was delicious spring weather in Oslo, cold but pleasant. One day it seemed as if the whole population was in the streets. We were riding in a droshsky and the friend who was with us told me to look at a smallish man on the sidewalk to our right. It was Henrik Ibsen. He wore a top hat and his hair was white. He was walking with his hands folded behind his back. Some things one sees never leave the eyes, never move into the back part of the mind. So Ibsen is in my eyes.

*

R.C. Would you try to recall which instrumentalists, singers, conductors impressed you most in your St Petersburg years?

I.S. Leopold Auer comes to mind first, probably because I saw him more often than any other performer, but also because he was very kind to me. Auer was 'Soloist to His Majesty', which meant that he was required to play the solos in *Swan Lake* at the Imperial Ballet. I remember seeing him walk into the Mariyinsky pit, play the violin solos, standing, as though for a concerto, and then walk out again. Auer's technique was masterful, but as so often with virtuosi, it was wasted on second-rate music, meaning the concertos of Vieuxtemps and Wieniawski. He is famous, of course, for having made Tchaikovsky's Concerto the most popular in the repertory. Auer enjoyed talking about the 'secrets' of his art, and he often boasted that his octaves had been a little false 'to help the audience realize I am in fact playing octaves'. Our relations were always good, and I continued to see him later in life on trips abroad – the last time in New York in 1925, when we were photographed together with Fritz Kreisler, and dined, together with Furtwängler, at Arthur Sachs's on Sixty-Ninth Street and Fifth Avenue.

Sophie Menter, Josef Hofmann, Reisenauer, Paderewski, Sarasate, Ysaÿe, and Casals were among the performers I remember from my youth, and of these I was most impressed by Ysaÿe and Hofmann. I visited Ysaÿe once, during a trip to Brussels in the 1920s, and told him I had been moved by his playing when I was a youth in St Petersburg. I did not meet Sarasate, but I did know his friend Granados, in Paris at the time of *Firebird*. Granados and Albéniz were then the lions of the Paris salons, and everyone seemed to regard them as a kind of Spanish Schiller and Goethe. A black, bushy-faced character, Granados reputedly carried a money-belt loaded with gold, which no doubt helped to sink him on the SS *Sussex,* though, of course, as he was a neutral subject, the Germans had to pay. Josef Hofmann I knew well, and his playing was a real point of enthusiasm for me during the years when I cared about my own pianism. We came to the United States on the SS *Rex* together in 1935, at which time I discovered that he had a querulous character and drank heavily, and that the latter made the former worse. He disliked my music, of course, but I did not expect him to attack me to my face about it, as he did one evening, full of alcoholic rectitude, after he had heard me conduct my *Capriccio.*[25] I never saw him during our mutual years in California.

I remember hardly any concerts by solo singers in St Petersburg, probably for the reason that vocal recitals are torture for me. I did go to hear Adelina Patti, out of curiosity, for at that time this tiny woman with the bright orange wig sounded like a bicycle pump. The singers I remember were all from the opera, and the only famous name among them is Chaliapin. A man of large musical and histrionic talents, Chaliapin at his best was an astonishing performer. I was more impressed by him in Rimsky's *Pskovityanka* than in anything else, but Rimsky did not agree. ('What shall I do? I am the author, and he pays absolutely no attention to anything I say.') Chaliapin's bad characteristics began to appear only when he repeated a role too often, as in *Boris*, where his exaggerations increased with each performance. (I do not know the Russian equivalent for 'ham'.) Chaliapin was also a gifted storyteller, and in my twenty-first, twenty-second and twenty-third years I saw him frequently at Rimsky's and listened to his tales with much pleasure.

Chaliapin succeeded my father as the leading basso of the Mariyinsky Theatre, and I remember the performance of *Prince Igor* in which my father explained this succession to the public by a gesture, as he and Chaliapin took their bows together, my father as the Drunkard and Chaliapin as the Prince. Three tenors of the Mariyinsky come to my memory: Sobinov, who was light and lyric, an ideal Lensky; Yershov, a 'heroic' tenor,

25 In Rio de Janeiro, in 1936.

and an outstanding Siegfried (he later sang the Fisherman in the Petrograd production of my *Nightingale*); and Nicolas Figner, the friend of Tchaikovsky, and the operatic king of St Petersburg. The leading female singers were Félia Litvinne, who sang a surprisingly brilliant Brünnhilde, surprising because she had such a tiny mouth; and Maria Kusnetsov, a dramatic soprano who was very appetizing to see as well as hear.

R.C. Were you impressed by any visiting foreign musicians in your student days in St Petersburg?

I.S. In the early years of the twentieth century most of the distinguished foreign artists who came to St Petersburg called on Rimsky-Korsakov in homage. I was in his home so frequently in 1903, 1904 and 1905 that I met many composers, conductors and virtuosi there. Rimsky spoke French and English, having learned the latter language during his term as a naval officer, but he did not know German. Since I spoke the language fluently from my childhood, he sometimes asked me to translate for him and a German-speaking guest. I remember meeting the conductors Hans Richter and Arthur Nikisch in this way. When Richter saw me he scowled and asked, '*Wer ist dieser Jüngling?*' ['Who's the kid?'] I remember meeting Max Reger in those years, at a rehearsal, I think. Since he and his music repelled me in equal measure, I became wary of the important critic Vyacheslav Karatïgin, who referred to Reger in print as a 'divine master'. Alfredo Casella also came to Russia then, at the beginning of his career. I did not meet him at that time, but heard about him from Rimsky: 'A certain Alfredo Casella, an Italian musician, came to see me today. He brought a complicated score of incredible size, his instrumentation of Balakirev's *Islamey*, and asked me to comment on it and to advise him. What could one say about such a thing? I felt like a poor little child. By saying so, I seemed to humiliate him.'

I remember seeing Mahler in St Petersburg, too. His concert there was a triumph. Rimsky was still alive, I believe, but he wouldn't have attended because a work by Tchaikovsky was on the programme, *Manfred*, I think, the dullest piece possible. Mahler also played some Wagner fragments and, if I remember correctly, a symphony of his own. Mahler impressed me greatly, himself and his conducting. I attribute the latter to his training as a composer. The most interesting (though, of course, not necessarily the prettiest or the most rousing) conductors *are* composers, for the reason that they are the only ones who can have new insights into music itself. The conductors of my period who have most advanced the art of conducting are Mahler, Strauss, Zemlinsky, Klemperer, all of them composers.

There were other good conductors, of course – Mottl, whose *Siegfried* impressed me, and Hans Richter – but conducting is very close to the circus, whose acrobats are often indistinguishable from the musicians. Nikisch, for one, performed more for the audience than for the music, and his programmes were always planned to ensure his personal success. I encountered Nikisch in the street by the Conservatory after I had been introduced to him. He must have recognized something about me, probably my big nose, for he took a chance and said, '*Es freut mich so Sie zu sehen, Herr Bakst.*' ['I'm so pleased to see you, Herr Bakst.'] But the star among the local St Petersburg conductors was Nápravník. As I have already said, the Nápravníks and the Stravinskys lived in adjoining apartment houses, and so I saw the eminent conductor almost every day and knew him well. My father had sung in his opera *Dubrovsky*, and we had been quite friendly with him at that time. But like most professional conductors, Nápravník's culture was primitive and his taste undeveloped. A small, hard man with a good ear and a good memory, he was the absolute boss of the Mariyinsky Theatre. His entrance on the concert stage or in the opera pit was very grand indeed, but more exciting still was his removal of his left glove. (Conductors wore white gloves then, to enhance the visibility of their beats – or so they said; Nápravník's left hand was employed chiefly in adjusting his pince-nez.) No ecdysiast at the moment of the final fall was ever regarded more attentively than Nápravník as he peeled this left glove.

R.C. Did you ever meet Balakirev?

I.S. I saw him once, standing with his pupil, Liapunov, at a concert in the St Petersburg Conservatory. He was a large man, bald, with a Kalmuck head and the shrewd, sharp-eyed look of Lenin. He was not greatly admired musically at this time – it was 1904 or 1905 – and, politically, because of his orthodoxy, the liberals considered him a hypocrite. His reputation as a pianist was firmly established by numerous pupils, all of them, like Balakirev himself, ardent Lisztians. Whereas Rimsky-Korsakov kept a portrait of Wagner over his desk, Balakirev had one of Liszt. I pitied Balakirev because I knew from Rimsky that he suffered cruel fits of depression.

R.C. You often mention the St Petersburg concert series 'Evenings of Contemporary Music'. What music did you hear there?
I.S. My own, first of all. Mme Petrenko sang my Gorodetsky song 'Monastery Spring' on 27 December 1907, accompanied by a Mr Ivanovich. But I did not hear Prokofiev's performance of two of the *Three Pieces* for piano from Schoenberg's opus 11, since this took place in the spring of 1911 when I was in Rome finishing *Petrushka*. A plethora of works by young Russian composers was performed, of course, but French music was also promoted, the quartets and songs of Debussy and Ravel, and pieces by Dukas and d'Indy. Brahms was played, too, and Reger. Like the 'Monday Evening Concerts' in Los Angeles, these St Petersburg concerts, in spite of their name, tried to match the new with the old. This was important and rare. So many organizations are dedicated to new music, and so few to the centuries before Bach. I heard Monteverdi there for the first time – in an arrangement by d'Indy, and, I think, Couperin and Montéclair. Bach was performed in quantity. When I met d'Indy at a rehearsal of *The Rite* in Paris in December 1920, I told him I had heard a generous amount of his music in St Petersburg in my youth. No doubt he understood that it had been part of the background that had provoked me into composing the *Rite*, for he said nothing.

R.C. Did any orchestral concerts in St Petersburg promote new music?
I.S. No. The programmes of the Imperial Symphony were very much like the programmes of American orchestras today: standard repertory, and from time to time a piece of second-rate local music. The symphonies of Bruckner and Brahms were categorized as new music and therefore rarely and very timidly played. Belyayev's 'Russian Symphony Concerts' were more

interesting, but they concentrated too much on the Russian 'Five'. Incidentally, I knew Belyayev and met him at concerts. He was the great music patron of his time – a violin-playing Russian Rockefeller. His 'Editions M. B. Belyayev' in Leipzig had published my *Faune et bergère* – probably on Rimsky's recommendation, since Glazunov, the other adviser, would not have endorsed the choice. Once I saw Belyayev stand up in his box – he was a tall man with very artistic hair – and stare with amazement at the stage, where Koussevitzky had just appeared carrying his double-bass to play a solo. Belyayev turned to me and said, 'Until now, such things have been seen only in circuses.'

R.C. How often do you remember hearing the works of Richard Strauss, Mahler, Debussy, Ravel?

I.S. I was exposed to Strauss's music for the first time in, I think, 1905, or 1904, with *Heldenleben*. *Zarathustra*, *Till Eulenspiegel* and *Tod und Verklärung* followed in St Petersburg in the next year, but this inverse order of acquaintanceship destroyed whatever sympathetic appreciation I might otherwise have had. The rodomontade of that first *Heldenleben* was too much for me. I heard *Elektra* in London in January 1913, conducted by Strauss himself, and was enthusiastic about it, but I saw no other Strauss operas until after the war, when I happened upon *Der Rosenkavalier* and *Ariadne* in Germany. I greatly admired the music expressing Elektra's high spirits, just before the entrance of Chrysothemis, and again at her '*Orest, Orest*'. I respect the stagecraft of all the Strauss operas I know (especially, perhaps, of *Capriccio*), but I do not like the treacly music, and I think I am just in denying Strauss any role in my own musical make-up.

Mahler conducted his Fifth Symphony in St Petersburg in October or November 1907. As aforesaid, I was impressed by him and by the symphony. But the Fourth, considered as a whole, is my favourite among his works in this form, along with the first movement of the Ninth. Debussy and Ravel were rarely played in St Petersburg in the decade before *Firebird*. Whatever performances took place were due to the efforts of Alexander Siloti, a champion of new music who deserves to be remembered. It was Siloti who brought Schoenberg to St Petersburg in 1912 to conduct his *Pelleas und Melisande*, and Siloti's performances of Debussy's *Nocturnes* and *L'Après-midi d'un faune* were among the major events of my early years. *L'Après-midi d'un faune* was played amidst hoots, whistles and laughter, but this did not destroy the effect of that lovely flute solo, of the long silence, of the harp arpeggios and the horns, especially after all the post-Wagnerian noise.

My acquaintance with Debussy's piano music and songs in my St Petersburg days was very slight, and, surprisingly, I heard *La Mer* for the first time as late as 1911 or 1912 in Paris, conducted by, I think, Monteux. Debussy took me to this performance. I remember that he called for me in a new automobile whose chassis was covered with osier wickerwork, and that a chauffeur stood by and held his hat for him as he entered the car. Ravel made great fun of this, but Debussy's style of living after his Bardac marriage was very grand. I remember, too, that during the intermission Debussy talked about the first performance of *La Mer*. He said that the violinists flagged the tips of their bows with handkerchiefs at the rehearsals, to express their ridicule and protest.

Ravel's music was better known, and most musicians of my generation regarded the *Rhapsodie espagnole,* also conducted by Siloti, as the *dernier cri* in harmonic subtlety and orchestral brilliance, incredible as this seems now. Not Ravel, or Mahler, or Debussy, or Strauss was esteemed so highly for the qualities of quintessential modernity, as Alexander Skryabin. The *Poème divin*, *Prometheus*, and the *Poème de l'extase*,[26] as well as the more interesting Seventh Sonata, were thought to be as up to date as the Paris Métro. Diaghilev was very interested in him, and in 1907 presented his Piano Concerto and Second Symphony in Paris in a series called 'From Glinka to Skryabin'. Skryabin's father was the Russian Consul in Switzerland in the years before World War I, and the composer lived in Lausanne in the autumn of 1913. We spent some time together and, I thought, parted on good terms. His sudden, unexpected death in 1915 was a terrible shock and a great loss to music. Incidentally,

---

26 One of Stravinsky's sketchbooks for May 1917 contains the statement: 'Sometimes we think that "taste" is meaningless, but when you listen to Skryabin you change your mind.' [R.C.]

my elder son, on a recent visit to me in New York [November 1969], reminded me that when he was a child his mother used to frighten him from picking pimples on his face by saying, 'That was how poor Monsieur Skryabin died.'

But performances of exploratory new music of this kind were great exceptions. The 'new' pieces fed to us more regularly were the symphonies and tone poems of Vincent d'Indy, Saint-Saëns, Chausson, Franck, Bizet. In the realm of chamber music, the 'modern' French composers most often performed were Dukas and Fauré. I met the latter at the time of his *Pénélope*, which I heard in May 1913, shortly before the première of *The Rite*. Ravel introduced me to him at a concert in the Salle Gaveau. I saw a white-haired, deaf, very kind-faced old man – indeed, he was compared for gentleness and simplicity to Bruckner.

The repertory of the St Petersburg orchestras in those years would make a depressing list. The classics of our concerts were the tone poems of Liszt, Raff, Smetana, the overtures of Litolff (*Maximilian Robespierre*), Berlioz, Mendelssohn, Weber, Ambroise Thomas, and the concertos of Chopin, Grieg, Bruch, Vieuxtemps, Wieniawski. Haydn, Mozart and Beethoven were played, of course, but badly played, and always the same few pieces over and over. Incidentally, I remember a description of Berlioz by Rimsky-Korsakov, who had met the French master after one of the famous Berlioz concerts in St Petersburg in the late 1860s. Rimsky-Korsakov, then in his twenties, had attended the concert with other young composers. They saw Berlioz – in a tailcoat cut very short in the back, so Rimsky said – conduct his own music and Beethoven's. Then they were shepherded backstage by Stasov, the patriarch of St Petersburg musical life. They found a small man – Rimsky's words were 'a little white bird with a pince-nez' – shivering in a fur coat and huddled under a hot pipe that crossed the room just over his head. He addressed Rimsky very kindly: 'And you compose music too?', but kept his hands in his coat sleeves as in a muffler.

I did not hear in Russia the Haydn symphonies I now delectate, or the Mozart wind serenades and the C minor Mass – indeed, Mozart performances were limited to the same three or four symphonies. Of the later symphonists, too, Rimsky's *Antar* and Borodin's Second were played a dozen times for every performance of a symphony by Brahms or Bruckner. I learned Bruckner's music at an early age by playing it four-hands with my uncle Yelachich, but I did not learn to like it, and I still have not, but I have come to respect the composer, and I think that the *Adagio* of the Ninth Symphony must be ranked as one of the most truly inspired of all works in symphonic form.

Performances of opera sometimes attained high standards in St Petersburg, and the operatic season was far more interesting than the symphonic, but though I heard *Figaro* and *Don Giovanni* in St Petersburg, I never heard a note of *The Seraglio*, *Così*, or *The Magic Flute*. The *Don Giovanni* was badly performed, too, but I was never inspired by a Mozart performance until many years later when I heard Alexander von Zemlinsky conduct *Figaro* in Prague. Of Rossini I knew only *The Barber*. My father had often sung Gessler in *William Tell*, but I did not hear the opera in Russia (or anywhere, in fact, before the 1930s, when it was performed in Paris, at about the same time as the *Italiana in Algeri*, the latter sung by Supervia). *Norma* was the only Bellini opera performed in St Petersburg in my youth, and *Lucia* and *Don Pasquale* were the only Donizetti operas. I remembered the trumpet solo in *Don Pasquale* – that far back! – when I wrote *The Rake*. Donizetti I still regard as a neglected composer who at his best – the last scene of *Anna Bolena* – is as good as the best Verdi *de l'époque*. Of Verdi's operas, *Traviata*, *Trovatore*, *Rigoletto*, *Aida*, and – this was unusual luck – *Otello*, were performed, but not *Falstaff* or *Don Carlo*, or *Un ballo in maschera* or *La Forza*. Verdi was always a controversial subject in St Petersburg. Tchaikovsky admired him, but the Rimsky group did not. None of the operas I have named was as popular as Nicolai's *Merry Wives*, in which I heard my father sing many times. Debussy surprised me years later by defending this piece of confection. *The Bartered Bride*, *Der Freischütz*, *Carmen*, Gounod's *Faust*, *Cav.* and *Pag.* were no less popular, and those Victor Emmanuel III monuments of music, *Les Huguenots*, *L'Africaine*, and *Le Prophète*. Wagner's operas (except *Parsifal*, which was at that time performed only in Bayreuth) were mounted, of course, and sung in Russian. I knew *Parsifal* from the score and was influenced by it as late as 1908. The slow section of my *Scherzo fantastique* derives from the

'Good Friday music'. *Tristan*, I might add, was a favourite opera of Tsar Nicholas II. Who knows why? I had heard of this unexpected taste of the Tsar from the brother of the Tsarina, at a dinner in Mainz, in 1931 or 1932.

The livelier and more exciting opera productions were of works of the Russian school: Glinka's operas above all, but also Dargomïzhsky's, Rimsky's, Tchaikovsky's, Borodin's and Musorgsky's. I heard *Boris* many times, of course, but not in the original version. Something of *Boris* survives in my own first opera, in the Emperor's deathbed scene, which is the best part of *The Nightingale*, as Death's aria and the folk-like *Berceuse* are certainly the best music. Perhaps *The Nightingale* only proves that I was right to compose ballets, since I was not yet ready for an opera – in spite of the male duet idea (Chamberlain and Bonze) that I was to develop later in *Renard*, *Oedipus Rex*, the *Canticum Sacrum* and *Threni*. Next to it in popularity was *Prince Igor*. (Borodin was a good friend of my father.) Of the Tchaikovsky operas, I remember most clearly *Eugene Onegin*, *The Golden Slippers* and *Pikovaya Dama* [*The Queen of Spades*]. The best performance of *Pikovaya Dama* that I have ever heard was in Dresden in the 1920s, conducted by Fritz Busch. I must have seen all of Rimsky's operas, but I remember seeing *Sadko*, *Mlada*, *Pskovityanka*, *Snegurochka*, *Mozart and Salieri*, *Christmas Eve*, *Kitezh*, *Tsar Saltan*, *Pan Voyevoda* and *Le Coq d'or*. This last is still vivid for me for the reason that I was at Rimsky's side.

Le Coq d'or had become a rallying point for students and liberals because it had been banned several times by the Tsarist censor. When the performance finally materialized, it was not in the Mariyinsky, but in the Conservatory. Rimsky did not show his great concern with the politics of the affair, I think because he was too hopelessly in love with the soprano Zabela, who sang the Queen of Shymakhan, to care about anything else. Nadezhda Zabela was the wife of the painter Vrubel. When she sang songs at Rimsky's *jours fixes*, he would almost swoon with pleasure.

A special condition of musical life in St Petersburg was the closing of the theatres during Lent, which then became open season for oratorios. Lent and oratorios, they deserve each other. *The Damnation of Faust*, Mendelssohn's *St Paul*,

Schumann's *Peri,* Brahms's *Requiem, The Seasons* and *The Creation* – these were annual offerings. I was surprised and disappointed at a recent performance of *The Creation* in Los Angeles. In spite of choruses that anticipate *Fidelio,* and in spite of the lucidity, the monotony of form, the limitation of the type of piece, and the emptiness of *ancien régime* art when it reaches for the grandiose, are too much even for Haydn. Of the Handel oratorios performed, I remember best *Messiah* and *Judas Maccabaeus.* Handel's reputation is another puzzle to me, and I have thought much about him recently, after listening to *Belshazzar.* The performance was at fault in many respects, above all because it had only two tempi, one fast and one slow. But apart from the performance, the music relies over and over on the same fugato exposition, the same obvious semicircle of keys, the same small harmonic compass. When a piece begins with a more interesting chromatic subject, Handel consistently fails to develop and exploit it. As soon as all the voices have entered, regularity, harmonic and otherwise, rules every episode. In two hours of music I experienced only 'style', but none of the wonderful jolts, the sudden modulations, the unexpected harmonic changes, the unexpected cadences that are the joy of Bach cantatas. The only major work of Bach's that I heard in St Petersburg was a single performance of the *St Matthew Passion.*

This catalogue of St Petersburg musical life is incomplete, but if it were fuller it would not be less depressing. Some of the inclusions are more remarkable than the omissions. I heard *Hänsel und Gretel* many times but never *Fidelio, Prince Igor* but not *The Magic Flute.* Grieg, Sinding, and Svendsen were performed in concerts, but only three or four Haydn symphonies. Mendelssohn's *Lobgesang* and Liszt's *St Elisabeth* were staples, but the *St John Passion* and the *Trauer-Ode* were never performed. My horizons were broadened as a child by trips to Germany, but this was chiefly in the domain of light music. I remember *Die Fledermaus* and *Der Zigeunerbaron* in Frankfurt, when my uncle Yelachich took me there, but not until I began to travel with Diaghilev did I have an opportunity to hear a variety of new works, and in one year under his always eager aegis I must have seen more theatre pieces than in a decade in St Petersburg. Diaghilev was a Gilbert and Sullivan amateur, incidentally, and on our visits to London before the war, in 1913 and 1914, we would steal off together to *The Pirates of Penzance*, *Patience* and *Iolanthe*.

When I compare the musical world of my youth with that of the present, in which recordings of new music can be issued within a few months of the completion of the composition, and in which the whole repertory is available at arm's length, I do not regret my own past. My more limited experience in St Petersburg was directly experienced, which made it rarer and more precious. Sitting in the dark of the Mariyinsky Theatre, I saw and heard everything at first hand, and my impressions were immediate and indelible. St Petersburg in the decade before *Firebird* was an exciting place to be.

*

R.C. What was your opinion of Musorgsky when you were Rimsky-Korsakov's student? Do you remember anything your father may have said about him? How do you consider him today?

I.S. I have little to say about Musorgsky in connection with my Rimsky years. Influenced by my teacher who, after all, recomposed so much of Musorgsky's *œuvre*, I repeated what was usually said about his 'big talent' and 'poor musicianship', and about the 'important services' rendered by Rimsky to Musorgsky's 'embarrassing' and 'unpresentable' scores. But I soon realized the partiality of this kind of mind, and changed my attitude toward Musorgsky. This was before my contact with French composers, who fiercely opposed Rimsky's 'transcriptions'. It was too obvious, even to an influenced mind, that Rimsky's Meyerbeerization of Musorgsky's 'technically imperfect' music could no longer be tolerated.

As to my own feeling, although I have little contact with Musorgsky's music today, I think that in spite of his limited technical means and 'awkward writing', his original scores show infinitely greater musical interest and intuition than the 'perfection' of Rimsky's arrangements. My parents often told me that Musorgsky was a connoisseur of Italian operatic music, in which he accompanied singers extremely well. They also said that Musorgsky's manners were always ceremonious, and that he was the most fastidious of men in his personal relations.

He was a time-to-time guest in our St Petersburg apartment.

R.C. Did you know César Cui in your Rimsky-Korsakov years?

I.S. I must have known him very early in my life, for he was a great admirer of my father and probably spent time in our home. My father had sung in Cui's operas, and I remember being sent to Cui in 1901 with a special invitation to an opera performance celebrating my father's jubilee – my father wished to pay Cui a mark of attention. But though I saw him frequently at concerts, I do not remember him dressed otherwise than in military uniform – trousers with a stripe on the side, and a tunic that on special occasions had a little balcony of medals. Cui continued to lecture at the Military Academy in St Petersburg until the end of his life. He was said to be an authority on fortifications. He was stiff and military, too, and one felt half inclined to stand at attention when talking to him. He could be seen at concerts and other musical functions in St Petersburg quite regularly, in spite of his age, and the musicians of my generation came to stare at him as at a great curiosity.

Cui was rabidly anti-Wagner, but as a composer he had little to advance in Wagner's stead, a case of 'more substance in our enmities than in our love'. Nor could I take his orientalism seriously. 'Russian music', or 'Hungarian', or 'Spanish', or any other of the nineteenth-century national kind is as thin as local colour and as boring. But Cui helped me to discover Dargomïzhsky, and I am grateful for that. *Rusalka* was the most popular Dargomïzhsky opera at the time, but Cui convinced me that *The Stone Guest* is the superior work. He drew my attention to the remarkable quality of the recitatives in it, and though I do not know what I would think of this music today, it had an influence on my subsequent operatic thinking.

Did Cui hear *Firebird*? I do not know, and though I think he was present at the first performances of *Scherzo fantastique* and *Fireworks*, I recall no hint of his reactions to these pieces.

R.C. And Anton Arensky?

I.S. Arensky was a composer of the Moscow school – in other words, a follower of Tchaikovsky. As a pupil of Rimsky-Korsakov, I could not know him well. And, in all that concerned Arensky, Rimsky was, I thought, unjustifiably harsh and unkind. He criticized Arensky's music captiously and unnecessarily, and one of his comments about it, which he allowed to be printed after Arensky's death, was cruel: 'Arensky did very little, and that little will soon be forgotten.' I attended a performance of Arensky's opera *Dream on the Volga* with Rimsky. The music was dull, and Arensky's attempt to evoke a sinister atmosphere with the bass clarinet was horse-opera farce. But Rimsky's exclamation to me that 'the noble bass clarinet should not be put to such ignominious use' must have been overheard several rows in front of us, and later, of course, throughout the theatre.

Arensky had been friendly, interested and helpful to me, and in spite of Rimsky I always liked him and at least one of his works, the famous Piano Trio. He meant something to me also by the mere fact of his being a direct personal link with Tchaikovsky.

R.C. And Sergey Taneyev?

I.S. I saw him from time to time – as often, that is, as he came to St Petersburg, for he, too, was a Muscovite. He was a Tchaikovsky disciple, and he sometimes took Tchaikovsky's classes for him at the Moscow Conservatory. Taneyev was a good teacher, and in my youth I highly valued his treatise on counterpoint, one of the best books of its kind. I respected him as a composer for certain passages in his opera *The Oresteya*, and I admired him greatly as a pianist. But the same hostility prevailed on the Rimsky-Korsakov side, and poor Taneyev was unjustly treated in St Petersburg. I might add that he was held in some awe by us for an extra-musical reason: he was reputed to be the Countess Tolstoy's lover.

R.C. What were your relations with Anatoly Lyadov, especially after you had accepted the *Firebird* commission he had failed to fulfil?

I.S. Lyadov was a darling man, as sweet and charming as his own *Musical Snuff Box*. We called him 'the blacksmith', but I cannot think why, unless it was because he was so soft and gentle and so very unlike a blacksmith. A small man with a sympathetic, squinting face and a few hairs on his head, he always carried books under his arm – Maeterlinck, E. T. A. Hoffmann, Andersen: he liked tender, fantastical things. He was a short-winded, *pianissimo* composer, who never could have written a long and noisy ballet like *Firebird*. I suspect that he was more relieved than offended when I accepted the commission.

I liked Lyadov's music, especially *Kikimora* and *Baba-yaga*. His harmonic sense was acute, and he presented his music well instrumentally. Perhaps I was aware of the *Musical Snuff Box* when I composed a similar piece of my own, the 'ice-cream wagon' *Valse* in my Second Suite for small orchestra. I often accompanied him to concerts, but if we were not together and he happened to see me in the hall, he would invite me to come and follow a score with him. I do not know if he heard *Firebird* in later years, but am certain he would have defended it if he had. He championed my first pieces and was the most progressive of the musicians of his generation. Early in Skryabin's career, when the public's resistance to him was still general, someone referred to him in Lyadov's (and my) presence as a fool, whereupon Lyadov said, 'I like fools.'

When I think of Lyadov, I remember another composer, and since it will not occur to you to ask me about him, I will mention him myself, Iosif Wihtol. He had collaborated with Rimsky in one or two works and was a colleague of Lyadov's in that horrible musical prison, the St Petersburg Conservatory. A jovial man, with a round face and round hands, like a cat's paws, he was helpful to me. He moved to Riga, and when I visited that city on a concert tour in 1938, his affection and hospitality to me were princely.

*

R.C. What were your associations with Skryabin, in St Petersburg, and later, when Diaghilev had become interested in him? Did he have any influence on you?

I.S. I do not remember my first meeting with Skryabin, but it must have been in Rimsky-Korsakov's house; at any rate we encountered each other there occasionally in the years of my Rimsky tutelage. He was personally so maladroit, and his way of treating me and Rimsky's other pupils *von oben bis unten* was so detestable, that I had no desire to cultivate his company. Rimsky disliked him, too, and whenever he mentioned Skryabin to me, referred to him as 'the narcissist'. Rimsky did not value Skryabin's gifts as a composer very highly either: '*Mais, c'est du Rubinstein,*' – 'Anton Rubinstein' being a term of abuse.

As a pupil of Taneyev, Skryabin was better grounded in counterpoint and harmony than most of the Russians – much better equipped in these respects than, say, Prokofiev, whose gifts seemed to be more brilliant. Skryabin's own materials were derived in part from Liszt, which was natural for the age. I had nothing against Liszt, but I did not care for Skryabin's way of continually arguing for a Chopin–Liszt line as against a German tradition. I have elsewhere described his shock when I expressed my admiration for Schubert. The F minor Fantasia for piano four-hands was '*la musique pour les jeunes demoiselles*' to Skryabin. Most of his musical opinions were on the same level. I last saw him in Ouchy, where he had just arrived from Paris. He talked to me about Debussy and Ravel, and about my own music, but he showed no insight, and he did not tell me, as he told others, that he was horrified by *The Rite of Spring.* Since he had not been able to follow either *Petrushka* or *Firebird,* I should not have been surprised.

I was influenced by Skryabin in one insignificant respect, the piano writing of my Etudes, op. 7. But one is influenced by what one loves, and I never could love a bar of his bombastic music. As for Skryabin's short career with Diaghilev, I know only why it was short: Skryabin was 'morbid' (i.e., not homosexual). Diaghilev had mistakenly assumed the contrary, and had decided to take him to Paris, telling me, 'I will show Skryabin's music to Paris.' The show, of the Piano Concerto and the Second Symphony, as aforementioned, did not succeed.

Skryabin was literary-minded. His rages were Villiers de l'Isle Adam, Huysmans, and the whole company of the 'decadents'. It was the age of Symbolism, and in Russia he and Konstantin Balmont were its chief disciples. A follower of Mme Blavatsky, he was a serious Theosophist himself. I do not understand this, for in my generation Blavatsky was *démodé*, but I respected Skryabin's beliefs. He was an arrogant-looking man with thick blond hair and a blond *barbiche*. Although his death was tragic and premature, I have sometimes wondered about the music such a man would have written had he survived into the 1920s.

*

R.C. What are your personal memories of Prokofiev, and what did you think of his music?

I.S. I met Prokofiev in St Petersburg in the winter of 1906–7. He was a teenager at the time, but he had been given part of a concert in Walter Nouvel's 'Evenings of Contemporary Music' in which to play a group of his piano pieces. His performance was remarkable – I have always liked his music when he played it – and the music had personality. I do not know if Rimsky was there, though I do remember from a conversation with him about Prokofiev that he regarded him sceptically. But Lyadov, not Rimsky, had been Prokofiev's protector.

I did not know Prokofiev well until several years later, in Milan, in 1915. Diaghilev was busy introducing him to the Futurists and to 'leftist' circles in general. Diaghilev wanted him to exchange ideas with other artists, but the attempt failed, as it always did thereafter, because Prokofiev was full of splinters, as he says about his music in a letter to me, with people who were more cultivated than he was – and a good many were. On this Milan visit *The Rite of Spring* was his only subject of conversation. It had struck him like lightning, and he was for many years quite unable to recover from the experience.

Prokofiev was the contrary of a musical thinker. In fact, he was startlingly naïve in matters of musical construction. He had some technique and could do certain things very well, but more than that, he had personality – biological personality let us call it – as one saw in his every gesture. But his musical judgements were usually commonplace and often wrong. An example of the latter comes to mind in relation to *Petrushka*. Once when he was seated next to me at a performance of it, he turned to me at the climax of the Russian dances in the Fourth Tableau, and said, 'You should have ended here.' But to a perceptive musician the best pages in *Petrushka* are obviously the last.

I do not know what Prokofiev liked of my music beyond the early Russian pieces, especially *The Rite*, *Renard*, *The Wedding*, but I doubt if he knew very much of what I wrote in the 1930s, and I am quite sure he would not have liked it if he did. The fact that we were not really in accord musically did not seem to matter. We were always on good terms, there was never any incident between us, and I believe he was as friendly toward me as he was to any musician. Yet one could see Prokofiev a thousand times without establishing any deep connection with him, and we rarely talked about music when we were together. I used to think that his depths were engaged only when he played chess. He was a master at the game and he played with celebrated partners, as well as with my wife, Vera.

Diaghilev had believed at first that Prokofiev would develop into a 'great' composer, and he persisted in this belief for several years, before confiding to me that he had begun to think him 'stupid'. Of Prokofiev's Diaghilev ballets, I preferred *The Prodigal Son*, as choreographed by Balanchine. But I do not wish to criticize Prokofiev, and should be silent if I can say nothing good about him. Prokofiev had great merits, and that rare thing, the instant imprint of personality. Nor was he cheap; facility is not the same thing as cheapness.

Prokofiev was always very Russian-minded and always anti-clerical. But in my opinion these dispositions had little to do with his return to Russia. The reason for this was a sacrifice to the bitch goddess. He had not reaped any considerable success in the United States and Europe. When I saw him for the last time in New York, in 1937, he was despondent about his material and artistic fate in France. But his visit to the USSR was a triumph. Politically naïve, he had learned nothing from the example of his good friend Mayakovsky, so he decided to return to Russia to live. When he finally understood his situation there, it was too late. A few weeks before his premature death, in 1953, a friend of mine in New York, Nicolas Nabokov, received a letter from him enquiring about me, which greatly touched me.

*

R.C. Were you aware in your St Petersburg years of the work of such Russian experimental composers as Vladimir Rebikov, with his whole-tone structures and unresolved dissonances; Mikhail Gnesin, with his *Sprechgesang*; and Roslavetz, with his 'non-dodecaphonic serial sets'?

I.S. I was indeed acquainted with the work of these stepping-stone composers, and though I did not meet Roslavetz, I was much interested in the compositions of his that I heard in St Petersburg. The now so-called serial-set music, such as *Three*

Compositions for Piano, was written after I left Russia, and I have seen it only recently. Roslavetz came from Chernigov, my father's birthplace. ('*Cherni*' means 'black', and '*gov*' means 'soil'.) I did not know Rebikov personally, either, but his innovations were familiar to me in my Rimsky years, and I admired at least one of his works, the ballet *Yelka*.

Roslavetz and Rebikov were 'Moscow composers', but Gnesin was a St Petersburg pupil of Rimsky. I knew him well. I do not think his composer's gifts were strong or original – at least, everything of his that I heard sounded anonymous – but he was the liveliest and most open-minded spirit of the Rimsky group, except when I consider that the others were Steinberg, Glazunov, Grechaninov and Alexander Tcherepnin, the compliment sounds less generous than I intend it to be. Gnesin's *Sprechgesang* was only of passing interest because, unlike Schoenberg's, it did not grow out of a musical necessity. But Gnesin himself was a striking character. He dressed as an Orthodox Hebrew, but at the same time was identified with radically anti-sectarian political and social views. I once sent him a note, after we had dined together, saying that I was delighted by our 'sympathetic understanding'. He answered me in a surprised and slightly shocked tone, saying that he was very sorry but I had been mistaken: he had felt no such sympathy. That was typical of Gnesin, and probably it explains why I remember him.

R.C. You have often conducted Glinka overtures, as well as *Kamarinskaya*, in Bologna, in 1935. Have you always been fond of his music?

I.S. His music is minor, but he is not, since all music in Russia stems from him. In 1906, shortly after my marriage, I went with my wife and Nikolsky, my civics professor at the University of St Petersburg, to pay a visit of respect to Glinka's sister, Lyudmila Shestakova. An old lady in her nineties, she was surrounded by servants almost as old as herself, and she did not attempt to get up from her chair. As the widow of an admiral, she had to be addressed as 'Excellency'. I was thrilled to meet her simply because she had been close to Glinka. She talked to me about him, about my late father, whom she had known very well, and about the rabid anti-Wagnerism of the Cui–

Dargomïzhsky circle. Afterwards, as a memento of my visit she sent me a silver leaf of edelweiss.

R.C. What do you recollect of the authors of your first song texts, Sergey Gorodetsky and Konstantin Balmont?

I.S. I knew Gorodetsky well in 1906–7, when I was composing the music to his songs, but we did not 'collaborate' in them, and after hearing them at a concert in St Petersburg, he confided to me that 'the music is very pretty, but it really does not interpret my texts accurately, since I describe a time-to-time ringing of long, slow bells and your music is a kind of jingle bells'. He was a tall, blond, sickle-nosed man who, in Tiflis during the Revolution, became a good friend to my future wife Vera.

I did not meet Balmont, though once I saw him at one of our concerts in St Petersburg: he had bright red hair and a goatee, and he was dead drunk, his normal condition. But I was never close to any Russian literary group, and in fact the only Russian literary intellectuals I ever knew – Dmitri Merezhkovsky and Prince Mirsky – I met in Paris. Balmont also lived in Paris in the 1920s, but I did not encounter him there. His poetry is more significant than Gorodetsky's, and slightly less faded, though, as a nature poet, he was easily overshadowed by the revolutionaries, and especially by Alexander Blok. Balmont's *Zvezdolikiy* ('The Star-Faced One') is obscure as poetry and as mysticism, but its words are good, and words were what I needed, not meanings. I couldn't tell you even now what the poem means.

*

Many of my later memories of St Petersburg are associated with Diaghilev. I recall the first time I saw his apartment on the Zamiatine Pereulok and how disturbed I was by the perversely large number of mirrors on his walls. I remember him, too, as we went together to visit Alexander Benois in his rooms in the Vassilievsky Ostrov; or took a boat to one of the island nightclubs – the 'Aquarium', or the 'Village Rogie Vue' – in the Neva; and I can see Diaghilev now, entering the Leiner restaurant on the Nevsky Prospect, where Tchaikovsky had caught cholera, and bowing to people right and left like Baron de Charlus; or as we would dine together after a concert, in a little sawdust delicatessen, on marinated fish, caviar, Black Sea oysters, and the most delicious mushrooms in the world.

R.C. What ballet dancer did you most admire in your student years?
I.S. Anna Pavlova. She was never a member of Diaghilev's company, though he had very much wanted her. I met her in December 1909 in her home in St Petersburg. Diaghilev had asked her to invite me to a party, hoping that after she had met me she might agree to dance the part of the Firebird. Benois and Fokine were also there that night, and I remember that we drank champagne copiously. But whatever Pavlova thought of me personally, she did not dance in *Firebird*. I think the reasons for her refusal were my *Scherzo fantastique* and *Fireworks*. She considered these pieces 'decadent', a synonym for 'modern' then, whereas today 'decadent' often means not modern enough.

The lines of Pavlova's form and her mobile expression were ever beautiful to behold, but her dancing was always the same and quite devoid of constructive interest. In fact, I remember no difference in her dance from the first time I saw her in St Petersburg in 1905 or 1906, to the last time, which was in Paris in the 1930s. Pavlova was an *artiste*, but of an art far removed from the world of the Diaghilev ballet.

As I grew up, I became aware that the ballet was petrifying, that it had already become quite conventional. I could not regard it as an exploitable musical medium, and I would have been quite incredulous had anyone suggested that a modern movement in the arts was to be born through it. But would that movement have taken place without Diaghilev? I do not think so.

*

When I returned to St Petersburg from Ustilug in the fall of 1909, the gestation of *Firebird* had already begun, even though I was not yet certain of the commission, which, in fact, did not materialize until December, more than a month after I had started to compose. I remember the day Diaghilev telephoned to say 'go ahead', and I recall his surprise when I said that I already had. Early in November I moved from St Petersburg to a *dacha* belonging to the Rimsky-Korsakov family about seventy miles south-east of the city. I went there for a vacation in the birch forests and snow-fresh air, but instead began to work on *Firebird*. Andrey Rimsky-Korsakov was with me at the time, as he often was during the following months, for which reason *Firebird* is dedicated to him. The Introduction up to the bassoon-and-clarinet figure at bar 7 was composed in the country, as were notations for later parts. I returned to St Petersburg in December and remained there until March, when the composition was finished. The orchestral score was ready a month later, and the complete music mailed to Paris by mid-April. The score is dated 18 May, but by that time I was merely retouching details.

Firebird did not attract me as a subject. Like all story ballets, it demanded descriptive music of a kind I did not want to write. I had not yet proved myself as a composer, and I had not earned the right to criticize the aesthetics of my collaborators, but I did criticize them, and arrogantly, though perhaps my *age* (twenty-seven) was more arrogant than I was. Above all, I could not abide the assumption that my music would be imitation Rimsky-Korsakov, especially as by that time I was in revolt against poor Rimsky. It seems to me now that the two strains of Rimsky and Tchaikovsky appear in *Firebird* in about equal measure. The Tchaikovsky element is more 'operatic' and more 'vocal' (see nos. 12, 45, 71), though at least two Tchaikovskian dance pieces appear as well, 'The Princesses and the Golden Apples' and the short dance at no. 12. The Rimsky strain is more pronounced in harmony and orchestral colour, though I tried to surpass him with *ponticello*, *col legno*, *flautando*, *glissando* and flutter-tongue effects. If I say I was less than eager to fulfil the commission, I know that in truth my reservations about the subject were an advance defence for my not being sure I could. But Diaghilev, the diplomat, arranged everything. He came to call on me one day, with Fokine, Nijinsky, Bakst and Benois. When the five of them had proclaimed their belief in my talent, I began to believe, too, and accepted.

Fokine is usually credited as the librettist of *Firebird*, but I remember that all of us, and especially Bakst, who was Diaghilev's principal adviser, contributed ideas to the plan of the scenario. I should add that Bakst designed the two most important costumes, those of the Firebird and the Crown Prince. The others, by Golovine, were lost or destroyed during the 1914–18 war. His sets were like Persian carpets. To speak of my own collaboration with Fokine means nothing more than to say that we studied the libretto together, episode by episode, until I knew the exact musical measurements required. In spite of his wearying homilies, repeated at each meeting, on the role of music as accompaniment to dance, Fokine taught me much, and I have worked with choreographers in the same way ever since. I like exact requirements.

I was flattered, of course, at the promise of a performance of my music in Paris, and my excitement on arriving in that city, from Ustilug, towards the end of May, could hardly have been greater. These ardours were somewhat cooled at the first full rehearsal. The words 'For Russian Export' seemed to have been stamped everywhere, both on the stage and on the music. The mimic scenes were especially crude in this sense, but since Fokine liked them best, I could say nothing about them. I was also deflated to discover that not all of my interdictions on the musical performance were accepted as oracular. Gabriel Pierné, the conductor, even disagreed with me once in front of the whole orchestra. I had written *non crescendo* at several places, a sensible precaution, I thought, but Pierné said, 'Young man, if you do not want a *crescendo,* do not write anything.'

The first-night audience glittered indeed, but the fact that it was heavily perfumed is more vivid in my memory; the greyly elegant London audience, when I came to know it later, seemed almost deodorized by comparison. I sat in Diaghilev's loge, where, at intermissions, a path of celebrities, artists, dowagers, aged Egerias of the Ballet, writers, balletomanes, appeared. I met for the first time Proust, Giraudoux, Paul Morand, St John Perse, Claudel (with whom, years later, I nearly collaborated on a musical treatment of the Book of Tobit), though whether at the première or at subsequent performances I do not remember. I was also introduced to Sarah Bernhardt, who sat in a wheelchair in her private box, thickly veiled, and apprehensive lest anyone should recognize her. After a month of such society, I was happy to retire to a sleepy village in Brittany.

A moment of unexpected comedy occurred near the beginning of the performance. Diaghilev had wanted two real horses to cross the stage, a black one at the beginning, in step with the last six quavers of bar 8, and a white one near the end. The poor animals entered on cue all right, but when one of them began to whinny and capriole, and the other, a better critic than an actor, left a malodorous calling card, the audience tittered; Diaghilev did not risk a repetition in future performances. That he could have tried it even once seems incredible to me now, but the incident was forgotten in the general acclaim for the new ballet.

I was called to the stage to bow at the conclusion, and was recalled several times. I was still on stage when the final curtain came down, and I saw Diaghilev and a dark man with a double forehead coming toward me, whom Diaghilev introduced as Claude Debussy. The great composer spoke kindly about the music, ending his words with an invitation to dine with him. Some time later, sitting together in his loge at a performance of *Pelléas et Mélisande,* I asked him what he had really thought of *Firebird*, and he said, '*Que voulez-vous, il fallait bien commencer par quelque chose.*' Honest, but not extremely flattering. Yet shortly after the *Firebird* he gave his well-known photograph in profile to me with a dedication: '*à Igor Stravinsky en toute sympathie artistique*'. I was not so honest about the work we were then hearing. I thought *Pelléas* boring as a whole, and in spite of many wonderful pages. I remember that in the intermissions of the opera the people in the foyers were making fun of the *récit* style and intoning little sentences *à la Pelléas* to each other.

Ravel, who liked *Firebird*, though less than *Petrushka* and *The Rite of Spring*, explained its success to me as having been paved, in part, by the musical dullness of Diaghilev's last new production, *Pavillon d'Armide* (Benois–Nijinsky–Tcherepnin). The Parisian audience wanted a taste of the avant-garde, and, so Ravel said, *Firebird* satisfied this perfectly. To this explanation I would add that *Firebird* belongs to the style of its time. It is more vigorous than most of the composed folk music of the period, but it is also not very original. These are all good conditions for a success, a success that was not only Parisian. When I had selected a suite of the best numbers, and provided them with concert endings, *Firebird* was played all over Europe, and, indeed, became one of the most popular works in the whole orchestral repertory.

I was more proud of some of the instrumentation than of the

music itself. The horn *glissandi* produced the biggest sensation with the audience, of course, but this effect did not originate with me. (The now famous trombone-slide nose-thumbing in Kastchei's dance was added in 1919.) Rimsky had used trombone slides, I think in *Mlada*, Schoenberg used them in *Gurre-Lieder* and *Pelleas und Melisande*, and Ravel in *L'Heure espagnole*. For me, the most striking effect in *Firebird* originated with Rimsky, the natural-harmonic string *glissando* near the beginning, which the bass chord touches off like a Catherine wheel. I remember Richard Strauss's astonishment when he heard it two years later in Berlin.

But how am I to talk like a confessing author about *Firebird* when my feelings towards it are purely those of a critic? Still, to be honest, I was criticizing it even when I was composing it. The Mendelssohnian–Tchaikovskian Scherzo ('The Princesses and the Golden Apples'), for instance, failed to satisfy me. I laboured again and again on that piece, but could do no better, and an awkward orchestral handicap remains, though I cannot say exactly what it is. I have already criticized *Firebird* twice, in my revised versions of 1919 and 1945, and these purely musical criticisms are stronger than words.

Am I too critical? Does *Firebird* contain more real musical invention than I am able or willing to see? I wish this were the case. It was in some respects a fecund score for my own development in the next four years,[27] but the few scraps of counterpoint to be found in it – in the Kastchei scene, for example – are derived from chord notes, and this is not real counterpoint but Wagner's idea of counterpoint in *Die Meistersinger*. If an interesting construction exists in *Firebird*, it will be found in the treatment of intervals, in the major and minor thirds in the *Berceuse*, in the Introduction, and in the Kastchei music. The most successful piece in the score, in my opinion, is the Firebird's first dance, in 6/8 time. Rhythmically, too, the Finale might be cited as the first appearance in my music of metrical

27 Compare no. 191 with the Moor's music in *Petrushka*; the use of the Wagner *Tuben* at no. 105, the arrival of Kastchei, with the use of those instruments in *The Rite of Spring*; and the music at no. 193 at the second bar of no. 47 in *The Nightingale*.

irregularity – the 7/4 bars subdivided into 1, 2, 3; 1, 2; 1, 2/1, 2; 1, 2; 1, 2, 3, etc.

The remainder of *Firebird*'s history is uneventful. I sold the manuscript in 1919 to one Jean Bartholoni, an oil millionaire who lived in retirement in Geneva. He eventually presented it to the Geneva Conservatory. He also gave a generous sum of money to a London publishing house for the purchase of the music I composed during the war years, *The Wedding*, *Renard* and *The Soldier's Tale* included. The Diaghilev 1926 revival of *Firebird*, with décor and costumes by Goncharova, pleased me less than the original production, and subsequent productions. I should add that *Firebird* has been a mainstay of my life as a conductor. My conducting début occurred in a cut version of the ballet at a Red Cross benefit in the Paris Opéra in December 1915, and since then I have performed it perhaps two hundred times, though ten thousand would not erase the memory of the terrible *trac* I suffered that first night. And, oh yes, to complete the picture, I was once addressed by a man in an American railway dining car as 'Mr Fireberg'.

R.C. Do you remember Golovine's décor for the first *Firebird*?
I.S. I remember only that his costume designs pleased me at the time. I do not remember his set designs, but am certain that if transported back to June 1910, I would find them very opulent. Golovine, several years my senior, was not our first choice. Diaghilev wanted Michail Alexandrovich Vrubel, the most talented of all the Russian painters of the epoch, but he was dying or going mad. We also considered Benois, but Diaghilev chose Golovine because of his realization of the fantastic scenes in *Ruslan*. Furthermore, Golovine's orientalism conformed to the ideals of Diaghilev's magazine, *Mir iskustva,* rather than to the academic orientalism then so popular. As an easel painter, Golovine was a Russian pointillist. I do not remember him at the first *Firebird* performance. Probably Diaghilev did not want to pay for his trip. I myself received only 1,000 roubles for the commission, travel expenses, and the stay in Paris.

The first *Firebird*! The stage and the whole Opéra glittered. But I have a better memory of Pierné's eight orchestra rehearsals.

*

At the beginning of July 1910, I returned to Ustilug to fetch my wife and two children in order to let them see one of the extra *Firebird* performances that Diaghilev had been compelled to add. After it we went to a beachside hotel in La Baule, Brittany, where I composed, and partly orchestrated, my Verlaine songs. The only other event I can remember from that *vacance* in Brittany is that while sitting on a rock by the sea one day I caught a lobster. I heard a peculiar, fine scraping noise and discovered red antennae exploring the side of the rock near my foot. I grabbed them and, though the creature tried to scuttle, I held fast and, two hours later, ate a fine *homard à la mayonnaise*.

At the end of August we moved to a *pension* in Chardon Jogny, a village two stops on the funicular above Vevey, and in September to a clinic in Lausanne for my wife's confinement. I lived in the clinic, too, but rented an attic studio across the street where I began to compose *Petrushka*. On 23 September I witnessed the birth of my younger son, a blue blob coiled in placenta, like the breathing apparatus of some creature from outer space. By this time I had written most of the Second Tableau, the first part to be completed. I remember that when Diaghilev and Nijinsky visited me a few days later, in Lausanne, not Clarens, as stated in my autobiography, I was able to play a considerable portion of it for them. As soon as my wife could be moved, we installed ourselves in Clarens, where I composed the *Danse russe* from the First Tableau. The name 'Petrushka' came to me one day while I was walking along the quai at Clarens.

In October we moved again, this time to Beaulieu (Nice). The rest of the First Tableau, the whole of the Third, and most of the Fourth were composed there. By the end of the following March I had completed the orchestral score of three-fourths of the ballet and sent it to Koussevitzky, who had agreed to publish whatever music of mine I would give to him. Of the months in Beaulieu I remember little. I worked hard at *Petrushka* in spite of a debilitating and almost continual *Föhn*. In December I returned to St Petersburg to study the scenario with Benois, an upsetting visit. *Firebird* had radically altered my life, and the city I had known only a few months before as the grandest in the world now seemed sadly small and provincial.

One night after my return to Beaulieu I had a horripilating

dream. I thought I had become a hunchback and awoke in great pain to discover that I was unable to stand or even sit in an erect position. Whatever the role of dreams in relating memory and perception, I believe them to have been the ground for innumerable solutions in my composing activity. One characteristic of me in my dreams is that I am forever trying to tell the time and forever looking at my wristwatch, only to find that it isn't there. My dreams are my psychological digestive system. The illness was diagnosed as intercostal neuralgia caused by nicotine poisoning. I was many months recovering my strength.

From Beaulieu, too, I wrote to Andrey Rimsky-Korsakov, asking him to send a copy of the popular Russian *chanson* I was to use in *Petrushka* [at nos. 18, 22, 26–9, in clarinets and celesta]. He did send the music, but with words of his own fitted to it, facetious in intent, but in fact questioning my right to use such 'trash'. When *Petrushka* was performed in Russia, the Rimsky-Korsakov clan vilified it, especially Andrey, who went so far as to write a hostile letter. (Andrey later became editor of the *Musical Contemporary*, a review founded by my friend Pierre Souvtchinsky in 1915. Its editorial tone was hostile to me.) I saw him only once again after this incident. That was in June 1914, when he came to Paris with my brother Guriy, he to see Diaghilev's production of Rimsky-Korsakov's *Coq d'or* ballet, Guriy to see *The Nightingale*. This was the last time I saw Guriy.

R.C. How did you happen to use the *Jambe en bois* melody in *Petrushka*?

I.S. A hurdy-gurdy played it every afternoon beneath my window in Beaulieu, and since it struck me as a good tune for the scene I was then composing, I wrote it in, not dreaming that the composer might be alive and the music protected by copyright. Maurice Delage was with me at the time, and his opinion was that 'the melody must be very old'. Then, several months after the première, someone informed Diaghilev that the tune had been composed by a Mr Spencer, a gentleman very much alive and resident in France. In consequence, a share of *Petrushka*'s royalties has gone to Mr Spencer or his heirs since 1911. I do not cite this to grieve about it, since I should pay for the use of someone else's property, but I do not think it fair that I must pay one-sixth of all royalties deriving from the concert (non-staged) performances of *Petrushka*, even of excerpts, such as the *Russian Dance*, to my co-author of the libretto, Alexandre Benois.

The *Jambe en bois* incident might have had a sequel years later with the 'Happy Birthday' melody in the *Greeting Prelude* that I wrote for Pierre Monteux's eightieth birthday. I must have assumed this melody to be in the category of folk music, too, or, at least, to be very old and dim in origin. As it turned out, the author was alive, but graciously did not ask for an indemnity.

In April 1911 my wife returned to Russia with the children while I joined Diaghilev, Nijinsky, Fokine, Benois and Serov in Rome. These collaborators were enthusiastic about the music when I played it to them (except Fokine, of course), and with their encouragement I composed the end of the ballet. The resurrection of Petrushka's ghost was my idea, not Benois's. As I conceived it, the music in two keys in the Second Tableau is Petrushka's insult to the public, and I wanted the dialogue for trumpets in two keys at the end of the ballet to signify that his ghost is still insulting it. I was, and am, more proud of these last pages than of anything else in the score, though I still like the latter part of the Third Tableau (the Moor's scene), and the beginning of the First Tableau. But *Petrushka*, like *Firebird* and *The Rite of Spring*, has already survived a half-century of destructive popularity, and if it does not sound as fresh today as, for example, Schoenberg's *Five Pieces for Orchestra*, the reason is partly that the Viennese opus has been protected by fifty years of neglect. Diaghilev wanted me to change the last four *pizzicato* notes in favour of 'a tonal ending', as he so quaintly put it, though two months later, when *Petrushka* was one of the Ballets' all-time greatest successes, he denied having made his original criticism.

The success of *Petrushka* was an agreeable surprise. We were afraid that its placement at the beginning of the programme, because of problems in setting the stage properties, would be ruinous. I also feared that French musicians, Ravel especially, who resented any criticism of the Russian 'Five', would consider the music as just such a criticism, which, of course, it was. But the success of *Petrushka* was exactly what I needed in that it gave me the absolute conviction of my ear as I was about to begin *The Rite of Spring*.

*

I was introduced to Giacomo Puccini for the first time at a performance of *Petrushka* in the Théâtre du Châtelet. Puccini, a big, handsome, dandified man, was very kind and cordial. He had told Diaghilev and others, in his thick Italian–French accent, that my music was horrible, but that it was also very talented. In any case the musical distance between us was no obstacle to our friendship. When I was in bed with typhus after *The Rite*, first in a hotel and then in a hospital in Neuilly, Puccini was one of the first people to visit me. (Ravel also came, and wept, which frightened me. Diaghilev, terrified of catching the disease, did not do that, but he paid my hospital bill.) I have sometimes thought that Puccini may have half-consciously recalled the tuba solo in *Petrushka* when he wrote the music of *Gianni Schicchi*, seven bars before rehearsal number 78.

*

R.C. Do you remember Fokine's choreography for the original *Firebird* and *Petrushka*?

I.S. I do, but I didn't really like the dance movement of either ballet. The female dancers in *Firebird*, the princesses, were insipidly sweet, while the male dancers were the *ne plus ultra* of brute masculinity: in the Kastchei scene they sat on the floor kicking their legs in an incredibly stupid manner. I prefer Balanchine's choreography of the 1945 suite to the whole Fokine ballet.

Nor did Fokine realize my ideas for *Petrushka*, though I suspect that this time the fault was rather with Diaghilev than with Fokine. I conceived the Charlatan as a character out of E. T. A. Hoffmann, a lackey in a tightly modelled blue *frac* with gold stars, and not at all as a Russian Metropolitan. The flute music, too, is Weber-like, or Hoffmann-like, not Russian-'Five'. I had thought of the Moor as a kind of Wilhelm Busch caricature and not as the merely mechanical comic-relief character he is usually made out to be. Another of my ideas was that Petrushka should watch the dances of the Fourth Tableau (the Coachmen, the Nurses, et al.) from a peep-hole in his cell and that we, the audience, should watch them, too, from the perspective of his cell. I never did like the full-stage dance carousel at this point of the drama. Finally, Fokine's choreography was ambiguous at the most important moment. Petrushka's ghost, as I conceived the story, is the real Petrushka, and his appearance at the end makes the Petrushka of the preceding play a mere doll. His gesture is not one of triumph or protest, as is so often said, but a nose-thumbing addressed to the audience. The significance of this gesture is not and never was clear in Fokine's staging. One great invention of Fokine's was the rigid arm movement that Nijinsky was to make such an unforgettable gesture.

Fokine, with Glazunov, was one of the two most disagreeable men I have ever known. But Glazunov was a time-to-time drunkard, which redeemed him – from time to time; he would lock his door for two-week binges on Château Yquem! (Imagine bingeing on Château Yquem!) I was never a friend of Fokine's, not even in our first years together, but was a partisan of Enrico Cecchetti, a mere academician in Fokine's eyes. Diaghilev decided that Fokine's dances for *Prince Igor* certified him as the best qualified of our choreographers to stage *Firebird*. After *Firebird* and *Petrushka*, I had little to do with him. He was spoiled by his success in America, and thereafter wore the 'I-have-made-an-American-kill' look. I saw him last with Ida Rubinstein. He was to have choreographed my *Fairy's Kiss* for her, but eventually Bronislava Nijinska did it, to my relief. After that and until the end of his life (1940), I received complaints from him about business or royalty matters connected with *Firebird*, which he would actually refer to as *my* 'musical accompaniment' to *his* 'choreographic poem'.

*

R.C. What are your recollections of Lev Bakst?
I.S. Nothing could describe him better than Cocteau's caricature. We were instant friends from our first meeting in St Petersburg, in 1909, though our conversation consisted largely of Bakst's accounts of his exploits in the conquest of women, and my incredulity: 'Now, Lev . . . you couldn't have done all that.' Bakst overdressed – hats, spats, canes – but this was meant to detract from his Venetian comedy-mask nose. Like other dandies, he was sensitive, and privately mysterious. Roerich told me that *'bakst'* was a Jewish word meaning 'little umbrella'. Roerich said he discovered this one day in Minsk, when he was caught in a thundershower and heard people sending their

children home for 'baksts', which then turned out to be what he said they were.

Bakst loved Greece and all things Greek. He travelled there with Serov, who was the conscience of our whole circle – even Diaghilev deferred to him in some matters – and a very important friend to me in my youth. Bakst published a book of travel diaries called *With Serov in Greece* (1922) that should have been translated into English long ago.

I had seen Bakst's easel painting before I knew any of his theatre work, but I could not admire it. In fact it represented everything in Russia against which *The Rite of Spring* is a revolt. I consider Bakst's *Sheherazade* a masterpiece, perhaps the perfect achievement of the Ballets Russes from the scenic point of view. The costumes, sets, the curtain, were colourful in an indescribable way – we are so much poorer in these things now. I remember, too, that Picasso regarded *Sheherazade* as a great achievement, no doubt for the voluptuousness of the costume of the title character. In fact, it was the one production of the ballet he really did admire: '*Vous savez, c'est très spécialiste, mais admirablement fait.*'

R.C. And Benois?

I.S. I knew him before Bakst, but my real friendship with him began in Rome in 1911, when I was finishing *Petrushka*. We stayed in the Albergo Italia near the Quattro Fontane and for two months were together every day. He was at that time the most cultivated Italophile I had ever met, and except for Eugene Berman, would be still. Benois and Berman are very alike in the fact of their Russian background, their Romantic theatre, their Italophilia. Benois knew more about music than any of the other painters, though the music he knew was nineteenth-century Italian opera. Nevertheless, I think he liked *Petrushka*.

Benois was very quickly up on his *amour propre*. The Ballets' greatest success at that time was the *Spectre de la rose* with Nijinsky, and Benois was plainly jealous of Bakst's role in that success. Jealousy accounts for an incident that occurred the following year. Benois was painting the backdrop of Petrushka's cell when Bakst happened on the set, picked up a brush, and started to help. Benois fairly flew at him.

*

R.C. You must have seen a great deal of José Maria Sert in the Diaghilev days.

I.S. Yes, but his wife Misia was much more of a friend to me, and in truth I could not help finding Sert somewhat ridiculous. The Serts – though they were not yet legally 'Serts' – were among the first people I met in Paris when I arrived there in 1910. He knew many 'interesting people', especially interesting *rich* people, and was very adept at procuring commissions from them. I believe that he became a 'painter of the Russian Ballet' chiefly because he knew Fürstner, Richard Strauss's publisher. Diaghilev wanted Strauss to compose a ballet, and the only way he could approach him was through Fürstner. Sert became the ambassador of the project and therefore its painter. The ballet was the *Legend of Joseph*. Sert's sets for it were crowded, Fokine's choreography was not very interesting, and the result was not one of Diaghilev's greatest successes, though Massine was perfect in the title role.

Sert might have figured more permanently in the history of painting as subject matter. A big, black-bearded man, *démodé–distingué*, he would have made an excellent portrait subject for Manet. His manner was very grand and he played at being Spanish, but he had a sense of humour that somehow redeemed these affectations. I remember asking him once how he intended to move one of his huge murals, and his sarcastic answer: 'You turn a little valve and it deflates to one-hundredth the size.' We came to the United States on the SS *Normandie* together in the 1930s, and the last time I saw him was in New York. Poor Sert, he wanted to be a painter, but his painting, alas, is *quelconque*.

In 1920 I presented my *Rite* sketches, handsomely bound, to Misia Sert, in gratitude for helping to underwrite the December 1920 revival of the ballet.

*

The idea of *The Rite of Spring* came to me while I was still composing *Firebird*. I had dreamed of a scene of pagan ritual in which a chosen sacrificial virgin danced herself to death. This vision was not accompanied by concrete musical ideas, and as I was soon impregnated with another and purely musical conception that began to develop into, as I thought, a *Konzertstück* for piano and orchestra; the latter piece was the one I started to compose. I had already told Diaghilev about *The Rite* before he came to see me in Lausanne at the end of September 1910, but he did not know about *Petrushka*, which is what I called the *Konzertstück*, thinking that the style of the piano part suggested the Russian puppet. Though Diaghilev may have been disappointed not to hear music for 'pagan rites', in his delight with *Petrushka*, which he encouraged me to develop into a ballet before undertaking *The Rite*, he did not show it.

In July 1911, after the first performances of *Petrushka*, I travelled to the Princess Tenisheva's country estate near Smolensk, to meet with Nicolay Roerich and plan the scenario of *The Rite of Spring*. Roerich knew the Princess well, and he was eager for me to see her collections of Russian ethnic art. I journeyed from Ustilug to Brest-Litovsk, only to find that I would have to wait two days for the next train to Smolensk. I therefore bribed the conductor of a freight train to let me ride in a cattle car, in which I was alone with a bull! The animal was leashed by a single not-very-reassuring rope, and, as he glowered and slavered, I barricaded myself behind my one small suitcase. I must have looked an odd sight in Smolensk as I stepped from that *corrida*, carrying my expensive, or, at least, not tramp-like, bag and brushing my clothes and hat, but I must also have looked relieved. The Princess Tenisheva gave me a guesthouse attended by servants in handsome white uniforms with red belts and black boots. I set to work with Roerich, and in a few days the plan of action and the titles of the dances were composed. Roerich also sketched his famous Polovtsian-type backdrops while we were there, and designed costumes after real costumes in the Princess's collection. At this time, our title for the ballet was *Vesna Sviaschennaia* ('Sacred Spring', or 'Holy Spring'). *Le Sacre du printemps* was Bakst's title. In English, 'The Coronation of Spring' is closer to my original meaning than 'The Rite of Spring'.

I became conscious of thematic ideas for *The Rite* immediately after returning to Ustilug, the themes being those of *Augurs of Spring*, the first dance I was to compose. Returning to Switzerland in the fall, I moved with my family to Les Tilleuls, a pension in Clarens, and continued work. Almost the entire

Rite of Spring was written in a tiny room of this house, in an eight-feet-by-eight closet, rather, whose only furniture was a small upright piano, which I kept muted (I always work at a muted piano), a table and two chairs. I composed from the *Augurs* to the end of Part One, then wrote the *Prelude* afterwards. My idea was that the *Prelude* should represent the awakening of nature, the scratching, gnawing, wiggling of birds and beasts. The dances of the second part were composed in the order in which they now appear, and composed very quickly, too, until *The Sacrificial Dance*, which I could play, but did not, at first, know how to write. The composition of the whole of *The Rite* was completed, in a state of exaltation and exhaustion, on 17 November 1912; I remember the day well because I was suffering from a raging toothache, which I then went to treat in Vevey. Most of the instrumentation – a mechanical job, largely, as I always compose the instrumentation when I compose the music – was written in score form by the end of March 1913.

I had pushed myself to finish *The Rite of Spring*, since I had originally wanted Diaghilev to produce it in the 1912 season. In Berlin, where the Ballets Russes was performing at the end of November, I found Diaghilev upset about Nijinsky's health. He would talk about Nijinsky by the hour, but all he ever said about *The Rite* was that, as had become evident, he could not mount it in 1912. Aware of my disappointment, he tried to console me by inviting me to accompany the Ballets to Budapest, Vienna, and London, its next stops. I did journey to these cities, all three new to me then, and all three greatly cherished ever since. But the real reason I so easily accepted the postponement of *The Rite* was that I had already begun to think about *The Wedding*. At this Berlin meeting Diaghilev encouraged me to use a huge orchestra for *The Rite of Spring*, promising that the size of our ballet orchestra would be greatly increased in the following season. I am not sure that my orchestra would have been as large otherwise.

R.C. What were Diaghilev's powers of musical judgement? What, in particular, was his response to *The Rite* when he first heard it?
I.S. His musical judgement was less astute and less important than his immense flair for recognizing the potentiality of success

in a piece of music or a work of art in general. In spite of his surprise when I played the beginning of *The Rite* for him at the piano, in spite of his at first ironic attitude to the long succession of repeated chords, he quickly realized that the reason was something other than my inability to compose more diversified music.

R.C. Did you choose Nicolay Roerich for the décor?

I.S. Yes. I admired his *Prince Igor* sets and imagined he might do something similar for *The Rite*. Above all, I knew he would not overload. I still have a good opinion of Roerich's *Rite*, though at the time I was far too busy with the music to be aware of anyone besides Debussy and Ravel, who were not then on speaking terms, and who sat on opposite sides of the house. I took my place directly behind Monteux to avoid a show of partiality for either of the feuding composers.

Roerich had designed a backdrop of steppes and sky, the terra incognita '*Hic sunt leones*' country of old mapmakers' imaginations. The row of twelve blond, square-shouldered girls against this landscape made a striking tableau. And Roerich's costumes were said to have been historically exact, as well as scenically satisfying. He came to Paris for the première, but received very little attention, and soon disappeared, slighted, I think, back to Russia. I never saw him again, but I was not surprised to hear during the last war of his secret activities and of his curious connection with Vice-President Wallace in Tibet. He looked as though he ought to have been either a mystic or a spy.

Everyone knows that the first performance of *The Rite of Spring* was attended by a scandal but, strange as it may seem, I had no intimation of it. The musicians who heard the orchestra rehearsals seemed intrigued by the work, and the stage spectacle did not appear likely to provoke a riot. Debussy, in spite of his later, ambivalent attitude ('*C'est une musique nègre*'), was enthusiastic at the rehearsals. Indeed, he might well have been pleased, for *The Rite of Spring* owes more to him than to any other composer, the best music (the *Prelude*) as well as the weakest (the music of Part Two between the first entrance of the muted-trumpet duos and *The Celebration of the Chosen One*). After rehearsing for months, the dancers knew what they were doing, even though this often had nothing to do with the music.

'I will count to forty while you play,' Nijinsky would say to me, 'and we will see where we come out.' He could not understand that though we might at some point come out together, this did not mean that we had been together on the way. The dancers followed Nijinsky's beat, rather than the musical beat. Nijinsky counted in Russian, of course, and since Russian numbers above ten are polysyllabic – eighteen, for example, is *vosemnádsat* – in fast tempos neither he nor they could keep pace with the music.

At the performance mild protests could be heard from the very beginning. When the curtain opened on the group of knock-kneed and long-braided Lolitas jumping up and down, the storm broke. Cries of '*Ta gueule*' came from behind me. I heard Florent Schmitt shout, '*Taisez-vous grues du seizième*', the '*grues*' of the sixteenth *arrondissement* being the most elegant ladies in Paris. But the uproar continued, and I left the hall in a fury; I was sitting on the right near the orchestra, and I remember slamming the door. I have never again been that angry. The music was so familiar to me, I loved it, and I could not understand why people who had not yet heard it wanted to protest in advance. Backstage I saw Diaghilev flickering the house lights in an effort to quiet the hall, and for the rest of the performance I stood in the wings behind Nijinsky holding the tails of his *frac*, while he stood on a chair shouting numbers to the dancers, like a coxswain.

R.C. Was the musical performance reasonably correct? Do you recall anything more about that night of 29 May 1913?

I.S. The image of Monteux's back is more vivid in my mind today than the stage picture. He stood there apparently impervious and as nerveless as a crocodile. It is still almost incredible to me that he actually brought the orchestra through to the end.

After the performance we were excited, angry, disgusted and . . . happy. So far from weeping and reciting Pushkin in the Bois de Boulogne as the legend is, Diaghilev's comment was: 'Exactly what I wanted.' He certainly looked contented. No one could have been quicker to understand the publicity value of what had happened. Quite probably he had thought about the possibility of a fracas when I played what was finished of the score for him in August 1912 in the east-corner ground room of the Grand Hotel in Venice.

I remember with infinitely more pleasure the first concert performance the following year, a triumph such as composers rarely enjoy. The acclaim of the young people who filled the Casino de Paris completely reversed the verdict of the year before. (Incidentally, Saint-Saëns, a sharp little man – I had a good view of him – attended *this* performance; whether or not he was at the première and walked out during the opening bassoon solo I do not know.) Monteux again conducted, and the musical realization was ideal. He was doubtful about playing it on a programme that included a Mozart concerto played by George Enescu, and the Bach Double Concerto played by Enescu and a violinist whose name I forget. Shortly before his 1914 *Rite* revival, Monteux had enjoyed a great success performing *Petrushka* in concert, and he was proud of his prestige among avant-garde musicians. I argued that *Spring* was more symphonic, more of a concert piece, than *Petrushka*. Let me say here that Monteux, almost alone among conductors, never cheapened *The Rite* or looked for his own glory in it, and he continued to play it all his life with the greatest fidelity. At the end, the entire audience jumped to its feet and cheered. I came on stage and hugged Monteux, who was a river of perspiration; it was the saltiest hug of my life. A crowd swept backstage. I was hoisted to anonymous shoulders and carried into the street and up to the Place de la Trinité. A policeman pushed his way to my side in an effort to protect me, and it was this guardian of the law whom Diaghilev later fixed upon in his account of the story: 'Our little Igor now requires police escorts out of his concerts, like a prize fighter.' Diaghilev was always verdantly envious of any success of mine outside of his Ballets Russes.

I have seen only one stage version of *The Rite* since 1913, Diaghilev's 1920 revival. Music and dancing were better coordinated this time than in 1913, but the choreography (by Massine) was too gymnastic and Dalcrozean to please me. I realized then that I prefer the work as a concert piece.

I first conducted *The Rite* myself in 1926, in Amsterdam, and then in 1928 for a recording by English Columbia.[28] I was

28 The recording actually took place in Paris during the second week of May 1929. [R.C.]

nervous about doing it at first, in view of its reputed difficulties, but these, actually no more than the simple alternation of twos and threes, proved to be a conductors' myth. *Spring* is strenuous but not difficult, and the *chef d'orchestre* is hardly more than a mechanical agent, a time-beater who fires a pistol at the beginning of each section but lets the music run by itself. After conducting *The Rite* publicly with the Concertgebouw, I did it regularly throughout Europe. One of my most memorable performances of these years was in the Salle Pleyel, in the presence of M. Poincaré, the President of the Republic, and his First Minister, M. Herriot.

I have revised large portions of *The Rite* three times, first for the Diaghilev revival in 1920 [see the 1921–22 miniature score], second in 1926 for my own first performance of it, in Amsterdam, and third in 1943 for a performance (unrealized) by the Boston Symphony Orchestra. The differences between these rewrites have been much discussed, though they are not well known or even often perceived. In at least two of the dances the lengths of the bars are now very different than in the 1913 original; I tried to adjust the metrical units to the musical phrasing. But by 1926, my performance experience had led me to prefer smaller metrical divisions (cf. *The Evocation of the Ancestors*). The smaller metres proved more manageable for both conductor and orchestra, and they greatly simplified the scansion of the music. (I was thinking of a similar question recently while reading a quatrain from one of the *Sonnets to Orpheus*. Did the poet write the lines at this length, or, as I think, did he cut them in half later?) Though my main purpose in revising *The Sacrificial Dance* was to facilitate performance by means of an easier-to-read unit of beat, the instrumentation has been changed, too – improved, I think – in many ways. The music of the second horn group, for example, is considerably amended in the later version – I was never satisfied with the horn parts – and the muted horn note following the five-note trombone solo is much stronger in the bass trumpet of the 1943 version. The string parts have also been radically rewritten. Amateurs of the older version claim to be disturbed by the change of the last chord, but I was never satisfied with it. A noise before, it is now an aggregation of distinctly voiced pitches.

But I would go on eternally revising my music were I not too busy composing more of it, and I am still far from content with everything in *The Rite*. (The first violin and flute parts in *The Procession of the Elder*, for example, are badly overbalanced.)

I was guided by no system whatever in *The Rite of Spring*. When I think of the other composers of that time who interest me, Schoenberg, Berg, and Webern, their music seems much more *theoretical*. And it is supported by a great tradition. Composing *The Rite*, I had only my ear to help me. I heard and I wrote what I heard.

*

R.C. Your *Autobiography* does not contain any information about the première of *The Nightingale*, which followed the sensational *Rite of Spring*. What do you remember of the performance and its reception, and why was the production so quickly eclipsed?
I.S. The eclipse, as you call it, must be attributed primarily to budgetary rather than to artistic reasons. The forty-minute opera required three sets and many costly costumes. The neglect of *The Nightingale* is in part due to the necessity of performing it on a double bill, and suitable companion pieces have been difficult to find. (When I conducted it myself at La Scala in the 1920s – a performance efficiently prepared by Toscanini, incidentally – the other half of the bill was *Hänsel und Gretel*!) Diaghilev coupled it with ballets, especially with *Petrushka*, a logical choice, but he wanted to stage *The Nightingale* as opera-ballet, with dancers miming the sung roles, and the singers nicely out of sight in the orchestra pit.

The première was unsuccessful only in the sense that it failed to provoke a protest. Musically and visually, the production was excellent. Monteux conducted capably; the singers – particularly Death and The Nightingale – were good; and Alexander Benois's costumes and sets were stunning. Boris Romanov composed the dances, and Alexander Sanin was the *metteur en scène*. The opera was sung in Russian, and that is all I remember about the première.

As to its reception, the 'advanced' musicians seemed genuinely enthusiastic. That Ravel liked it, I am certain, but I am almost as convinced that Debussy did not, for I heard nothing whatever from him about it. I remember this well, since I expected him to question me about the great difference between the music of Act I and the later acts. Though I knew he would have liked the Musorgsky–Debussy beginning, he probably would have said, 'Young man, I do it better.' On my last trip to Russia I remember reading a remark in my diary – I kept a diary from 1906 to 1910 – written when I was composing the first act of *The Nightingale*: 'Why should I be following Debussy so closely, when the real originator of this operatic style was Musorgsky?' But in justice to Debussy I should add that I saw him only very infrequently in the weeks after *The Nightingale*, and perhaps he simply had no opportunity to tell me his true impressions.

The Nightingale was put together in a great hurry, and in fact I was still composing the music only a few weeks before the première. The London performances in June were probably superior to the Paris première in May, if only because the singers and dancers would have had more time with their parts. I immensely enjoyed the London performance, at any rate, thanks also to the generosity of Sir Thomas Beecham.

Alexander Benois was in Russia and I in Switzerland during the latter stages of the opera's planning and composition. Since my wife was ill with tuberculosis, we moved to Leysin – to be near the sanatorium. I could not meet with Benois, therefore, and anyway Diaghilev tended to favour Roerich, not Benois, as the opera's designer. My great respect for Benois prevailed.

*

R.C. The early 1910 group photo taken at the English Club in St Petersburg and including you and Vaslav Nijinsky shows you positioned apart from the members and widely separated from each other. I imagine you became close during *Petrushka*.

I.S. When Diaghilev introduced me to Nijinsky, in St Petersburg in 1909, I was aware of him as an extraordinary physical being with curious absences in his personality. I liked his shy manner and his soft, Polish speech, and he was immediately very open and affectionate with me. When I knew him better, I thought him childishly spoiled and impulsive. Later, too, I came to understand the absences as a kind of stigmata. I could not imagine that they would so soon and so tragically destroy him. I often think of Nijinsky in his final years, a captive in his own mind, his perfect gift of expression in movement stricken, immobile.

Already a celebrity when I met him, Nijinsky would soon become even more widely known as a subject of scandal. Diaghilev had taken charge of his costuming – they were living together – with the result that Nijinsky appeared at the Imperial Theatre in the tightest tights anyone had ever seen, and little else. Diaghilev had padded the dancer's athletic support with handkerchiefs. The Tsar's mother saw a performance and was shocked. Diaghilev and the director of the theatre, a man who shared the same sexual proclivities, were thought to have conspired against public decency. When the Tsar alluded to the matter in a conversation with Diaghilev, he answered so curtly that he was never in good odour at court thereafter. I discovered this for myself when Diaghilev asked me to approach Ambassador Izvolsky in an attempt to secure a passport for a dancer of conscription age. When Izvolsky understood my request to be on Diaghilev's behalf, he became coldly diplomatic. (I was often Diaghilev's ambassador in later years, especially his 'financial' ambassador, or, as he used to call me, his tax-collector.)

The truth of the Imperial Theatre scandal is that the exhibitionist was not Nijinsky but Diaghilev. Nijinsky was always serious and high-minded and, in my judgement, never conscious of his performances from Diaghilev's point of view. I was even more certain of this later, in Paris, when he danced *The Afternoon of a Faun*. This ballet's famous representation of masturbation was Diaghilev's idea. Even so, Nijinsky's performance was such marvellously concentrated art that only a fool could have been shocked by it – but then, I loved the ballet myself.

Nijinsky was innocently honest and wholly without guile. He never understood that in society one does not always say all that one thinks. At a dinner party in London, in January 1913, Lady Ripon proposed a parlour game in which we were all to decide what sort of animal each of us most resembled – a dangerous game. Lady Ripon initiated it herself by saying, 'Diaghilev looks like a bulldog and Stravinsky like a *renard*. Now, M. Nijinsky, what do you think I look like?' Nijinsky thought a moment, then spoke the awful, exact truth: '*Vous, Madame – chameau*' – just the three words; Nijinsky did not know much French.

Lady Ripon did not expect that, of course, and in spite of her repeating 'A camel? How amusing! I declare. Really? A camel?', she was flustered all evening.

My own disappointment with Nijinsky was that he did not know the musical alphabet. He never understood musical metres and did not have a very certain sense of tempo. In truth, *The Rite of Spring* was rhythmic chaos on stage, especially the last dance. Poor Mlle Piltz, the sacrificial maiden, was not even aware of the scrambled bars. Nor did Nijinsky understand my own choreographic ideas for *The Rite*. I do not say that his creative imagination lacked abundance; on the contrary, it was almost too rich. The point is simply that he did not know music, and therefore his notion of the relation between music and dance was primitive. To some extent this might have been remedied by education, for of course he was musical. But at the time he was made chief choreographer of the Ballets Russes he was hopelessly unprepared with regard to musical technique. He believed that choreography should re-emphasize the musical beat and pattern in constant co-ordination, which, in effect, restricted the dance to rhythmic duplication and an imitation of the music. Choreography, as I see it, must realize its own form, independent of the musical form, but measured to the musical unit. Its construction will be based on whatever correspondences the choreographer may invent, but it must not seek merely to duplicate the line and beat of the music. I do not see how one can be a choreographer unless, like Balanchine, one is a musician first.

Nijinsky was not the least capable musically of my choreographic collaborators, but his talent was elsewhere. To call him a dancer is not enough, for he was an even greater dramatic actor. His beautiful, but certainly not handsome, face could become the most powerful actor's mask I have ever seen, and, as Petrushka, he was the most exciting human being I have ever seen on a stage.

I recently discovered a letter from him addressed to me in Russia and forwarded to Switzerland. It is a document of such astounding innocence that if Nijinsky hadn't written it, I think only a character in Dostoyevsky might have done. It seems incredible to me even now that he was so unaware of the politics, the sexual jealousies, and the ulterior motives within the Ballets Russes.

Tuesday, 9th December 1913
1 Hidegkuti ut 51 (Budapest)

Dear Igor:

I cannot hide from you what has happened to me these last months. You know that I went to South America and have not been in Europe for four months. These four months cost me dearly in money and health. My room with board costs 150 francs daily. I did not receive this money from Serge, but was obliged to take it from my own capital. What did Serge do all this time while we were in South America? I do not know. I wrote to him many times without receiving any answer. And I needed an answer, too, as I had worked on two new ballets – *Joseph and Potiphar*, by Strauss,[29] and another one, with Bach's music. All the preparatory work for these ballets was completed and I had only to put them in rehearsal. I could not rehearse in America because of the terrible heat, from which we almost died. How I managed to stay in good health up to the last evening there I do not know. But though I was lucky in America, here I have been ill for two months. Now I am all right.

I did not send you an invitation to my wedding as I knew you would not come,[30] and I did not write to you because I had so much to do. Please excuse me. I went with my wife to her parents' home in Budapest and there I immediately sent a telegram to Serge asking him when we could see each other. The answer to my telegram was a letter from Grigoriev[31] informing me that I shall not be asked to stage any ballets this season, and that I am not needed as an artist.

Please write to me whether this is true. I do not believe that Serge can act so meanly to me. Serge owes me a lot of money. I have received nothing for two years, neither for my dancing nor for my staging of *Faune*, *Jeux*, and *Sacre du printemps*. I worked for the Ballet without a contract. If it is true that Serge does not want to work with me – then I have lost everything. You understand the situation I am in. I cannot imagine what has happened, what is the reason for his behaviour. Please ask Serge what is the matter, and write to me about it. In all the newspapers of Germany, Paris, and London, etc., it is reported that I am not working any more with Diaghilev. But the whole press is against him (including the *feuilletons*). They also say that I am gathering a company of my own. In truth, I am receiving propositions from

29 *Josephslegende*, first performed in Paris in May 1914.
30 The wedding took place in Montevideo.
31 Serge Grigoriev, the *régisseur* of the Ballets Russes.

every side, and the biggest of these comes from a very rich businessman, who offers one million francs to organize a new Diaghilev Russian Ballet – they wish me to have sole artistic direction and large sums of money to commission décor, music, etc. But I won't give them a definite answer before I have news from you.

My numerous friends send me letters of revolt and rage against Diaghilev – and propositions to help me and join me in my new enterprise. I hope you will not forget me and will answer my letter immediately.

Your loving

VASLAV

Regards to your wife and to all I know. v.

I never saw Nijinsky again after *The Rite of Spring*, so, in fact, I knew him for only four years. But those four years were the great age of the Ballets Russes and from September 1910 to June 1913 I was with him most of the time. I do not recall what I answered, but Diaghilev had already returned to Russia, and when he was next in Paris, Leonid Massine had 'replaced' poor Nijinsky.

*

R.C. What are your memories of Bronislava Nijinska?

I.S. Her choreography for the original productions of *Renard* (1922) and *The Wedding* (1923) pleased me more than any other of my works performed by Diaghilev's troupe in the 1920s, except Balanchine's *Apollo*. Her conception of *The Wedding* in blocks and masses, and her acrobatic *Renard*, coincided with my ideas, as well as with the décor. The set for *The Wedding* was beeswax yellow, and the costumes were peasant brown, in contrast to the hideously non-Russian reds, greens and blues one usually sees in foreign stagings of Russian plays and operas. *Renard* was a real Russian satire. The animals saluted very like the Russian Army (Orwell would have been amused by this), and there was always an underlying significance to their movements. Nijinska's *Renard* was superior in every way to the 1929 Lifar revival, though the latter was ruined by some jugglers Diaghilev had borrowed from a circus – one of many whims that failed.

Poor Bronia was luckless with Diaghilev. Since her face was bony and interesting, and not at all doll-like, Diaghilev opposed the idea that she dance the Ballerina in *Petrushka*, even though as a dancer she was second to none. Indeed, the Nijinskys – brother and sister together – were the greatest dancing pair imaginable. Later, after Nijinsky's marriage, Diaghilev could not overcome his prejudice against her. She looked like Nijinsky, was shaped like him bodily, with the same big shoulders, and was a constant reminder of him. It pained Diaghilev doubly that this person who dared to look like Nijinsky was a woman. Diaghilev's sexual prejudice was indomitable. He had argued for years to convince me that the exclusive love of women was morbid (though I don't know how he could have known very much about it), that I was an incomplete artist because morbid. He would draw cartoons on restaurant tablecloths of steatopygous and gourd-geously mammiferous women – Dubuffet madonnas – and he would argue about Socrates, Jesus, Leonardo da Vinci, Michelangelo, Caravaggio (what a monument of pederasty is his *Conversion of St Paul* – even including the horse – and how unnecessary, in any case, for the conversion), and go on about 'all great artists', etc. His own latest *mignon* was always described in the most gratifying terms, and Verlaine was quoted: '*Démon femelle . . .*' At the same time, this supreme showman knew how to exploit the beauty of the female body in the ballet.

In sum, Bronia's sex, looks, and name were against her, though only she, Fokine and Balanchine were true choreographers, as distinguished from dance performers who had been elevated to the position of choreographer not by education or experience but by being Diaghilev's *eromenoi.*

The perversity of Diaghilev's entourage – a kind of homosexual Swiss Guard – and the incidents and stories concerning it, are beyond my descriptive powers. I recall a rehearsal for the revival of *Renard*, in Monaco in 1929, at which our pianist – a handsome *fificus* of Diaghilev's – suddenly began looking intently beyond the music rack. I followed his gaze to a Monegasque soldier in a tricorne, then asked what was the matter. He answered, 'I long to surrender myself to him.'

While attempting to remember the dancers of the Russian Ballet, I see that I have actually said more about Diaghilev himself and his abnormal psychology (which I have not exaggerated) than about the Terpsichorean arts and artists in his company.

But this was inevitable. Diaghilev was stronger-willed than all of his artists, and he controlled every detail of every ballet he produced.

Diaghilev was sometimes possessed by very odd and impractical ideas, and, as he was a stubborn man, many hours of my life were spent in trying to argue him out of what I thought were eccentric notions. That I was not always successful is illustrated by his use of jugglers in *Renard*. I did win one important case, though, in *The Soldier's Tale*. Diaghilev could not bear to hear of this opus because his company had not produced it, as indeed it could not have done in 1918, temporarily dissolved as it was by the war. But when he suddenly decided to stage it, in 1924, his concept was eccentric. The dancers were to go about wearing advertisements, American sidewalk-walking-advertisements, 'sandwich men', as they were called. Massine would eventually have been blamed for the choreography of this undanceable ballet, but it was all Diaghilev's idea.

Diaghilev was in no sense an intellectual. He was much too intelligent for that. Besides, intellectuals never have any real taste, and no one has ever had such great taste as Diaghilev. He was a deeply cultured man, an art-history scholar, and an authority on Russian painting. He once told me about his visit to Yasnaya Polyana to see Tolstoy's old family portraits. The old man received him cordially and showed him around his gallery with a big lantern, but his real interest in Diaghilev was as a draughts opponent. When Tolstoy asked Diaghilev if he played draughts and Diaghilev answered in the affirmative, Sergey Pavlovich was terrified, never having played the game, and of course did everything wrong. Tolstoy said, 'Young man, you should have told the truth right away; now go upstairs and take tea.' Diaghilev had been a bibliophile all his life, also, and his Russian library was one of the finest in the world. But his mind was so preyed upon by superstition that he was incapable of true self-examination. I thought him pathologically superstitious. He carried amulets, pronounced talismanic formulas and, like Dr Johnson, counted paving stones. He avoided thirteens, black cats, open ladders. His domestic, Vassili, who was always by his side holding Turkish towels, or hairbrushes – but you know Cocteau's caricature – was made to perform what

Diaghilev regarded as the more orthodox superstition of prayer. Which is not to say that Diaghilev was a believer, but he did not want to exclude the Christian possibility altogether. Vassili told me that when they were *en route* to America in 1916, Diaghilev was so frightened by rough seas that he made him go down on his knees and pray, while he, Diaghilev, lay on his bed worrying for both of them – a real division of labour.

Diaghilev was also self-destructively vain. I remember him – it was the next to last time I saw him – opening his overcoat and proudly showing me how slender he had become – for the benefit of Igor Markevitch, his last *protégé* – a modest, self-effacing, and utterly ruthless careerist who was about as fond of Diaghilev as Herod was of children.

R.C. Do you remember any other dancers and choreographers?
I.S. I should mention Woizikovsky and Idzikovsky. The latter, after Nijinsky, was the greatest jumper and the greatest Petrushka. Tamara Karsavina was the first lady of the ballet, the first ballerina in *Petrushka* and the first Firebird (though she should have been the Princess and Pavlova the Firebird). Tchernicheva, a beautiful *Firebird* Princess and a beautiful woman, too, had infatuated Alfonso XIII and was the only woman who ever attracted Ravel; Lopukhova had good technique and was a flirt; Piltz, the Russian with the German name who danced with Fokina and Tchernicheva and was the prima ballerina of the first *Rite of Spring*; Lydia Sokolova, who danced the same part in the revival of *The Rite*; Lifar, who was a beautiful Apollo; Adolph Bolm, who danced in the first *Firebird* and became my close friend in Hollywood; and, finally, George Balanchine, who choreographed the first European *Apollo* (I met him in 1925, in Nice, as he was preparing a revival of the *Song of the Nightingale*).

THE EUROPEAN YEARS

1910–1939

Switzerland
1910–1920
Renard, The Wedding, The Soldier's Tale, Pulcinella

In May 1910 I left St Petersburg and my apartment on the English Prospekt, where *Firebird* was composed. At that time I could not have imagined that I would see my native city again only during two brief visits, both of them on Diaghilev business. Nor could I have been made to believe that I would be living in Switzerland for the next decade, though I remembered the country fondly from my childhood. I had accompanied my parents to Interlaken in the summer of 1895, and we had returned to Switzerland in succeeding years. My parents were simply following the Russian fashion of the time.

After the première of *Firebird*, I wanted to return to the Switzerland I had known in early years, and accordingly, at the end of August 1910, we moved, as I have already mentioned, to Chardon Jogny, near Vevey. After a short time there, we moved to a pension, Les Tilleuls, in Clarens, where most of *The Rite of Spring* was composed. At the beginning of 1914 we spent two months in Leysin, where the higher altitude was considered beneficial for my wife's health. Cocteau visited us there, with Paul Thévenaz, a young Swiss artist in whom he was interested at the time, and who painted a portrait of me and my wife. In July of that year we moved to a '*bois de Mélèze*' chalet near Salvan, in the Valais du Rhône, rented from peasants. Here I composed *Pribaoutki* and the *Three Pieces for String Quartet*. At the end of August [1914] we returned to Clarens and La Pervenche, a cottage owned by Ernest Ansermet, where I began to compose *The Wedding*.

We moved again in the spring of 1915, this time to Château d'Oex, high in the mountains. This new change was intended as a holiday, but while there I began to compose *Renard*. The Avezzano earthquake occurred during our stay, and I remember being shaken out of my sleep and seeing my armoire hop toward me like a man whose hands and feet are bound. Our next home was the Villa Rogie Vue in Morges. We stayed there until 1917. At the beginning of that year we transferred to a second-floor flat in the Maison Bornand, also in Morges (2 rue St-Louis), a seventeenth-century building which has since – I saw it a few years ago [1965] – added a statue of Paderewski to its court-yard. This piano-playing future President of Poland lived at the opposite end of the same building, but we never met. I was once told that when someone asked him if he wished to meet me, his answer was: '*Non, merci: Stravinsky et moi, nous nageons dans les lacs bien différents.*'

*

R.C. Do you recall your first meeting with Ernest Ansermet?
I.S. He introduced himself to me in a street in Clarens one day in 1911 and invited me to his home for dinner. I had heard of him as a schoolmaster and a musician, but his beard startled me, like an apparition of the Charlatan in *Petrushka,* which I was composing at this time. He became the conductor of the Kursaal Orchestra in Montreux shortly after. Our next meeting was at the home of the *chanson* composer Henri Duparc, a morose old gentleman living in retirement near Vevey. At this same time I also made the acquaintance of the Geneva composer Ernest Bloch, whom I next saw many years later in Portland, Oregon.

When Gabriel Pierné and Pierre Monteux left the Russian Ballet at the outbreak of war in 1914, I persuaded Diaghilev to replace them with Ansermet, who had a good understanding of Franco-Russian new music, and a special gift for regulating orchestral balances. I was on close terms with him from that time and throughout the Diaghilev period. After he conducted the première of the *Symphony of Psalms*, in Brussels in 1930, we saw each other less frequently, and in 1938, when he cut a section of *The Card Game*, we quarrelled. After World War II he criticized my revised version of *Petrushka*[1] and other early

---

1 I rewrote *Petrushka* in 1946–47 with the dual purpose of copyrighting it and

uary 27, 1886, St Petersburg: Igor, aged three-and-a-half. In the summer of this year,
ld was taken to Pavlovka in the Samara district, to the estate of his uncle Alexander
ich, the husband of Stravinsky's mother's sister Sofiya.

5, 1895: the thirteen-year-old Stravinsky with his parents at the Elizabeth Spa,
rg. The picture is a detail from a large group photo in which the Stravinskys are
g at the front-centre.

vinsky's drawings (London, August 11, 1957) of Tsar Alexander III and the Shah of
during a state visit by the latter to St Petersburg.

4 The winter view from the Stravinsky apartment at 66 Kryukov Canal, in a painting by the composer's sister-in-law, Elena Nikolayevna, wife of the composer's brother Yuriy. According to Stravinsky, the background dome is that of a synagogue, and the large entranceway on the left led to a food market.

5 Spring 1910: the composer on the Nevsky Prospekt.

6 1892, St Petersburg: Stravinsky's family at dinner. From the left foreground: Igor, R Anna (mother), Simon Ivanovich (serving), Fyodor (father), Yuriy, and Guriy.

Stravinsky's corrections on a proof copy of *Firebird*, 1911.

8 October 1913: the last photograph of Stravinsky in St Petersburg.

1910: with Debussy in his Paris home, photographed by Erik Satie.

ng 1911: with Diaghilev in Beaulieu-sur-Mer. Stravinsky is carrying his sketchbooks
res of *Petrushka*.

: 1912: 'Ravel, Wazlav Nijinsky, Bronislava Nijinska on Ravel's balcony, M. Ravel,
not.' Photograph and caption by Stravinsky.

12 Spring 1914: Stravinsky on the balcony of Ravel's residence in Paris. Photograph Maurice Ravel.

13 Autumn 1920, Paris: with Coco Chanel (lower right) and Misia and José Maria Se

oupe du jubilé Steinway à New-York

1925

...uary 1925, Steinway Hall, New York: Wilhelm Furtwängler, Joseph Steinway, and ...ofmann are at the composer's left; Serge Rakhmaninov is seated behind Hofmann, ...tz Kreisler is seated to Rakhmaninov's right. The man wearing the white tie to ...'s right in the third row is Alexander Ziloti, pupil of Liszt and friend of Tchaikovsky, ...d conducted the first performance of Stravinsky's *Fireworks* in St Petersburg sixteen ...arlier.

15 January 1925, Aeolian Hall, New York: piano practice apparently interrupted.

16 Summer 1925: Cocteau, Picasso, Stravinsky and Mme Olga Kokhlova Picasso in Juan-les-Pins.

pieces, forgetting that he had been the first to perform the 1919 revision of *Firebird*. Still later, he campaigned against my new music, publishing a tome full of *a priori* arguments and up-to-date phrases ('*conscience logarithmique*') but only proving, and sadly, that he could not hear or follow the music. Still, I can never forget the many merry hours we shared together – the time, for instance, in my Pleyel studio in Paris, when we imbibed a whole bottle of Framboise, after which he pretended to be a dog and even began barking like one under my piano.

*

R.C. Have you any notion where the manuscript of your instrumentation of [Musorgsky's] *Khovanshchina* might be found?
I.S. I left it in Ustilug on my last trip there [in the summer of 1913] and must assume it has been lost or destroyed. I feel certain that [the music publisher] Bessel had already engraved it in Russia just before the 1914–18 war. The plates could exist with the inheritors of Bessel's Russian firm. I remember a quarrel about money with Bessel, who said that [Ravel and I] were demanding too much, and argued that 'Musorgsky received only a fraction of what you are asking'. I replied that because they had succeeded in starving poor Musorgsky was reason to pay us more.

The idea of asking Ravel to collaborate with me on reorchestrating *Khovanshchina* was mine. I was afraid not to be ready for the spring season of 1913 and I needed help. Unfortunately, Diaghilev cared less about establishing a worthy instrumentation of the opera and rescuing it from Rimsky-Korsakov than about providing a vehicle for Chaliapin, who did not understand the value of our work and refused to sing it. I orchestrated Shaklovity's famous and banal aria, and *composed* as well as orchestrated the hundred bars of the final chorus; Musorgsky had left only a few sketches for this. I began with these sketches and composed the whole piece from them, ignoring Rimsky.

Ravel and I worked together in Clarens in late March–April

—

adapting it to the resources of medium-sized orchestras. Ever since the first 1911 performance of the score, I had wanted to balance the orchestral sound more clearly in some places. I think that the 1947 orchestration improves it.

1913. At that same time, he composed the *Trois Poèmes de Mallarmé*, which is still my favourite music by him. I remember an excursion that Ravel and I made from Clarens to Varese, near Lago Maggiore, to buy Varese paper, which was of the highest quality. The village was so crowded that we could not find two hotel rooms or even two beds, so we slept together in one.[2]

When I think of Ravel, in comparison to, for example, Satie, Ravel appears quite ordinary, but his musical judgement was very acute. Certainly he was the only musician who immediately understood *The Rite of Spring*. His manner was dry and reserved, and sometimes little darts were hidden in his remarks, but he was always a very good friend to me. He drove a truck or ambulance in the war, as you know, and I admired him for it, because at his age and with his name he could have found an easier place, or done nothing. He looked pathetically small in his uniform; he was an inch or two shorter than I am.

I think Ravel knew when he entered the hospital for his last operation that he would go to sleep for the last time. He said to me, 'They can do as they wish with my cranium as long as the ether works.' It didn't work, and the poor man felt the incision. I did not visit him in the hospital, and my last view of him was in a funeral home. The top part of his skull was still bandaged. His final years were cruel, for he was gradually losing his memory and some of his co-ordinating powers, and of course was quite aware of it. Gogol died screaming, and Diaghilev died laughing, and singing *La Bohème*, which he loved as much as any music, but Ravel died gradually. That is the worst.

*

R.C. What are your recollections of Lord Berners?
I.S. I met him – Gerald Tyrwhitt, not yet Lord Berners – in Rome in 1911. He was attached to the British Embassy there, and introduced himself to me as a friend of my St Petersburg friend Klukovsky. He was delightful company. I saw him often after that and on every trip to Rome during the 1914–18 war.

2 When this was first published, Stravinsky's friends jokingly asked, 'How was it?' He invariably answered, 'You will have to ask Ravel.' Stravinsky always maintained that Ravel was sexually neuter. [R.C.]

In 1916 he visited me in Morges, and thereafter became an intermediary in my wranglings over money with Diaghilev. His remarks about music were perceptive, and though I considered him an amateur, he was certainly not amateurish, as we now use the word. When we knew each other better, he began to come to me for criticism and advice in his composition. I often looked through his scores with him at the piano, or listened to them together with him in the theatre, and I thought his *Wedding Bouquet* and *Neptune* at least as good as the French works of the kind produced by Diaghilev, which I intend – though it may not be so construed – as a compliment.

Tyrwhitt aided me when I was detained by Italian border police on a train from Rome to Switzerland in 1917, and accused of trying to smuggle a plan of fortifications, in fact my portrait by Picasso,[3] out of the country. I suddenly thought of Berners because of some Mandorlati figs he had given to me to eat on the train. A policeman had confiscated the figs and begun to split them open with his sabre, in search of contraband. I telegraphed to Tyrwhitt at the British Embassy and had the portrait sent to him to be forwarded to me in Switzerland as an official paper.

After the war, when he became Lord Berners, I was a guest of his on each of my English visits. I remember with special pleasure an October weekend in the late 1930s at Faringdon, his estate in Berkshire. Here one slept in a crystal bed, walked in deep meadows, and sat by brick fireplaces in Hepplewhite chairs. At Faringdon, meals were served in which all the food was of one colour pedigree. If Berners was in a certain mood, lunch might consist of beet soup, lobster, tomatoes, strawberries, while a flock of pink doves flew overhead. The pigeons were sprayed with (harmless) cosmetic dyes; Vera Sudeykina used to send him saffron dye from France, and a blue powder that he used for making blue mayonnaise. I remember receiving a letter

3 The first one, with the 'monocle'. The armchair portrait was done in Picasso's Paris studio on 24 May 1920, and the third, in profile with arms folded, in the same place on 31 December 1920. The 'monocle' portrait was drawn in the Hôtel de la Russie, Rome, near the Piazza del Popolo, where many of Diaghilev's dancers, including Picasso's future wife Olga Kokhlova, were staying. Stravinsky owned a dozen paintings and drawings by Picasso, as well as some beautiful ink designs of horses drawn on letter envelopes. [R.C.]

from him a little later, the only one ever from anybody in which greetings were extended both to my wife and to Mme Sudeykina.

Berners knew of my interest in old English music and promised to send the complete works of Purcell to me. I think if he were to visit my home today nothing would please him more than the discovery that my library contains so much Purcell, Tallis, the complete Byrd, and the complete sets of madrigals and lute songs.

*

R.C. How did you meet Romain Rolland?

I.S. At the beginning of the war, before the scandal of his *Au dessus de la mêlée,* he wrote asking me to contribute a statement to a book he was then preparing, an indictment of German 'barbarism'. I replied as follows:

Mon cher confrère!

I hasten to answer your appeal for a protest against the barbarism of the German armies. But is 'barbarism' the right word? What is a barbarian? It seems to me that by definition he is someone belonging to a conception of culture new or different from our own; and though this culture might be radically different or antithetical to ours, we do not for that reason deny its value, or the possibility that this value might be greater than our own.

But the *present* Germany cannot be considered as a manifestation of a 'new culture'. Germany, *as a country*, belongs to the old world, and the culture of the country is as old as that of the other nations of Western Europe. However, a nation which, in time of peace, erects a series of monuments such as those of the Siegesallee in Berlin and which, in time of war, sends her armies to destroy a city like Louvain and a cathedral like Rheims is not a barbarian in the proper sense or civilized in any sense. If 'renewal' is what Germany really seeks, she might better start at home with her Berlin monuments. It is the highest common interest of all those peoples who still feel the need to breathe the air of their ancient culture to put themselves on the side of the enemies of the present Germany, and to flee for ever the unbearable spirit of this colossal, obese, and morally putrefying Germania.

IGOR STRAWINSKY

P.S. Throughout these terrible days – to which we are the living witnesses – your appeal *L'union fait la force* has been our one encouragement.

Shortly after sending this letter, I met Rolland on, of all places, a *lac de quatre Cantons* excursion boat. I was with my wife and children enjoying a day's outing when a tall, spectacled gentleman, evidently doing the same thing, came up to me and shyly introduced himself as my correspondent.[4] I was taken by his personal charm and intellectual honesty. Though his literature – *Jean-Christophe* and *Beethoven the Creator* – was and is exactly what I most abhor, these books have not affected my feeling for the man. I saw him occasionally after that in company with Claudel and Jules Romains, if I remember correctly, at Ramuz's home near Lausanne. Later, he wrote an enthusiastic article about *Petrushka*, after hearing it at a concert in Geneva. I wrote to thank him, and we became friends.

*

I would also like to record my associations with other writers and artists, most of them associated with Diaghilev and the Ballets Russes. I think, for example, of Alexej von Jawlensky. Diaghilev had described him to me in St Petersburg days as a committed follower of the new Munich school and a contributor to the *Blaue Reiter*, as well as to *Mir iskustva*. Diaghilev, of course, considered the Munich school to be the ultimate in 'Boche' bad taste. I did not meet Jawlensky in Russia but in Switzerland. At the beginning of the war I was living in Morges and he in Saint-Prex, a nearby village on the shore of Lake Geneva. I remember walking with my children from Morges to his house. He was hospitable, and his studio was a little island of Russian colour that delighted my children. He last visited me in Morges in 1915, at a time when he became a friend and supporter of Paul Klee, who was living in Freiburg.

Max Liebermann was another friend, especially during the first period of our Ballets Russes in Berlin. I made his acquaintance, together with Gerhardt Hauptmann's, after a performance of *Petrushka*, and I saw him often thereafter. Liebermann was a celebrated wit. In a story then circulating, a portrait painter commissioned to do Hindenburg complains to Liebermann of

4 Rolland's *Journal* describes a chat with the composer in the writer's home on 26 September 1914. [R.C.]

his inability to draw Hindenburg's features, whereupon Lieber-mann exclaims, '*Ich kann den Alten in den Schnee pissen.*' As you know, Liebermann nominated me to the Prussian Academy.

Jacques-Emile Blanche was another friend of my early Diaghilev years, a keen observer and an intellectual. He painted two portraits of me that are now in the Luxembourg. I remember sitting for him, and how he drew my head and features after a great deal of modelling, while everything else, the body and the background, was added *in absentia*. This meant that one's legs might turn out too long and one's middle too capacious, or that one might find oneself promenading on the beach at Deauville, as I am made to do in one of these portraits. Blanche's faces were accurately characterized as a rule, and that was the impor-tant thing. Blanche had a *fine mouche* for celebrities; he came to make my portrait the morning after the première of *Firebird*.[5]

*

R.C. Was Henri Matisse your choice of painter for the *Chant du Rossignol* sets?

I.S. No. He was Diaghilev's idea. In fact, I opposed it, but too directly. (Amiel: 'Every direct resistance ends in disaster.') The production, as I have said, and especially Matisse's part in it, were failures. Diaghilev hoped Matisse would do something Chinese and charming, but all he did was to copy the China of the shops in the rue La Boëtie. Matisse designed the costumes and the curtain as well as the sets.

Matisse's art had never inspired me, but at the time of *The Song of the Nightingale* [1920] I saw him often and was attracted to his somewhat acidulous personality. I remember an afternoon with him in the Louvre. He was not a rousing conversationalist, but he stopped in front of a Rembrandt and started to talk excitedly about it. At one point he took a white handkerchief from his pocket: 'Which is white, this handkerchief or the white in that picture? Even the absence of colour does not exist, but only "white" or each and every white.'

Our Matisse collaboration made Picasso very angry:

5 Blanche had been painting portraits of Nijinsky throughout the *Firebird* rehearsal period.

'Matisse! What is a Matisse? A balcony with a big red flower-pot falling all over it.'

Here is a letter from Matisse concerning the 1925 revival of *The Song of the Nightingale*:

Nice, 1, Place Charles Félix
May 28, 1925

My dear friend,

I have your letter in front of me – forgive me for not having replied sooner. I couldn't. I am very pleased about the revival of *The Nightingale*. But I hope that the stage will not be too small because of the proportions of the pillars – that the friezes will be visible – and that you will not eliminate the major props which are an indispensable part of the décors. As for the costume of the young female dancer, I don't see the need for any great alteration. I hope that Karsavina's is still around, and that we are still inspired by it. It must be white, in any case, and the feathers formed by white silk petals bordered with a thin black thread, but probably larger. I hope that you will employ Marie Muelle, or her father, who will do it very well . . . This costume had a happy effect of crystalline lightness, like the song of a bird and the sound of the flute. I don't foresee any other problems – it is important to keep the hips from being too heavy, although a young girl of twelve often has no hips at all.[6]

As for the costume of the mechanical nightingale, the one that I made can serve as a reasonably good example. The colours should remain as they are. Replace the stiff lining by a slightly padded, supple costume; the feet, I think, should remain the same Chinese rose colour – but smaller. (That depends on the turns, and it will be necessary to modify them according to the mobility of the dancer.) The same for the headpiece, which, I hope, still exists.

I will return to Paris on about the 5th of June and will be able to see you then if you think it will be useful.

In the meantime, dear friend, tireless worker, I wish you all the best.

HENRI MATISSE

*

R.C. Do you remember Balla's set for your *Fireworks*?
I.S. Vaguely, but I couldn't have described it even at the time [Rome, 1917] as anything more than a few splashes of paint on

6 Alicia Markova, who danced this part in 1925, now (2002) aged ninety-two, recalls that Balanchine rehearsed her for the performance to Stravinsky's transcription for pianola. [R.C.]

an empty backcloth. I remember that it baffled the audience, and that when Balla came out to bow there was no applause: the public didn't know who he was, what he had done, why he was bowing. Balla then reached into his pocket and squeezed a device that made his *papillon* necktie do tricks. Diaghilev and I, sharing a loge, began to laugh, but the audience remained dumb.

Balla was amusing and likeable, and some of my drollest hours were spent in his and his fellow Futurists' company. The idea of doing a Futurist ballet was Diaghilev's, but we decided together on my *Fireworks* music: it was 'Modern', only four minutes long, and Balla had impressed us as a gifted painter. We asked him to design a set, after which I made fast friends with him, visiting him often in his apartment in Rome. He lived near the zoo, so near in fact that his balcony overhung a large cage. One heard animal noises in his rooms as one hears street noises in New York hotel rooms.

But Milan was the centre of Futurism, and it was there that I met with Balla, Carrà, Boccioni, Depero, the noisemaker Russolo, and Marinetti. It was easier then to take the train from Switzerland to the Italian city for an evening performance than it is now to drive from Beverly Hills to downtown Los Angeles and back. And in wartime Milan my few Swiss francs made me feel agreeably affluent.

On one of my Milanese visits Marinetti and Russolo, a genial, quiet man but with wild hair and beard, and Pratella, another noisemaker, demonstrated their 'Futurist Music' for me. Five phonographs standing on five tables in a large and otherwise empty room emitted an assortment of noises, static, whooshings, and so forth remarkably like the *musique concrète* of some years ago (so perhaps they were Futurists after all; or perhaps Futurisms aren't progressive enough). I pretended to be enthusiastic and told them that sets of five phonographs with such music, mass-produced, would surely sell like Steinway grand pianos.

Some time after this demonstration Marinetti invented what he called 'discreet noises', to be associated with objects. I remember one such sound (not at all discreet, to be truthful) and the object it accompanied, a substance that looked like velvet but had a rough surface. Balla must have participated in the 'noise' movement, too. As an Easter present he once gave a papier-mâché Paskha cake to me that sighed peculiarly when sliced.

The most memorable event in my years of friendship with the Futurists was a performance we saw together at the Milan puppet theatre of *The Chinese Pirates*, a 'drama in three acts'. The theatre itself was puppet-sized. An invisible orchestra, clarinet, piano, violin, bass, played an overture and bits of incidental music. There were tiny windows on either side of the tiny stage. In the last act we heard singing and were terrified to see that it came from giants standing behind these windows – the pirates. They were normal-statured people, of course, but we were accustomed to the puppet scale.

The Futurists were 'absurdists' but sympathetic, and they were much less pretentious than some of the later movements that borrowed from them – Surrealism, for one, which had more substance. Unlike the Surrealists, they were able to laugh at their own pose of artist-contra-Gentiles. Marinetti himself was a flibbertigibbet but also companionable. I regret that he seemed to me the least gifted of the whole group – compared to Boccioni, Balla and Carrà, who were able painters. The Futurists were not the airplanes they wanted to be, but they were at any rate a pack of nice, noisy Vespas.

*

R.C. What attracted you to the medium of four-hand and two-piano music, and what were the circumstances of composition and performance in the case of the *Eight Easy Pieces*?

I.S. The *Easy Pieces* were composed in Morges – the *Polka*, *March* and *Valse* just before *Renard*, in 1914–15, the others just after. The *Polka* was written first, as a caricature of Diaghilev, whom I saw as a circus animal-trainer cracking a whip. The idea of the four-hand duet was an aspect of the caricature also, because Diaghilev was fond of four-hand piano playing, which he had done with his lifelong friend Walter Nouvel[7] for as long as I had known him. The simplicity of one of the parts was designed in order not to embarrass Diaghilev's limited technique.

7 Nouvel had been a composer in his youth, a member of the St Petersburg avant-garde whose Modernist tendencies so annoyed Rimsky-Korsakov. Another of Nouvel's piano partners was the poet Kusmin, whom I met with Diaghilev at Nouvel's St Petersburg home. [Kusmin was also a close friend of Vera Sudeykina.]

I played the *Polka* for him and Alfredo Casella in a hotel room in Milan in 1915, and I remember the amazement of both men that the composer of *The Rite of Spring* should have produced such a piece of popcorn. But for Casella a new path had been indicated, and he was not slow to follow it; so-called neo-classicism was born in that moment. Casella was so enthusiastic about the *Polka* that I promised to write a little piece for him, too. I composed the *March* for him immediately on my return to Morges, and a little later added the ice-cream-wagon *Valse* in homage to Erik Satie, a souvenir of a visit to him in Paris. Satie, a very touching and attractive personality, suddenly had become old and white, though not less witty and gay. I tried to portray something of his *esprit* in the *Valse*. I orchestrated it for seven solo instruments immediately after composing it, and at the same time prepared a version of the *Polka* for cimbalom and small ensemble, and another of the *March* for eight solo players, but the two pieces have never been published in this form.

The other five pieces were composed as music lessons for my children Theodore and Mika. I wished to cultivate a love of music in them and to disguise my piano pedagogy by composing very easy parts for them to play, reserving the more difficult parts for the teacher, in this case myself, hoping thereby to give them a sense of performance participation. The *Española* was joined to the album after a trip to Spain, the *Napolitana* after a trip to Naples. Two of the Russian souvenirs, the *Balalaika*, which I like best of all the eight pieces, and the *Galop*, were added at a later date. And the *Andante*, like many preludes, was tacked on last. (Pascal: 'The last thing one discovers in composing a work is what to put first.') The *Galop* is a caricature of the St Petersburg version of the Folies Bergères, which I had watched in the Tumpakov, a demi-respectable night-club in the Astrava (the islands of the Neva, on one of which my second wife Vera was born). Hearing me conduct the *Galop* in the orchestral version, Ravel advised me to play it at a faster, the fastest possible, tempo, but I think he had mistaken it for a cancan. The first concert performance of the eight piano pieces was sponsored by Werner Reinhardt, in Lausanne. My co-pianist was the young José Iturbi.

R.C. What were the origins, textual, instrumental and theatrical, of *Renard*?

I.S. Afanasiev's collection of Russian folklore contains at least five different 'Renard' stories in which that Rabelaisian liar is caught and brought to justice by a cat and a goat. I chose one of the stories and fashioned my own libretto from it. Then, starting to compose the music, I discovered that my text was too short, whereupon I conceived the idea of repeating the '*salto mortale*' episode. In my version, the cock, twice seduced, jumps twice into Renard's clutches; this repetition was a successful accident, the reprise being the principal element in the fun. My original title of the barnyard fable was 'Tale about the Cock, the Fox, the Cat, and the Ram'. I finished the libretto early in 1916, and the music before the end of the summer.

Renard was inspired by the *guzla*, the extraordinary instrument carried by the goat in the last part of the play, and imitated in the orchestra with good but less than perfect success by the cimbalom. The *guzla*, a museum piece now, was rare even in my childhood in St Petersburg. A kind of metal-stringed balalaika, it is strapped over the player's head like the tray of a cigarette girl in a night-club. The sound produced is deliciously live and bright, but it is preciously tiny, too, and who now plays the *guzla*? '*Guzli*' means 'string music played by human touch'. Part of the fun in *Renard* is that this extremely nimble-fingered instrument should be played by the cloven-hoofed goat. Incidentally, the *guzla* music – 'plink, plink . . .' – was the first part of *Renard* composed.

I heard a cimbalom for the first time in a Geneva café with Ansermet one evening in January 1915, and decided it could be used as a substitute for the *guzla*. The cimbalomist, a Mr Racz, kindly helped me find an instrument, which I purchased and kept with me throughout my Swiss and French years. I learned to play it, and to love it, and I composed *Renard* 'on' it (as I normally compose 'on' a piano), with two sticks in my hand, writing down as I composed. I also used the cimbalom in my *Ragtime*, in the *Chant dissident*, and in the half-finished 1919 version of *The Wedding*.

The music of *Renard* begins in the verse. I had already discovered a new technique, while composing songs on popular

Russian texts: *Pribaoutki*;[8] *Berceuses du chat*; *The Bear* (a nursery rhyme); *Tilimbom*; *The Drake, Geese and Swans*; *The Flea*; *Chanson pour compter*.[9] In the spring of 1914 my sketchbook began to fill with notations for songs, as well as for *Renard*, *The Wedding* and the *Three Pieces for String Quartet*. The mockoperatic accompaniment figure played by the cello (sustained harmonics and simultaneous *pizzicato*) in the cock's aria in *Renard* was composed at this early date, and by autumn the profusion of material was so great that many bits and pieces were left over and never fashioned at all. The *Pribaoutki* songs, composed during and just before the early days of the 1914–18 war, are the immediate ancestors of *Renard*. The word '*pribaoutki*' identifies a form of popular Russian verse, to which the nearest English parallel is the limerick. It means 'a telling', '*pri*' being the Latin '*pre*' and '*baout*' deriving from the Old Russian infinitive 'to say'. *Pribaoutki* are always short – usually not more than four lines. According to popular tradition, they derive from a type of game in which someone says a word, to which someone else adds another, and which third and fourth persons develop further, with utmost speed. *Tilimbom* – which I orchestrated in 1923 for a concert with the singer Vera Janacopulos – the *Chanson pour compter* and *Chicher-Yatcher* are counting-game songs of this sort. One important characteristic of Russian popular verse is that the accents of the spoken verse are ignored when the verse is sung. The recognition of the musical possibilities inherent in this fact was one of the most rejoicing discoveries of my life. It was like finding that one's finger can be bent from the second joint as well as from the first. We all

8 *Pribaoutki* should be sung only by a man's voice. I composed it with my brother Guriy's baritone in mind, and I have sung the cycle myself for small gatherings of friends; I had to take the lower octave in places, and my voice is not orotund, but tone quality apart, my performance was at least authentic. I sing all my vocal music as I compose it, incidentally, and it is all composed 'on' my voice. I am sure that Lasso and Gombert and Isaac and Josquin all did the same. Weren't they all singers first?

9 The ancestor of this group of songs is the *Trois Souvenirs de mon enfance* of 1906. I remember playing them for Rimsky-Korsakov in that year. The *Souvenirs* employed popular texts, the third song pure onomatopoeic nonsense words. They were published in 1913, and in orchestra score in 1933 for a French film that was never released.

know parlour games in which the same sentence can be made to mean something different when different words are emphasized. In *Renard*, the syllable sounds within the word itself, as well as the emphasis of the word in the sentence are so treated.

Renard is phoneme music, and phonemes are untranslatable. All four texts are from Afanasiev's *Popular Russian Tales* [vol. III, pp. 338, 339, 547]. The melody of the second part of the first song (Afanasiev's no. 543) came to my ear in London in June 1914, an octave higher than I ultimately wrote it. Next to these two bars in my sketchbook are three variant notations of the bells of St Paul's, and all three, in my irregular metres, look remarkably Russian. Do these songs betray my homesickness for Russia? What I can say is that I greatly regretted being unable to spend that summer of 1914 at my home in Ustilug.

The outward career of *Renard* is quickly told. In December 1915 the Princesse Edmond de Polignac commissioned it for performance in her salon. This remarkable American lady, née Winaretta Singer, daughter of Isaac Singer, the Palm Beach sewing-machine magnet, was to play an important part in my life as patroness and friend. She looked like Dante and was very masculine and imposing, rumoured to be fond of whipping young women. Her ambition was to have her bust next to Richelieu's at the Louvre. I met her at the time of my visit to Paris to conduct *Firebird* for the Red Cross. The circumstances of the commission helped to determine the size of the performing ensemble, but even that requirement was adjustable. The music was quickly composed, with the *March* as the last part of the score to be completed. I planned the staging myself, always bearing in mind that *Renard* was a burlesque. The players must be dancing acrobats with whom the singers are only partly identified. The relationship between the vocal roles and the stage characters is the same as it is in *The Wedding* and, again as in that work, the performers, musical and mimetic, should be on the stage together with the singers in the centre of the instrumental ensemble. *Renard* does not have symbolic overtones. It is a banal moral tale, no more. The religious satire, the fox disguised as a nun – nuns were untouchables in Russia – is merely gentle mockery.

Renard was never performed in the Princess's salon, nor did I ever play it there on the piano for a gathering of guests, as I did my Piano Concerto and *Oedipus Rex*. When the composition was finished, the Princess came to visit me, bringing a gift, a cigarette-holder made of ostrich feathers and gold. Many years later she wrote the following account of the visit:

Stravinsky asked me to dine one night and came to fetch me in Lausanne for the half-hour's journey by train from Lausanne to Morges. He had taken a house in Morges, where he lived with his wife and family and numerous pale, fair-haired young children. Everything was covered with snow and it was a quiet, clear, moonlit night, very still, and not very cold. I shall always remember the happy impression I had as Stravinsky took me into his house, which looked like a Christmas tree, brilliantly lighted up and decorated in the warm colours that the Russian Ballet had brought to Paris.

Madame Stravinsky was a striking figure: pale, thin, full of dignity and grace; she at once gave me the impression of nobility of race and grace that was confirmed by all she did in the following years. In the warmth of her charming house she looked like a princess in a Russian fairy tale: surrounded by her delicate children, then, of course, very young. But although everything was so friendly and kind, there was an atmosphere of tragedy about the whole family which turned out to be only too justified, for all were more or less inclined to suffer from lung trouble, which ended pitifully for Madame Stravinsky and one of her daughters quite recently [1938–39].

I can never forget the delight of that evening at Morges: the table brilliantly lighted with coloured candles, and covered with fruit, flowers, and desserts of every hue. The supper was a wonderful example of Russian cuisine, carefully prepared by Madame Stravinsky and composed of every form of *zakousky*, then borsch, tender sterlets covered with delicious jelly and served with a perfect sauce, various dishes of fowls and every sort of sweet, making it a feast always to be remembered.

*

R.C. To what extent does your Russian music, especially *Renard* and *The Wedding*, make use of folk melody?
I.S. There is no conscious use of folk melody in *Renard*, and only one of the themes of *The Wedding* is folk-derived, though not really a folk melody, but a workers' melody, a proletarian song. This theme was given to me by my friend Stepan Mitusov four years before I made use of it in the final tableau of *The Wedding*. Excellent collections of Russian folk music by Tchaikovsky and Lyadov, and a more or less good one by Rimsky-Korsakov, had

been published. All of these were familiar to me, and while I did not actually turn to folk music as source material, I was undoubtedly influenced by it. The song 'Down St Peter's Road' in *Petrushka* (St Petersburg was called simply 'Peter' in the peasant villages – 'Are you going to Peter?') was taken from Tchaikovsky's collection. There are also three folk melodies in *Firebird*, the two 'Khorovod' themes and the theme of the *Finale*, which has a dotted rhythm in the original. I do not remember which of the three collections supplied which themes.

The opening bassoon melody in *The Rite of Spring* is the only true folk melody in that work. It came from a recently published anthology of Lithuanian folk music that I found in Warsaw,[10] and not from Borodin or Cui, as some critics have suggested. To my knowledge, none of my Russian songs – *Pribaoutki*, the *Four Peasant Choruses*, the *Four Russian Songs*, the *Berceuses du Chat* – contains folk material. If any of these pieces sounds like aboriginal folk music, it may be because my powers of fabrication tapped some unconscious 'folk' memory.

R.C. What are the textual sources of your Russian choruses, 'The Saucers'?

I.S. For most of us, the word 'saucers' refers to UFOs, 'unidentified flying objects', but the Russian title, '*Podbludnyeh*', lacks an English equivalent. 'Saucer-readings' or 'Saucer-riddles' are closer in meaning, but suggestive of tea leaves. Short choruses of this sort were sung by peasants while fortune-tellers read their fingerprints on the smoke-blackened bottoms of saucers. The texts I used are from Afanasiev. I was attracted to them for their musico-rhythmic qualities. Judging from the place names, Tchigissy and Bielozero, I assume the texts to be North Russian in origin.[11] Probably they are from the neighbourhood of Pskov, but whether saucer sorcery was peculiar to that part of Russia, I am unable to say. I composed one of the choruses immediately after finishing *Pribaoutki* and just before beginning *The Wedding*. The four of them were performed in Geneva in 1917, conducted by Vasily Kibalchich, a Russian consular official who

10 It is the Lithuanian National Anthem, in fact. [R.C.]
11 The texts actually originated in central Russia. [R.C.]

was also a scrupulous musician and the director of the chorus of the Geneva Russian Church. He visited me in California in the early 1940s.

*

R.C. Had you ever planned a Russian 'liturgical ballet'? If so, did any of it become *The Wedding*?

I.S. The 'liturgical ballet' was entirely Diaghilev's idea. He knew that a Russian church spectacle in a Paris theatre would be enormously successful. He possessed a rich collection of icons and costumes that he wanted to exhibit, and he kept pestering me to give him music. Diaghilev was not really religious, not really a believer, but only a very superstitious man. He wasn't at all shocked by the idea of the church in the theatre. I began to conceive *The Wedding*, and its form was already clear in my mind, from about the beginning of 1914. I was in Clarens at the time of Sarajevo, and I needed Kireyevsky's book of Russian folk poetry in order to construct a libretto. I took a train to Kiev, stayed with my father-in-law, Dr Nosenko, and found the all-important book there after a few days. I regret that on this trip, which was to be my last view of Russia for forty-eight years, I did not see the Vydubitsky Monastery, which I knew and loved. On the return trip the German border police were already very tense, and I reached Switzerland only a few days before war was declared. Incidentally, Kireyevsky had asked Pushkin to send him his collection of folk verse. Pushkin sent some verses with a note reading: 'Some of these are my own verses; can you tell the difference?' Kireyevsky could not, but took them all for his collection, so perhaps a line of Pushkin's is in *The Wedding*.

R.C. When did you begin to compose the *The Wedding*, and why did it take so long to complete? Can you say more about the textual sources, and how would you describe the style of the libretto?

I.S. As you know, I became aware of an idea for a choral work on the subject of a Russian peasant wedding early in 1912; the title *Svádyebka*, *The Wedding*, occurred to me almost at the same time as the idea itself. As my conception developed, I began to see that it did not indicate the dramatization of a wedding or the accompaniment of a staged wedding spectacle with descriptive music. My wish was, instead, to present actual wedding material through direct quotations of popular, non-literary, verse. I waited two years before discovering my source in the nineteenth-century anthologies of Afanasiev and Kireyevsky, as I have already related, but this wait was well rewarded, as the dance-cantata form of the music was also suggested to me by my reading of these two great treasures of the Russian language and spirit. *Renard* and *The Soldier's Tale* were, as you know, adapted from Afanasiev, *The Wedding* almost entirely from Kireyevsky.

The Wedding is a suite of typical wedding episodes told through quotations of typical talk. The latter, whether the bride's, the groom's, the parents', or the guests', is always ritualistic. As a collection of clichés and quotations of typical wedding sayings it might be compared to one of those scenes in *Ulysses* in which the reader seems to be hearing scraps of conversation without the connecting thread of narrative.

Individual roles do not exist in *The Wedding*, but only solo voices that impersonate now one type of character and now another. Thus the soprano in the first scene is not the bride, but a bride's voice. The same voice is associated with the goose in the last scene. Similarly, the fiancé's words are sung by a tenor in the grooming scene, but by a bass at the end; and the two unaccompanied bass voices in the second scene, though their music may suggest the actual chanting of the marriage service, should not be identified with two priests. Even the proper names in the text, such as Palagai or Saveliushka, belong to no one in particular. They were chosen for their sound, their syllables, and their Russian typicality.

The Wedding is also, perhaps primarily, a product of the Russian Church. Consider the bells in the pianos throughout the second part of the second scene, and the bells at the end. Further, invocations to the Virgin and the saints occur throughout the work, and prominent among the latter are the names of Cosmos and Damian, who were recognized as wedding saints in Russia, and even worshipped as deities of a fertility cult. (I have read that in certain southern Italian churches, peasant-made phallic objects are found associated with images of Cosmos and

Damian.) The binding of the bride's tresses with red and blue ribbons was a religio-sexual custom, and the tying of the tresses around her head signified the married state. In the period of the *Wedding* texts (early nineteenth century), such customs were hardly more than ritual for ritual's sake. The bride weeps in the first scene not out of real sorrow at her imminent loss of virginity, but because, ritualistically, she *must* weep.

A knowledge not only of the cultural customs but also of the language of *The Wedding* is indispensable to anyone aspiring to a true appreciation of the work. For example, the word 'red' in the last tableau is an exclamation for 'beautiful'; it does not refer purely to colour. 'The table is red' and 'the table is beautiful' are one and the same statement. *'Lushenki'*, too, is simply a rhyming word, or the diminutive of a rhyming word. It has no 'sense'. At one point, tradition requires someone to say, 'The wine is *gorko* [bitter].' Hearing this, the groom must kiss the bride, after which the whole company says, 'The wine is sweet.' This game develops in a bawdy way in actual peasant weddings, where a man may look in his wine glass and say, 'I see a bosom and it is *gorko*', after which he kisses the bosom to make it sweet, and so on, downwards. As for musical versification, a translation of the sound-sense of *The Wedding* is an impossibility, and an exact translation of word-sense, even if possible, would be through a glass darkly.

The Wedding Feast tableau is made up largely of quotations and scraps of conversation. The non-Russian listener should understand in this scene that the swan and the goose are folk characters, and that the solo voices who impersonate and quote them are enacting a traditional folk game. Swans and geese both fly and swim, hence they have fantastic stories to tell about the skies and the waters, stories that mirror peasant superstitions. I am referring, in *The Wedding*, to the soprano's lines beginning, 'I flew up high one day and saw the sea . . .' But 'swan' and 'goose' also refer to a bride and groom. They are popular terms of endearment, like 'my little dove' or 'my little mouse'.

The first staging of *The Wedding*, at the Théâtre de la Gaïté, Paris, in June 1923, was generally compatible with my conception of the ritualistic and non-personal. As I have already said, the choreography was expressed in blocks and masses: there are no individual personalities. The curtain was not used, and the dancers did not leave the stage even during the lamentation of the two mothers, a wailing ritual that presupposes an empty set. Changes of scene, from the bride's to the groom's to the church, are created solely by the music. Finally, although the bride and groom are always present, the guests talk about them as if they were not, a stylization not unlike Kabuki theatre.

At the first rehearsal, the four pianos were placed at the corners of the stage, thus being separated from the percussion ensemble, as well as from the chorus and solo singers in the pit. Diaghilev mistakenly argued for this arrangement on aesthetic grounds: the four black, elephantine shapes were a *coup de théâtre*. My original idea was that the whole company, musicians and dancers, share the stage as equal participants.

As I have already said, I began the composition in 1914, a year before *Renard*, in Clarens. The music was completed in short-score form by October 1917, but not finished in full score until three months before the première, six years later. No work of mine has undergone so many instrumental metamorphoses. I completed the First Tableau for an orchestra of instrumental groups – woodwinds, brass, percussion, two groups of solo strings, keyboard (cimbalom, harpsichord, piano) – planning to separate these groups on the stage. In another version I sought to combine pianolas with bands of instruments that included saxhorns and flügelhorns. Then one day in 1921, in Garches, where I was living as a guest of Gabrielle Chanel, I suddenly realized that an orchestra of four pianos and percussion would satisfy all of my concepts. It would be at the same time perfectly homogeneous, perfectly impersonal, and perfectly mechanical.

When I played the First Tableau for Diaghilev, in 1915, at his home in Bellerive, near Lausanne, he wept and said it was the most beautiful and most purely Russian of all the creations of our Ballets Russes. I think he did love *The Wedding* more than any other work of mine. That is why I dedicated it to him.

*

Hearing two of my discontinued preliminary versions of *The Wedding* for the first time recently, at a concert in the Los Angeles County Museum [September 1968], I was reminded of a unique but long-forgotten experience of music-making fifty years ago. I am no longer certain how many versions I may have begun, or how extensive each fragment may have been. But I have lately discovered a complete score for four pianos without vocal parts, of which I had no recollection, and other scores and sketches might still be excavated among the manuscripts I gave to people in return for monetary help during the war. Nor am I certain of the chronology, except that the ensembles dwindled over the years from a medium–large orchestra to one for two cimbaloms, harmonium, pianola and two percussion – requiring only six players in all.

This last, six-player version, composed in Morges in the spring and summer of 1919, is the most polished of the abandoned ones, and the most authentic, more so in some ways than the final score, which, though streamlined, stronger in volume, and instrumentally more homogeneous, is also, partly for the same reasons, something of a simplification. The manuscript of the six instruments is complete in detail to the end of the Second Tableau, except that repeated passages, in which the instrumentation is unchanged, are not written out. At this point I was interrupted by the rush-order commission for *Pulcinella*, but I must also have begun to realize that the problems of synchronization with the pianola, and the near impossibility of finding competent cimbalomists, had made my instrumentation impracticable.

Every note of this 1919 score was tested in my own proving grounds. I had packed all of the instruments into my little musical pantry and learned to play all of them myself, spending as much time experimenting with them, tinkering with, and tuning, the cimbalom, as I did composing. But what I did write came directly from the instruments, while the sound was still hot, so to speak. I am no mystic: I need to touch music as well as to think it, which is why I have always lived with a piano, why in this instance it was necessary for me to manipulate the cimbalom sticks, familiarize myself with the harmonium registrations (a two-manual instrument; I still have my receipt for a year's rental), try out flams and rim shots on the snare drum, and even shake the tambourine ('raaaaaaaise your voices'). Risky as my memory is in matters of dates and places, I am certain of the position of each of the instruments of this little orchestra in my studio, which must be because my acoustical reality – bilateral in my case, not circular, as I am aware when hit in the nape of the neck by 'spatial music' – is part of my biological reality.

The instrumentation exposes lines of descent from *The Nightingale*, which I had not hitherto noticed. The music from the first entrance of the tenor, for example, seems to devolve from the opera, not only in rhythm and harmony (parallel chords emphasizing fifths), but also in vocal style; and the twitterings in the pianola part during the bride's lament are unexpectedly revealed as an inheritance from the ornithological ornaments evoked in the opera. Both works employ orientalisms, too; in *The Wedding* most conspicuously during that same lament, where the cimbaloms might be Japanese plectrum instruments accompanying a scene from a Kabuki play.

The automated poltergeist exploits the superhuman (multi-digital) velocity of the mechanically programmed instrument to the extent that three pianists would be required to encompass all of the notes. (My *Etude for Pianola* would require the same number of players, incidentally, if read from the six-stave original score.) I did not choose the pianola only for economy, but also because the tinny, nickelodeon-like rattle of this primeval juke-box suited my scheme of sonorities. It compares with the glossy, emulsified 'tone' of a Chopin recitalist's Steinway as a Model-T Ford compares with a six-door limousine. What defeated me, as I said, was the problem of synchronization, in pitch as well as tempo, for the instrument can make one's flesh creep, partly because of the spooky absenteeism of the player, but mainly because it is always out of tune. The harmonium part was the most difficult to write. I did not trust the instrument acoustically, and in fact composed alternate versions for many passages, hoping to allow for the varying resources of different makes of instruments. Harmoniums were popular in that hymn-singing age, but are virtually extinct now, replaced by the electric organ, whose unctuous tone I cannot bear.

No substitute, no thumb-tacked or otherwise doctored piano is admissible for the cimbaloms, the scarcity of which constitutes the chief obstacle to performance. A rare animal, more rarely tamed – meaning played by people who read music – hence the chance of capturing *two* of the species, then of corralling a pair of competent players, is astronomically poor. But its sound is so winsome that a society for the preservation of musical wildlife must be persuaded to endow a school both with the instrument and with scholarships for its study. The cimbalom sound bounces, glittering delicately when articulated with felt sticks, and with wooden ones as compact as the click of billiard balls. Both timbres are effective antidotes to the murky harmonium, and both combine ideally with the wiry playerless piano, as it should have been named.

The role of the *batterie* was another novelty, at least in 1918. Percussion sections had long served the orchestra as arsenals and sound-prop departments, supplying it with extra colours, articulation, weight. Before *The Soldier's Tale* and this version of *The Wedding*, in which the percussion is a continuing and internally consistent element, the 'drums' had never really been given their heads. The music itself is percussive, and that character is another part of my biological profile. To bang a gong, bash a cymbal, clout a wood block has always given me the keenest satisfaction. In fact, I am still tempted at dinner tables to tap the drinking glasses with the cutlery. But surely this is natural in a musician. After all, the first musician in the Bible was a hammer-and-anvil player (despite the façade at Orvieto, which portrays him striking bells suspended from a rack), and the music of the same instruments is supposed to have inspired Pythagoras' discovery of the relationships of intervals, by tapping glasses filled to varying levels with water.

My recollections of *The Wedding* are happy, but the associated ones are painful. All of my friends of that time are dead, and I am the only and ever-lonelier survivor. Stepan Mitusov comes to mind first: he was closer to me than anyone else at the time, and among other debts of gratitude I owe to him the encouragement of my *Wedding* idea. The thought of Mitusov reminds me, in turn, of Rimsky-Korsakov. We were together at Rimsky's nearly every day at one time. Rimsky was as fond of him as I was myself, but did not accept him as a pupil. I should be ashamed to say that this gave me my first better opinion of myself: I had at least been accepted.

I do not know whether Mitusov ever heard *The Wedding*, or even whether the music was repatriated during his lifetime. (Has it been now?) And the world is so different now that the name Korsakov is less likely to remind me of my dear old teacher than of the dreaded syndrome of defective time-memory. 'Old men forget', of course, but, like everyone, they forget or remember selectively. It follows that these memories are a selection, but they are the only ones willing to be summoned today concerning a long-vanished episode in the making of my *Wedding*.

*

R.C. What were the origins of the *Three Pieces for String Quartet*,[12] and when did you orchestrate them?
I.S. The orchestrations were completed in 1917. The fourth began life as the *Etude for Pianola* [1917] and became the fourth etude for orchestra in 1928, at which time I called it *Madrid*, adding titles to the three earlier pieces as well. The first, a *Danse* for woodwinds, repeats a four-note chant – 'The Four Fingers', one might call it – in varying rhythmic positions. The second, *Excentrique*, was inspired, as I have already said, by the movements and postures of the clown Little Tich, whom I had seen in London in June 1914. The third, *Cantique*, which might have been titled 'Hymne', is choral and religious in character. I composed the string-quartet original of the *Danse* in April 1914, in Leysin, and gave the manuscript (fair copy) to Ernest Ansermet. The quartet original of *Excentrique* was composed in Salvan, 2 July (1914). My sketchbooks contain several versions of the six-note tune in cello harmonics. The quartet original of the *Cantique* was composed in Salvan, 25–26 July (1914), by a process of much trial and error, to judge from my sketchbook.

*

R.C. Did you have Maeterlinck's *La Vie des abeilles* in mind as a programme for your *Scherzo fantastique*?

12 The Boston Symphony programme book for 7 and 8 February 1969 includes a detailed account of the first American receptions of these *Pieces*, and reprints the verses by Amy Lowell said to have been inspired by them. To the information printed in this programme book I can add that I made a two-piano version of the *Three Pieces* in 1914 that has never been published, and that I revised and corrected the quartet versions in December 1918, no. 1 on 2 December, and no. 2 on 6 December. [Footnote added by Stravinsky in one of his copies of the book.]

I.S. No, I wrote the *Scherzo* as a piece of 'pure' symphonic music.[13] While I have always been fascinated by bees, awed by them after reading von Fritsch's book, and terrified after reading Gerald Heard's *Is Another World Watching*, I have never attempted to evoke them in my work. (As, indeed, what pupil of the composer of the *Flight of the Bumblebee* would have?) Nor have I been influenced by them, except that, defying Galen's advice to elderly people, I continue to eat a daily diet of honey.

But Maeterlinck's bees nearly gave me serious trouble. One morning in Morges I received a startling letter from him, accusing me of intent to cheat and fraud. My *Scherzo* had been entitled *Les Abeilles* – anyone's title, after all – and made the subject of a ballet then performing at the Paris Grand Opéra (1917). The ballet *Les Abeilles* was not authorized by me, and, of course, I had not seen it; but Maeterlinck's name was mentioned in the programme. The affair was settled, and to satisfy the publisher, who thought a story would help to sell the music, Maeterlinck was quoted on the flyleaf. I regretted the incident with Maeterlinck because I greatly respected the works of his that I had read in Russian translation.

Some time later I recounted this episode to Paul Claudel, who said that Maeterlinck had been unusually polite to me: 'He often starts suits against people who say *bonjour* to him. You were lucky not to have been sued for the "bird" part of *Firebird*, since he had written the *Bluebird* first.'

*

R.C. What are your recollections of the circumstances concerning the composition and first performance of *The Soldier's Tale*? What was the source of the libretto, and which of the staging ideas were yours and which C.-F. Ramuz's?
I.S. The idea came to me in the autumn of 1917, but I could not develop it, still being occupied with *The Wedding* and with the task of preparing a symphonic poem from *Nightingale*. The thought of composing a dramatic spectacle for a *'théâtre*

13 This statement has been challenged, but is undoubtedly true. Stravinsky added the quotation from Maeterlinck when he began to think of publishing the score. [R.C.]

ambulant' had occurred to me more than once since the beginning of the war. The sort of work I envisaged would have to be small enough in the complement of its players to allow for performances on a circuit of Swiss villages, and simple enough in the outlines of its story to be easily understood. I discovered my subject in one of Afanasiev's tales of the soldier and the Devil. In the story that attracted me, the soldier tricks the Devil into drinking too much vodka, then gives a handful of shot to him, saying it is caviar, which the Devil greedily swallows, then dies. Subsequently I found other Devil–soldier episodes and gradually pieced them together. But only the skeleton of the play is Afanasiev–Stravinsky. The final form of the libretto must be credited to my friend and collaborator, C.-F. Ramuz. I worked with him, translating my Russian text to him line by line.[14]

Afanasiev gathered his soldier stories from peasant recruits to the Russo-Turkish wars. The stories are Christian, therefore, and the Devil is the *diabolus* of Christianity, a *person*, as always in Russian popular literature, though a person of many disguises. My original idea was to transpose the period and style of our play to 1918, and to endow it with several nationalities and none, without destroying the religio-cultural status of the Devil. Thus, the soldier of the original production was dressed in the uniform of a Swiss army private of 1918, while the costume, and especially the tonsorial apparatus, of the lepidopterist were of the 1830 period. Thus, too, place names like Denges and Denezy are Vaudois in sound, but these and other imaginary regionalisms were intended to be changed with the locale of the performance. The actors in the first staging introduced bits of Canton de Vaud patois. I still encourage producers to localize the play and, if they wish, to dress the soldier in a uniform temporally remote from, but sympathetic to, the audience. *Our* soldier, in 1918, was very definitely understood to be the victim of the present world conflict, despite the neutrality of the play in other respects. *The Soldier's Tale* remains my one stage work with a contemporary reference. The narrator device was adopted to satisfy the need for a two-way go-between: an interpreter

---

14 Perhaps I prefer the piece in the German version. I regret not having seen the Vienna performances with Harold Kreuzberg as the Devil and Curt Jurgens as the Soldier.

between the characters themselves, as well as a commentator between the stage and the audience. The intercession of the narrator in the action of the play was a later development, an idea borrowed from Pirandello. The role of the dancer was also a later conception. We must have feared that without dancing the play would be monotonous.

The shoestring economics of the original *Soldier* production confined me to a handful of instruments, but my musical ideas were already directed towards a solo-instrument style. My choice of instruments was influenced by an important event in my life at that time, the discovery of American jazz. The *Soldier* ensemble resembles a jazz band in that each category – strings, woodwinds, brass, percussion – is represented by both treble and bass components. The instruments themselves are jazz legitimates, too, except the bassoon, my substitute for the saxophone. (I prefer the more turbid and louder saxophone in larger orchestral combinations, as used by Berg in *Lulu*, following Schoenberg in *Von Heute auf Morgen*.) The percussion part must also be considered as a manifestation of my enthusiasm for jazz. I purchased the instruments in a music shop in Lausanne, learning to play them myself as I composed. (NB, the *pitch* of the drums is extremely important, and the intervals between high, medium and low should be as nearly even as possible; the performer must also take care that no drum exerts its own 'tonality' on the whole ensemble.) The *Soldier* 'Ragtime' is a concert portrait, or snapshot of the genre, in the sense that Chopin's *Valses* are not dance waltzes, but portraits of waltzes. Since I had never heard any of the music in actual performance, I borrowed its rhythmic style not as played, but as written. The jazz element brought an entirely new sound to my music, and *The Soldier* marks my final break with the Russian orchestral school. (How unlike the jazz of *Lulu* and *Der Wein* mine is, though perhaps not so unlike that of, say, Ives's Third Violin Sonata, which I learned from Sol Babitz.) If every good piece of music is marked by its own characteristic sound, those of *The Soldier* are the scrape of the violin and the punctuation of the drums. The violin represents the soldier's soul, the drums the *diablerie*.

My first thematic idea for *The Soldier* was the trumpet–

trombone melody at the beginning of the march. I may have been influenced in composing it by the popular French song *Marietta*, but if so, it is the only borrowed melodic material in the piece. One of the chief motives is very close to the *Dies irae*, of course, but this resemblance did not occur to me during the composition, which is not to deny that the funereal tune may have been festering in my 'subconscious'. Nor was I dedicated to a plan for a work of an international character: an 'American' trombone melody at the beginning of the march; the American 'ragtime'; the French *valse*, the German [Lutheran] wedding chorale, which so resembles *Ein' feste Burg*; the Spanish *pasodoble*. This last was suggested by a real incident I witnessed in Madrid. I was standing in a street with Diaghilev during the Holy Week processions in 1917 and listening with much pleasure to a tiny 'bullfight' band consisting of a cornet, a trombone, and a bassoon. They were playing a *pasodoble*. Suddenly a large brass band came blaring down the street playing the Overture to *Tannhäuser*. The *pasodoble* was drowned out, but not without shouting and fighting. One of the *pasodoble* band had called the Madonna doll of the large band a whore. I never forgot the *pasodoble*.

During the composition of *The Soldier* Tristan Tzara and the other initiators of the Zurich Dada movement tried to persuade me to join them. But I could see no future in Dada, and no musical use for it at all; and though the word 'Dada' sounded like 'yes, yes' to my Russian ears, what the Dadaists themselves were saying amounted to something more like 'no, no'. After a year or two of Dadaism the movement seemed dead, its concocters mere sycophants of art.

The first performance of *The Soldier* took place in a small Victorian theatre in Lausanne. The production was sponsored by Werner Reinhardt, an altruistic gentleman who paid for everybody and everything, and who finally even commissioned my music. I gave him the manuscript in appreciation, and composed the *Three Pieces for Clarinet Solo* for him in gratitude; he was an amateur clarinettist. Reinhardt later purchased the sketches of *The Wedding* for 5,000 Swiss francs. But though the performance was financially guaranteed, we had no assurance it would be seen by an audience. For this reason I decided to seek the help of the Grand Duchess Helena, who was living in Ouchy. Her patronage and presence would require the attendance of Ouchy's colony of Russian aristocrats, as well as the leading members in the various diplomatic corps at Berne. Someone in Paderewski's entourage arranged the meeting, and when I reminded Her Highness of how her father the Grand Duke Vladimir (whom I had seen in the street in my childhood) had so generously given his patronage to Diaghilev, she accepted at once and purchased several loges. *The Soldier* suddenly became a *mondaine* affair, and the performance was a considerable success. But we had to be content with a single one, since Spanish influenza struck Lausanne the next day, and public halls were closed by law. I did not see *The Soldier* again until five years later, at the Bauhaus in Weimar.

The sets were designed and executed by René Auberjonois, a local painter, a friend of mine, and an intimate of Ramuz. The outer-stage curtain was a gauze on which were depicted two fountain jets with a boat rowing on top of each one. The curtains for the tiny inner stage were a series of painted oilcloths containing pictures deliberately unrelated in subject matter to *The Soldier* – a whale, a landscape, etc. These oilcloths were hand-pulleyed, like window shades or maps in a geography class. The ideas for the costumes were my own, as well as Auberjonois's. The Princess wore red stockings and a white tutu, the narrator a *frac*, and the soldier, as I have said, the uniform of a Swiss Army private. The Devil had four disguises. He appeared first as the lepidopterist, in a costume that included such paraphernalia as a green-visored *casquette* and a butterfly net. The idea of the disguise was that lepidopterists are supposed to be papilionaceous themselves, and so absorbed in the pursuit of their specimens that they do not notice anything else; the interest of this particular 'lepidopterist' in the soldier is therefore out of character and suspicious. The second disguise was that of a French–Swiss cattle merchant; in our production this costume was a knee-length blue jacket, with a dark blue hat. His third appearance was in the guise of an old woman, with a brown shawl and a *capuchine*. In fact, this old woman is a procuress, and the portraits she produces from her basket, which the audience does not see, are meant to be of her gallery-for-

hire. This was the original scenario, at any rate; the more inno-
cent old woman of subsequent productions deprives the episode
of its point. The fourth costume is the *frac* for the restaurant
scene. Here the Devil drinks himself into a stupor, while the
soldier steals back his violin, this being the original Afanasiev
episode upon which the work was conceived. At the end of the
play the Devil reveals himself in his true colours, and in his
forked tail and pointed ears.

The stage direction of the first performance was the work of
George and Lyudmilla Pitoëff, though the movements themselves had already been worked out by Ramuz and myself.
Pitoëff played the part of the Devil, and his wife mimed and
danced the Princess. Pitoëff had rather too much of a Russian
accent, I thought. His problems as director were all created by
the diminutive inner stage, which was hardly as large as two
armchairs together.

I was thirty-two and Ramuz was forty when we first met, in
a Lausanne restaurant. He introduced himself to me as an
admirer of *Petrushka*. Ramuz was a kind man – except to his
wife, whom he had been obliged to marry and whom he continued to call 'mademoiselle', in a strict, hard voice, in front of
his friends – and a very lively one, an impression not easily
deduced from his books. Our work together while preparing the
French versions of my Russian texts was one of the more enjoyable associations of my life.

In speaking of Ramuz, I must also mention another dear friend
and close companion of the same time and place, Charles-Albert
Cingria,[15] an itinerant scholar, a kind of bicycle troubadour,

15 Though highly esteemed by Claudel, Cocteau, Max Jacob, Jean Paulhan,
Jean Starobinski and others, Cingria was little known at the time of this
Stravinsky conversation. Cingria is now regarded as a 'great writer' by the
French literary world. He was a prolific one, in any case, his *Œuvres complètes*
having been published in seventeen volumes. He was also a musician (pianist)
and musicologist, as Stravinsky indicates. Geneva-born, of a French–Polish
mother and a Turkish-Yugoslavian father, he was a close friend of Stravinsky
from the composer's earliest years in Switzerland, and even during the composition of *Perséphone*, though Cingria's nemesis was Gide. I met him in Venice
in 1951 – he had bicycled there for the première of *The Rake's Progress* – and
again in Paris in May 1952. At the news of his death in 1954, Stravinsky
wept. [R.C.]

who would suddenly disappear in Greece or Italy and return as suddenly months later, poor and empty as Torricelli's vacuum. Cingria was nearly always drunk, and he was passionate only about neumes, but he was also the most affectionate companion imaginable. More than once I pedalled – Switzerland was the bicycle stage of my life – from Morges to Neuchâtel with him, stopping *en route* at Yverdon to drink the open *vin du pays*, and tottering somewhat from there on.

*

R.C. What were the jazz origins of *Ragtime for Eleven Instruments*, and how do you regard this music today?
I.S. A jazz influence, the blanket term, can be found throughout my music, for example in the *Bransle de Poitou* and the *Bransle Simple* in *Agon*, and in the *pas d'action* and *pas de deux* (middle section) in *Orpheus*. My *Ebony Concerto* is my contribution to 'blues', and the flute, harp and clarinet music of the slow movement of my *Symphony in Three* is my gift to boogie-woogie, as is the flute and clarinet music in the sarabande of *Perséphone*.

I began the *Ragtime* in October 1918 and finished it on the morning of the Armistice. I remember how, sitting at the cimbalom in my garret in Morges, I was aware of a buzzing in my ears that increased until I was afraid I had been stricken like Robert Schumann. I went down to the street and was told that everyone was hearing the same noise, and that it was from cannon along the French frontier signalling the end of the war.

When the *Ragtime* was completed, I asked Picasso to design a cover. I watched him draw six figures, each from a single, uninterrupted line. He chose the published one himself.

I have a vague recollection of meeting Picasso with Vollard at my friend Prince Argutinsky's in Paris in June 1910, but I did not know him until 1917, when we were together in Rome. I immediately liked his flat, unenthusiastic manner of speaking, and his Spanish way of accenting each syllable: '*Je ne suis pas musicien, je comprends rien dans la musique*', all said as though he couldn't care less. It was the moment of the Russian Revolution, and we could no longer precede our ballet programmes with the Imperial Anthem. I orchestrated 'The Song of the Volga

Boatmen' to replace it, and on the title page of my manuscript
Picasso painted a red circle as a symbol of the Revolution.

*

R.C. Would you discuss your recomposition of 'Pergolesi' in
Pulcinella? Also, what were the origins of the idea – why
Pergolesi? – and what do you recall of the history of the
work?

I.S. The suggestion that was to lead to *Pulcinella* came from
Diaghilev in September 1919, while we were walking together
in the Place de la Concorde: 'Don't protest at what I am about
to say. I know you are much taken by your Alpine colleagues' –
said with withering contempt – 'but I have an idea that I think
will amuse you more than anything they can propose. I want
you to look at some delightful eighteenth-century music with
the idea of orchestrating it for a ballet.' When he revealed
that the composer was Pergolesi,[16] I thought he must be
deranged. I knew Pergolesi only by the *Stabat Mater* and *La
serva padrona*, and though I had just seen a production of the
latter in Barcelona, Diaghilev knew I wasn't in the least excited
by it. But I promised to look at the music and to give him my
opinion.

I did look, and I fell in love. My ultimate selection of pieces
derived only partly from Diaghilev's examples, though I played
through the whole of them, and the other part from published
editions. My first step was to fix a plan of action and an accompanying sequence of pieces. Diaghilev had found a book of
'Pulcinella' stories in Rome. We read this book together and
selected certain episodes. The final construction of the plot and
ordering of the dance numbers was the work of Diaghilev,
Leonid Massine, and myself, all three of us working together.
But the libretto – or argument, for *Pulcinella* is more an *action
dansant* than a ballet – does not come from the same source as
the texts of the songs. The latter were borrowed from two
operas and a cantata. As in *The Wedding*, the singers are not

16 In truth, a letter from Ansermet in London to Stravinsky in Morges in
June 1919 informs him that Diaghilev has a Stravinsky–Pergolesi ballet in
mind. [R.C.]

identified with stage characters. They sing 'in character' songs, solo serenades, duets, trios as interpolated numbers.

Pulcinella was the swan-song of my Swiss years. I began by composing directly on the copies of Pergolesi's manuscripts, as though I were correcting an old work of my own. I had no preconceptions, no aesthetic attitudes, and I could have predicted nothing about the result. I knew that I could not produce a 'forgery' of Pergolesi because my motor habits are so different. At best, I could repeat him in my own accent. Probably it was inevitable that the result was a satire – who could have treated that material in 1919 otherwise? – but even this observation is hindsight. I did not set out to compose a satire, and Diaghilev hadn't considered the possibility of such a thing. A mannered orchestration of something very sweet was what Diaghilev wanted, nothing more, and my music so shocked him that he went about for a long time with a look that suggested The Offended Eighteenth Century. *Pulcinella* is remarkable, however, not for how much, but for how little has been added or changed.

My main problem was to convert operatic and concert pieces into dance pieces. I therefore began to look through Pergolesi for 'rhythmic' rather than 'melodic' numbers. I did not go far before discovering that this distinction does not exist. Instrumental or vocal, sacred or secular, eighteenth-century music is, in one sense, *all* dance music.

Pulcinella was my discovery of the past, the epiphany through which the whole of my late work became possible. It was a backward look, the first of many love affairs in that direction, as well as a look in the mirror. No critic understood this, and I was attacked for being a *pasticheur*, chided for composing 'simple' music, blamed for deserting 'modernism', accused of renouncing my 'true Russian heritage'. People who had never heard of, or cared about, the originals called it 'sacrilege': 'The classics are ours. Leave the classics alone.' To them my answer was and is the same: 'You "respect", but I love.'

When musicians talk among themselves about the masterpieces of their art, a moment always comes when someone will demonstrate what he means by singing it. Instead of saying 'three quavers of G followed by a minim E♭', he or she will sing the opening of Beethoven's Fifth. The limits of criticism could hardly be better defined. I, too, would rather 'sing' *Pulcinella* than try to talk about it.

R.C. Do you remember Massine's *Pulcinella* choreography?

I.S. I considered it good, on the whole, a bit mechanical perhaps, but only his dance for the Variations contradicted the music. This was because he had choreographed it before I wrote the orchestra score, and Diaghilev had told him I would use a large orchestra with harps. My orchestra in the Variations, as you know, is limited to solo wind instruments.

R.C. Have you any idea where Picasso's backdrop for *Pulcinella* might be found?

I.S. It was in the dome of the Paris Opéra when I last heard, but except for the moon, whose yellow had once been renewed by a cat, was severely faded. Diaghilev, I suppose, was in financial straits with the Director of the Opéra, and when our ballet company evacuated the building after the *Pulcinella* perfor- mances he kept the Picasso as collateral.

Picasso accepted the commission to design the décor for the same reason that I agreed to arrange the music, for the fun of it, and Diaghilev was as shocked by his set as he was by my sounds. Picasso's stage was a volumetric view of balconied, Spanish-style houses. It filled only part of the huge Paris Opéra stage, and a smaller frame had to be built for it. The costumes were simple. The six Pulcinellas who appear in the course of the piece were all dressed in baggy white costumes with red stockings. The women wore black corselets and red-and-white- striped shirts with black fringes and red pompoms.

In the spring of 1917 Diaghilev, Massine, Picasso and I had journeyed from Rome to Naples together – Picasso's portrait of Massine was drawn in the train – and spent some days in close company there. We were all agreeably entertained by the *com- media dell'arte* performance that we saw in a crowded little room reeking of garlic. The Pulcinella was a great drunken lout whose every gesture, and probably every word, if I had under- stood, was obscene. The only other incident of our Neapolitan holiday that I remember is that Picasso and I were arrested one night for urinating against a wall of the Galleria. I asked the policeman to escort us across the street to the Teatro San Carlo where someone would vouch for us. The request granted, the three of us proceeded backstage, where the policeman, hearing us being greeted as *'maestri'*, let us go.

Picasso's original *Pulcinella* was very different from the pure *commedia dell'arte* Diaghilev wanted. His first designs were for Offenbach-period costumes with side-whiskered faces instead of masks. When he showed them, Diaghilev said, brusquely, 'Oh, this isn't it at all' and proceeded to tell Picasso how to do it. The evening concluded with Diaghilev actually throwing the drawings on the floor, stamping on them, and slamming the door as he left. The next day he succeeded in persuading Picasso to do a *commedia dell'arte Pulcinella*, but all of Diaghilev's charm was needed to reconcile the deeply insulted painter.

France
1920–1939
Symphonies of Wind Instruments, Octet, Oedipus Rex,
Apollo, The Fairy's Kiss, Symphony of Psalms,
Perséphone, Concerto for Two Solo Pianos,
The Card Game, Concerto in E♭

We left Switzerland permanently in June 1920, moving first to
Carantec, a fishing village in Finisterre, and then, in the fall, to
Madame Gabrielle Chanel's home in Garches, near Versailles.
She was a very close friend at the time, as well as one of
Diaghilev's most generous supporters, and she had underwritten
the December 1920 revival of *The Rite of Spring* at the Théâtre
des Champs-Elysées. My family and I lived in her Garches home
from late autumn until the following spring.

The concluding chorale of the *Symphonies of Winds* was
composed 20 June 1920, in Carantec. I had leased a cottage
there for the summer before discovering the impossibility of
renting a piano locally, and that one would have to be carted
in from a neighbouring village. The remainder of the music
was finished in abbreviated-score form by 2 July, but not in
full score until 30 November, in Garches. On the 1st or 2nd
of December I added the first phrase of the chorale to the
body of the piece in two places. The earliest sketches contain
notations for string quartet, and the duets for alto flute and
alto clarinet were originally scored for violin and viola. Another
section in one of the same sketches was later developed as the
waltz variation in the Octet. Like my *Piano Rag-Music* and
Three Pieces for Clarinet Solo, both composed in 1919, the
sketch score is not fully metred, but in questions of phrasing,
the sketch score of the *Symphonies* differs strikingly from the
three published proof scores, which in turn are so different
from each other that the two versions will doubtless continue

to be played as two different pieces, or, more likely, as at present, continue *not* to be played.[1]

In the spring of 1921, we rented a beach house called Cottage L'Argenté in Anglet, near Biarritz, where I composed Three Movements from *Petrushka* for piano solo in August of that year. Artur Rubinstein, to whom I had dedicated my *Piano Rag-Music*, hoping to encourage him to play contemporary music, paid a generous 5,000 francs for it, but he played it only once, in Memphis, Tennessee, many years later, and never played the *Rag-Music*. Incidentally, the reason I have never performed the Three Movements publicly myself is quite simple: I lack the technique.

We liked the area so much that we rented a house, Villa des Rochers, in the centre of the city and remained there until 1924. I became an *aficionado* during my Biarritz period and went to the *corrida* in Bayonne several times. I was there with Rubinstein on the tragic occasion when a bull dislodged a *banderilla* and sent it through the air and into the heart of the Consul-General of Guatemala, who was standing by the railing and died instantly. In Biarritz I entered into a six-year contract with the Pleyel company in Paris, by which I agreed to transcribe my complete works for the Pleyela, their player-piano machine, in return for 3,000 francs a month and the use of one of their Paris studios in the rue Rochechouart, which then became my first Paris residence.

My transcriptions for the Pleyela, forgotten exercises to no purpose, represented hundreds of hours of work and were of

---

1 Stravinsky wrote to Gavril Païchadze, Director of the Editions Russes de Musique, Paris, 28 May 1932: 'Ansermet managed to call about the *Symphonies of Wind Instruments* before his departure for Switzerland. He asks that you immediately send the proof sheets, which he will soon have corrected for you.' On 4 July Stravinsky reminded Païchadze that Ansermet had agreed to correct the proofs, but on 11 August the composer was still asking the publisher to 'send the *Symphonies of Wind Instruments* to Ansermet immediately. This is the only time that he can work on it, and it would be a pity to let the opportunity pass.' More than a year later, Stravinsky again wrote that 'Ansermet asks me a number of questions concerning the *Symphonies of Wind Instruments,* which means that he has agreed to correct it [*korrecturit*, a non-existent form of the verb]' (originals in Russian). Still, the score was not published, and soon the Editions Russes de Musique, having declined an offer by Schott in April 1932 to bring it out, virtually ceased to function, other than to rent music. [R.C.]

major importance to me at the time. My interest in player-pianos dated from 1914, when I saw a demonstration of the pianola by the Aeolian Company in London. During the war, Aeolian commissioned an original piece from me. The idea of being performed by rolls of perforated paper amused me, and I was interested in the mechanics of the instrument. After composing an etude for pianola, I did not forget about the instrument, and six years later, when I began my transcription work for Pleyel, I borrowed one of their instruments for a study of the mechanism at first hand. The chief problem, I discovered, was in the restrictive application of the pedals caused by the division of the keyboard into two parts. Perhaps I can compare it to Cinerama, or a film shown half and half from two projectors. I overcame the difficulty by employing two assistants to sit, one on each side of me, as I stood facing the keyboard, dictating as I transcribed, from right to left and to each in turn. My experience with this schizoid instrument must have influenced the music I was composing then, at least where questions of tempo relationships and the absence of tempo nuances are concerned. I should add that many of my Pleyela arrangements, especially of vocal works like *The Wedding* and the Russian songs, were virtually recomposed for the medium.

We moved to Nice in 1924, to the *bel étage* of a house at 167 boulevard Carnot. We were barely installed there when my four children contracted diphtheria. I purchased an automobile in Nice, and though I began to think of myself as a competent driver, first in my Renault and later in my Hotchkiss, I never could drive in Paris, and I lacked the courage to drive in the United States. Nice was our family home until the spring of 1931, though we lived at Lac d'Annécy (Talloires) in the summers of 1927, 1928 and 1929, and at Echarvines les Bains (Dauphiné), in the Châlet des Echarvines, in the summer of 1930. At the beginning of 1931 we moved from Nice to the Château de la Vironnière, near Voreppe (Grenoble), living there for three years, except for the winter of 1933–34, which we spent in a furnished house in the rue Viet, Paris. Toward the end of 1934 we moved to 125 rue Faubourg St-Honoré, Paris, my last and, because of the deaths of my elder daughter, my wife, and my mother, unhappiest home.

I became a French citizen on 10 June 1934. The next year

Paul Dukas died, and my French friends urged me to canvass for election to his seat in the Institut de France. I opposed the idea, but Paul Valéry changed my mind by telling me of privileges that academicians enjoyed. I called dutifully on Maurice Denis, Charles-Marie Widor, and other elderly voters of the kind, but lost by a huge margin to Florent Schmitt, which upset my belief that academies are formed by bad artists who wish to distinguish themselves by subsequently electing a good one. Satie's witticism is right: 'To have turned down the Légion d'Honneur is not enough. One should never have deserved it.'

But to return to my work, I wrote *The Five Fingers* in 1921, one piece a day, on 24, 26, 29, 31 January and 4, 13, 17, 18 February, at Garches. Unlike the [*Eight*] *Easy Pieces* for piano duet, these studies were not written for my own children, but for all piano débutantes. My idea was to assign each finger of the right hand to a single note, thus limiting myself to a five-note series. (In the same way, in the *Gigue* of my Septet [1953], I confined each *instrument* to a single row of notes.) I orchestrated the last of *The Five Fingers* on 6 December 1961, for a concert in the Bellas Artes in Mexico City, at which time I called it 'Tango', though 'The Tijuana Blues' would have described it more aptly, since, being the Christmas season, the hall was empty. Having digressed this far, I should add that I went on to orchestrate the other seven pieces for different combinations of up to fifteen instruments, the *Andantino* on 21 March of 1962, the *Vivace* on 23 March, the *Lento* on the 25th, and the *Kosachok Variation*, which entailed an amount of adding and rewriting, on the 26th. The *Marcialetta* was written on 2 April, and I conducted the first performance of the *Eight Instrumental Miniatures*, as I called the suite, in Toronto later that month.

Also in 1921, at Diaghilev's request, I contributed two orchestrations to the revival of *The Sleeping Beauty*. Tchaikovsky had instituted certain cuts after the first performance, some of them at the suggestion of Tsar Alexander III himself, and the excised numbers did not appear in the only available full score. I therefore orchestrated them from the piano reduction, the *Variation d'Aurore* from Act II and the *Entr'acte symphonique* preceding the finale of the second act. In addition, I implemented several changes in Tchaikovsky's own orchestration of 'The Russian Dance' in the last act. The Tsar found the *Entr'acte symphonique* – a dream sequence danced before the curtain – dull, and I agree, but Diaghilev needed the piece for stage-setting time. My work on these numbers, whatever I thought of them as music, awakened my appetite to compose *The Fairy's Kiss*.

*

My next opus, *Mavra*, a one-act *opera buffa* dedicated 'to the memory of Tchaikovsky, Glinka, and Pushkin', was composed in Anglet and Biarritz. It was inspired in the spring of 1921 in Seville during the planning stage of *The Sleeping Beauty* revival. I had thought of Pushkin's *House of Kolomna* as a subject for an operatic skit, and I asked the young Boris Kochno – he was only seventeen – to compose a libretto based on it. Kochno had been one of Diaghilev's lovers a year before but by this time had fallen from the fickle favour. He was a gifted versifier, and his *Mavra* lyrics are musical. The scheme of the action, with the sequence of numbers, was worked out by the three of us together, in London, after which I retired to Anglet to await the libretto and compose the music. Parasha's aria was composed first, and the overture last. I used wind instruments principally because the music seemed to whistle as wind instruments do, and because there was a *démodé* 'jazz' element in it, in the quartet especially, that seemed to require a 'band' sound rather than an 'orchestra' sound.[2] When the little opera was finished, Diaghilev organized a preview performance in the Hôtel Continental. While accompanying the singers at the piano, I could see that my deliberately simple music horrified Diaghilev, and that he was desperately worried about the performance. In fact, it was a fiasco, but to the reason already suggested, I will add one more: Diaghilev's own inimical attitude to Bronislava Nijinska, the *metteur en scène*. The singers were unable to execute her choreographic ideas.

Mavra is Tchaikovskian in period and style (style in the sense

2 This 'jazz' element was perceived by Jack Hylton, the English jazz-band conductor, who subsequently acquired my permission to arrange the middle scene of the opera, the duet and quartet, for his own combination of saxophones-and-so-forth. Mr Hylton actually conducted this *Mavra* potpourri as part of a concert at the Paris Opéra (!) in 1932. It was a flop.

that it is *poméshchiks*', townspeople's or small landowners', music, which is the contrary of folk music), but the dedication to Tchaikovsky was also propaganda. I wanted to show a different Russia to my non-Russian, and especially my French, colleagues, who derided him as the master of the maudlin, a sentimental absurdity. The French, I thought, were saturated with the tourist-office orientalism of 'The Five', the *magucha kuchka*, 'The Mighty Handful', as Stasov used to call them. In essence, I was protesting against the picturesque in Russian music, and against those who failed to see that the picturesque is produced by gimmicks. Tchaikovsky's talent was the greatest of any Russian musician. His virtues, as I thought, were his elegance (in my view, Tchaikovsky's most successful music is in his ballets) and his wit (the animal variations in *The Sleeping Beauty*).

Léon Bakst was chosen to design *Mavra*, but he and Diaghilev quarrelled about money, and I sided with Diaghilev. Bakst never forgave me, which I regretted, especially when three years later, aboard the SS *Paris* on my first trip to the United States, I read a notice of his death in the ship's newspaper.

The failure of *Mavra* upset Diaghilev. He had been eager to impress Otto Kahn, who attended the première in Diaghilev's loge and was to have brought the company to America. Kahn's only comment was: 'I liked it all, then, "poop", it ends too quickly.' Diaghilev asked me to change the ending, but I refused. The principal factor in the failure was in the programming.

Imagine *Mavra* on the huge stage of the Opéra and performed next to *The Rite of Spring*!

*

R.C. Of your early contemporaries, you say that your greatest debt is to Debussy. Do you think his contact with you had any effect on his own music?

I.S. I do not perceive any change in his music resulting from our connection. After reading his friendly and complimentary letters to me – he really did like *Petrushka* – I was puzzled to find a different feeling concerning my subsequent music in some of his letters to his musician friends. Was it duplicity, or was he annoyed at his incapacity to digest the music of *The Rite of*

Spring when the younger generation received it enthusiastically? Such questions are difficult to judge at a distance of more than forty years.

Virgil Thomson once wrote that 'Stravinsky scared the daylights out of Claude Debussy.' Recently I came across an eyewitness account that I had not seen before of another of Debussy's reactions to me, or rather to a work of mine. Shortly after I first heard *Pelléas* – sitting with its composer – Debussy heard a performance of *The Rite*. The dramatist Lenormand was watching him, apparently with more attention than he was giving to the music. 'Debussy's face was distressed,' Lenormand wrote:

It showed a grief impossible either to master or to hide: that of the creator before whom opens a world wholly different from his own: the sadness of being left behind, the suffering of the artist in the presence of new forms which reveal his place and his limits.

Debussy did not sense that *The Rite* was the apex of the Ballets Russes musical revolution. Apart from that, it could not have been all that new to him, and he must have recognized the debt to him in it, particularly at the beginning of Part Two. Probably the premonitory newness to him was the tremendous groundswell at the end. I think Lenormand's reading of the composer's face was right.

I recall with particular pleasure a luncheon at Debussy's shortly after the first performance of *Petrushka*. 'Chou-chou' was there, and I noticed that her eye teeth were like her father's, which is to say like tusks. Debussy gave me a walking stick then, on which our initials were inscribed together like a monogram. Later, during my recovery from typhus, he gave a handsome cigarette case to me.

Debussy was only slightly taller than I am, but much heavier. He spoke in a low quiet voice, and his phrase endings were scarcely audible – which was to the good, since they could contain verbal booby traps. The first time I visited him in his house, after *Firebird*, we talked about Musorgsky's songs and agreed that they were the best music of the whole Russian school. Debussy said that he had discovered Musorgsky in a pile of music lying untouched on Mme von Meck's piano. Debussy did not like Rimsky, whom he called 'a voluntary academic, the worst kind'. He was especially interested in Japanese art at that time, and, I thought, *not* especially interested in new developments in music. In fact my own appearance on the musical scene must have been a shock to him. I saw him rarely during the war, and our few visits were probably painful for him. His subtle, grave smile had disappeared, and his skin was sallow and sunken; it was hard not to imagine him as a cadaver. I asked if he had heard my *Three Pieces for String Quartet*, which had just been played in Paris, thinking he would like the last twenty bars of the third piece, which are Debussyist, but he had not heard them, indeed, had heard almost no new music. Whereas Ravel was stimulated by what I had told him about *Pierrot Lunaire*, Debussy said nothing – but wrote to his friend Robert Godet that 'Stravinsky is inclining dangerously *du côté de Schoenberg*'.

I saw Debussy for the last time about nine months before his death [in 1918], a *triste* visit. Paris was grey, quiet, without lights and movement. He did not mention the piece from *En blanc et noir* that he had written for me, and when I received this music in Morges, late in 1919, I was moved by the dedication and equally pleased to see that it was such a good composition. I was moved, too, while composing my *Symphonies* to his memory, and, if I may say so, it, too, is 'a good composition'.

Lately [1968] I have been listening to a new recording of *Pelléas*, much inferior to Ansermet's old one, it must be said. The performance is stylistically questionable in over-accenting and over-articulating (the dotted notes in the *Interlude* between the first two scenes of Act Two are too short and bouncy, more in my style than in Debussy's), and in substituting *forte* for *pianissimo* (the winds at 35, Act Two). But the singers are the main problem. The child Yniold is the only one wholly free of a pitch-blurring vibrato, but his puling '*petit père*' – and everyone else's – is a penance. The mispronunciations – Mélisande's '*un*' and '*une*' are indistinguishably masculine; Golaud's '*vous*' rhymes too perfectly with the word used for the vocalizing of cows in children's books – attract too much attention to the words. And what words! How could Debussy, Mallarmé's friend, stomach Maeterlinck, let alone underline some of his most irritating mannerisms? Those interjections of '*loin, loin*', '*tous, tous*', '*où est-il, où est-il*', '*la verité, la verité*', '*ne me touchez pas, ne me touchez pas*', and other nervous-tic repetitions, which Debussy makes worse by separating the words with evenly measured rests. 'O [rest, rest] O' must occur a dozen whining times even before Mélisande drops her ring – and with it her second 'O'. Of the two inexactnesses of the singers, rhythm and intonation, the first is the more surprising. Not that exactness is all; but suppleness comes after, not before, fidelity to the written rhythmic values.

But what beautiful things the score contains! I limit my judgement to the music only because I am no longer able to 'see' the work as drama. My impression of the musical whole is of a decline in effectiveness after the 'hair' scene, when the quiet gloom of the earlier acts is shattered by Golaud's melodramatics. The idiom is too confining for an opera of this length, and it wears off like a drug. The music ranges from Wagner, without anything like Wagner's range, to *Petrushka* (the bassoons and clarinets in seconds in the *Interlude* to the second scene of Act II), a decade before *Petrushka* was written, but the later scenes are musically claustrophobic. Simplicity and restraint turn into limitation and constraint, beautiful monotony into just plain monotony. The opera is too long, even though the death scene in Act V is very beautiful.

*

R.C. What were the circumstances attending the composition of the Octet?

I.S. It began with a dream in which I saw myself in a small room surrounded by a small group of wind instrumentalists playing some very attractive music. Though I strained to hear the music, I could not, but I remember my curiosity – in the dream – to know how many the musicians were.[3] I remember, too, that after I had counted them to the number eight, I looked again and saw that they were playing bassoons, trombones, trumpets, flute, and a clarinet. I awoke from this silent concert in a state of delight

3 This confession exposes me to Minkowski's analysis of the counting mania as a time frustration, i.e., of the compulsion to count as a wish to force future time. But time dreams and counting dreams are common with me, and so are dreams in which people shout, but inaudibly, like a cinema when the sound-track fails, or talk out of hearing in the distance. I dream regularly now that I am able to walk without a cane, as I could five years ago.

and anticipation, and the next morning began to compose the Octet, which I had not thought of the day before, though for some time I had wanted to write an instrumental sonata.

The music was quickly composed, the first-movement *allegro* first, followed immediately by the waltz in the second movement. The *tema* of the second movement variations was taken from a *fugato* written in 1921, and used as the final variation, my favourite episode in the piece. Only after I had composed the waltz did I see that the first five notes of the *fugato* were an incipient subject for variations. I then wrote the 'ribbons of scales' variation as a prelude to each of the other variations.

The plan of the culminating variation was to present the theme in rotation by the instrumental pairs – bassoons, trumpets, trombones, flute–clarinet – the instrumental combinations at the root of my dream. The final movement developed from the bridge separating it from the *fugato*, and was intended as a contrast to its harmonic density. Bach's two-part inventions were somewhere in my mind while composing the last movement, as they were during the composition of the last movement of the Piano Sonata. The terseness and lucidity of the inventions were an ideal of mine at that time, and I sought to keep those qualities uppermost in my own composition. What could be more concise than the punctuation of the Octet's concluding chord, in which the first inversion suffices to indicate *finis* and at the same time gives more spirit than the flat-footed tonic?

My appetite was whetted by my rediscovery of sonata form, and by my pleasure in working with new instrumental combinations. I like the instrumental games in the Octet, and I can add that I achieved in it exactly what I set out to do. If I were to compile a textbook of instrumental usages, they would have to be chosen from my own works only, for the reason that I could never be certain of the exact intentions of any other composer and therefore of the degree of his success or failure.

In spite of a bad case of *trac* (nerves), I conducted the first performance, the first concert work of mine that I introduced myself. The Paris Opéra seemed a large frame for only eight players, but the group was set off by screens, and the sound was well balanced. The Octet was composed for, and is dedicated to, Vera Sudeykina.

*

R.C. You were on good terms with Erik Satie, and he wrote an affectionate article about you for American consumption.

I.S. Satie was certainly the oddest person I have ever known, and one of the wittiest. I had a great liking for him, and I believe that he appreciated and returned my friendship. With his pince-nez, umbrella and galoshes he looked like a schoolmaster, but he also looked like one without these accoutrements. He spoke very softly, hardly opening his mouth, but pronouncing each word in an inimitably precise way. His calligraphic handwriting recalls the immaculateness of his speech. His manuscripts were like him also, which is to say '*fin*'. No one ever saw him wash. He had a horror of soap and was forever rubbing his fingers with pumice. He was very poor, poor by conviction, living in the poorest *arrondissement*. His neighbours greatly respected him and seemed to appreciate his coming among them.[4] His apartment was very modest. It had a hammock instead of a bed, and in winter Satie would fill bottles with hot water and put them flat in a row underneath, where they looked like some exotic kind of marimba. I remember his reply when someone had promised him a gift of money: 'Monsieur, what you have said did not fall on a deaf ear.'

His sarcasm depended on French bourgeoisie usages. The first time I heard his *Socrate*, at a séance where he played it for a few of his friends, he turned around at the end and said, like the proprietor of a café or a store, '*Voilà, messieurs, dames.*' I was deeply moved by the gravitas and dignity of his music for Socrates' death, though the piece as a whole is rhythmically monotonous. I don't think he knew much about instruments; I prefer *Socrate* as he played it on the piano to the orchestra score.

I met Satie in June 1910 at Debussy's, where he photographed us, and where I photographed Debussy several times, alone and with his daughter 'Chou-chou'. In those early years Satie played many of his own compositions for me at the piano. The titles of the pieces were their most interesting part, but literary, of course, and limited by this, whereas Klee's titles are literary but of the essence of the picture.

4 He joined the French Communist Party in 1925 when it separated from the Socialists. [R.C.]

Satie's own sudden and mysterious death touched me, too. He had been turned towards religion near the end of his life and started going to Communion. When I saw him after a church service one morning, he remarked in that matter-of-fact way of his, '*Alors, j'ai un peu communiqué ce matin.*' He became ill very suddenly and died quickly and quietly.

R.C. What do you recall of Reynaldo Hahn?

I.S. He was a thin, elegant man with motherly manners. I saw him at concerts and ballets, which he reviewed for a publication. Occasionally he came in company with his closest friend, Marcel Proust. Diaghilev needed Hahn's favourable notices and therefore staged his ballet *Dieu Bleu*. After that, and to a lesser extent before, Hahn was a salon idol, and salon support was necessary to Diaghilev at the time. After the war, Diaghilev dropped him for the very reason that he had once found him important, the eclipse of his salon reputation. Hahn was pro-*Rite of Spring*, as indeed almost everyone in Paris was after Monteux's 1914 concert performances, and he remained a partisan of my music up to *Pulcinella*.

*

R.C. Would you say a few words about the painters you knew in the Paris years? For instance, was Michel Larionov your choice of painter for *Renard*?

I.S. Diaghilev suggested him, but he would have been my choice as well. A huge blond *muzhik* of a man, even bigger than Diaghilev – Larionov had an uncontrollable temper and once knocked Diaghilev down – he made a vocation of laziness, like Oblomov, and we always believed that his wife, Goncharova, did his work for him. He was a talented painter, nevertheless, and I still like his *Renard* set and costumes.

Another 'ballet' painter I saw a lot of at this time was Derain. I liked his *parigot* talk, liked him more than his pictures, in fact, though he was the best of the Fauves, superior in this genre to Matisse. He too was a man of large build – Balthus's portrait of him is good as a resemblance – and a sot, on which occasions furniture was sometimes smashed. I once mediated for him in a quarrel with Diaghilev, who wanted to change something in *La Boutique fantasque*. In his later years Derain was a solitary figure, no longer visible at concerts or spectacles. My last meeting with him was an extraordinary coincidence. Driving near Toulon one summer day, I stopped to walk in a pine wood and came upon a man standing before an easel who turned out to be Derain.

Robert Delauney was another painter I saw often in the early 1920s. He talked too much and too enthusiastically about 'modern art', but was affable, nevertheless. He painted my portrait, but I have no idea what became of it. It was certainly better than Albert Gleizes's Cubist one, which features my moustache. Delauney never designed a ballet for Diaghilev but was often with him, and in Madrid, in the spring of 1921, we were all three constantly together. In fact, Delauney and I once visited a brothel in Madrid together.

I first knew Pavel Tchelichev in Berlin in 1922, while waiting for my mother's boat from Russia. Tchelichev was talented, handsome and quick to understand the value of these assets in the Diaghilev *ambiance*. But though lively and attractive as a person, he had a difficult and morbidly superstitious character. He wore a mysterious red thread around his wrist and talked codswallop about the Golden Section and the true meaning of Horapollo. I was not attracted by his earliest 'Russian-style' paintings, but his sets for Nicolas Nabokov's ballet *Ode* convinced me of his abilities. I considered him more gifted as a theatrical designer than as a painter, but that is probably because he decorated my own ballets – *Apollo* as well as *Balustrade* – so extremely well. In fact, he made my *Balustrade* one of the most visually satisfying of all my stage works; his 1942 Buenos Aires *Apollo* was the most beautiful as décor of any production anywhere. I was also fond of his costumes for Giraudoux's *Ondine*, and I had a good opportunity to watch him work then, since my niece Ira Belline executed them for him.

R.C. Klee, Kandinsky and Ferruccio Busoni attended the 1923 Weimar performance of *The Soldier's Tale*. Do you remember anything of these artists at that time?

I.S. I was there only very briefly, just long enough for the rehearsals and the performance of *The Soldier*, admirably conducted by Hermann Scherchen, who also conducted the performances staged by Pirandello in Rome two years later. Of the three artists, I only remember meeting Busoni, who shared a loge with me. He had a noble, beautiful head, and I watched him as closely as I watched the production. He seemed to be deeply touched by the work. But whether it was the play by Ramuz, my music, or both, was not easy to determine, especially since I knew that until then I was his *bête noire* in music. Now, thirty-five years later, I have a great admiration for his vision, for his literary talent, and for at least one of his works, *Doktor Faust*. Unfortunately, I have no recollection of meeting Klee there or later in my life, and Klee's portrait of me must have been done from memory. I did not know Kandinsky until later, in Paris in the 1930s.[5]

R.C. How did your connection with Giacometti come about?
I.S. I met him at a party in Paris after I had conducted the French première of *Agon*. He said that he had done five or six portraits of me from photographs, did not like them, and asked if I would sit for an hour. I agreed and we fixed a time for the next day in my stuffy hotel room at the Rond Point des Champs-Elysées. He did a whole series, as you know, working very fast and with only a few minutes of actual drawing for each one. He said that in sculpture he also completes the final product very quickly, but does the sometimes hundreds of discarded preparatory ones slowly and over long periods of time. He drew with a very hard lead pencil, from time to time slightly smudging the lines with erasures and he was forever mumbling: '*Non . . . impossible . . . je ne peux pas . . . une tête violent . . . je n'ai pas de talent . . . je ne peux pas . . .*' He said he had just escaped from an automobile manufacturer, who had been offering him a considerable sum to say that automobiles and sculptures are the same things, meaning beautiful objects. In fact, one of Giacometti's favourite subjects was the difference between a sculpture and an object. 'Sculpture', he said, 'is a *matière* transformed into expression, expression in which nature counts for less than style.' 'Sculpture is expression in space, which means that it can never be complete, since to be complete is to be static . . . All busts are ridiculous; the whole body is the only subject for sculpture . . . Brancusi is not a sculptor but a maker of objects.'
His conversation about sculptors was sometimes surprising.

5 After the performance Stravinsky dined with the Kandinskys and Klee. [R.C.]

He thought Pigalle the greatest sculptor of the *dix-huitième*, especially in the memorial to the Maréchal de Saxe at Strasbourg,[6] and he preferred Pigalle's rejected 'nude Voltaire', 'because of its greater nervousness', to Houdon's famous official portrait. For him, Rodin was 'the last great sculptor and in the same line as Donatello' (not the Rodin of the Balzac or the Burghers, of course). I like Giacometti's work, I have one of those sculptural-space paintings of his on my dining-room wall, and I have a strong affection for him, for his own 'nervousness'. I like his character as revealed in a story he told me. He greatly admired Paul Klee, and one time in the 1930s, when both artists were living in Switzerland, he at last determined to go and call on the painter. He walked from the station to what he assumed was Klee's house, on a mountainside some distance from the town, but on arriving there was told that Klee actually lived farther up the slope. 'I lost all courage and didn't go. I had just enough courage to get that far.'

R.C. And Rodin?

I.S. I made the acquaintance of Auguste Rodin in the Grand Hotel in Rome at the time of finishing *Petrushka* in the nearby Albergo Italia in May 1911. I confess that I was more interested in him because of his fame than because of his art, for I partly agreed with the philistine view that some of his sculptures had been out in the rain too long. I met him again at the scandalous première of Nijinsky in *The Afternoon of a Faun*. He greeted me as if I were an old acquaintance, and at that moment I remembered the impression his fingers had made on me at our first handshaking: soft, squishy, quite contrary to what I had expected; they did not seem to belong to a male hand, especially not to a sculptor's hand. He had a white beard that reached to the navel of his long, buttoned-up *surtout*, and white hair covered his entire face. He sat reading a Ballets Russes programme through a pince-nez while people waited impatiently for the great old artist to stand up to permit them to pass him in his row. It has been said that Rodin drew a sketch of me, but if so it has

6 On this recommendation, the Stravinskys, David Oppenheimer and I drove there from Basel the following week. [R.C.]

not surfaced. Perhaps the author of that information was confusing him with Bonnard, who did in fact make a fine ink portrait of me in 1913, lost, unfortunately, with all of my belong-
ings, in my home in Ustilug. Modigliani also did a portrait, but
I have not seen it. I remember visiting him in company with Léon
Bakst in 1912 or 1913, with this in mind.[7]

R.C. One last artist question. I once heard you describe your
meeting with Claude Monet.
I.S. I do not know where Diaghilev found the old man, or how
he managed to lure him into a loge at one of our Ballets Russes
spectacles, but I saw him there and came to *serrer la main*. It
was after the war, in 1922 or 1923, I think, and of course no one
would believe it *was* Claude Monet. He had a white beard and
was nearly blind. I know now what I wouldn't have believed
then, that he was painting his greatest pictures at the time, those
huge, quasi-abstract canvases of pure colour and light that have
been ignored until recently. I go to the Museum of Modern Art
now primarily to see one of his beautiful *Water Lilies*.[8] Old
Monet, hoary and near blind, could not have impressed me
more if he had been Homer himself.

*

R.C. Do you have any recollections of Gabriele D'Annunzio?
I.S. He attended Ballets Russes performances quite regularly
just before the 1914–18 war, and I saw him frequently. Later,
after the war, he came to concerts of mine in Paris and in Italy.
Diaghilev had known him earlier. I think I met him for the first
time in Paris at Mme Golubev's, a Russian Mme Récamier, who
remained on a divan, elbow raised and head propped on her hand,
throughout one's entire audience. I seem to recall D'Annunzio
entering her salon, a small man, brisk, natty, perfumed and

---

7 Since these remarks were made, the Modigliani has been discovered. It is a
large picture in grey, black and ivory oils, undated but similar in period style
to the Max Jacob and Cocteau portraits. It has been certified by such experts
as Zborovsky, Schoeller and Georges Guillaume, and by a statement from
Picasso: '*Je pense que ce tableau est une portrait de Stravinsky. Cannes, le
18.9.57 (signé) Picasso.*' [R.C.]
8 Since this was first published, the painting has been destroyed by fire.

totally bald – Harold Nicolson's description of his head as an egg is perfect. A brilliant, fast and very amusing talker, he was much taken by my *Nightingale*, and when the French press trashed it after its première, he wrote an article in its defence, an article I would still like to have. I was present at the first *Martyre de Saint Sébastien*, but soon after it he vanished in Italy and his Mussolini period began. Of his novels I remember only the one about Mantua, *Forse sì, Forse non*, but some of his sonnets will survive.

As you know, I was more interested in painters than in writers at this time, but my recollections of the latter are clearer. After the première of *Renard* in 1922, I went to a party given by the Princesse Violette Murat, whom I had known in Switzerland. Most of the guests had come directly from my première at the Grand Opéra, but Marcel Proust arrived from his bed at the Ritz, getting up as usual late in the evening. Elegantly dressed, wearing gloves and carrying a cane, he was as pale as a mid-afternoon moon. I remember that he spoke ecstatically about the late Beethoven quartets, an enthusiasm I would have shared if it had not been a commonplace among the *literati* of the time, not a musical judgement but a pose. James Joyce was there that night, too, but in my ignorance I did not recognize him.

On a lower level, my memory of Mayakovsky during his visit to Paris in 1922 is vivid. A burly youth, twenty-eight or so at the time, he drank more than he should have and was deplorably dirty and unkempt. I admired some of his verses, but he insisted on talking to me about music, of which he understood nothing. Since he did not speak French, I acted as his translator on two or three occasions, becoming a kind of referee between him and Cocteau on one of them. I quickly found the French for everything Mayakovsky said, but not the Russian for Cocteau's remarks. Describing this later, Cocteau wrote that I had been more a barrier than a conduit. Mayakovsky's suicide after his return to Russia was the first of the shocks that were to come regularly from the Soviet Union thereafter.

I must have met Cocteau's prodigy Raymond Radiguet in May 1920, since his description in *Le Bal du Comte d'Orgel* of the party following the première of *Pulcinella* accurately details my outrageous behaviour. I saw him almost daily in Paris in

1922. A silent youth with a serene, childlike look, he also had something of the young bull in him. He was of medium build and very handsome. I seem to remember sitting with Diaghilev in a café when he appeared with Cocteau, and Diaghilev saying, '*Qu'est ce que c'est, ce nouveau truc?*' Seeing that Diaghilev was struck by him, I replied, '*Tu l'envies?*' It should be mentioned that Cocteau deserves credit for perceiving that this boy of twenty was a writer of genius, and for not interfering in his private life. ('*Bébé est vicieux, il aime les femmes.*') I recognized Radiguet's great gifts, and that he had the other intelligence, too, the *machine à penser* kind. His opinions were immediate and they were his, unlike the opinions of most of those around him. I still think his poems very good indeed, and the novels have not faded. They were *romans à clef*, of course, and everyone in Paris recognized the *clés*. I recall that when he died, even the man effigied as the Comte d'Orgel, Etienne de Beaumont, was greatly grieved.

R.C. Finally, what are your recollections of Cocteau?
I.S. I think I was introduced to him at a rehearsal of *Firebird*. But it might have been some time after, in the street. At any rate, I seem to remember someone calling my name in the street – '*C'est vous, IgOR?*' – and turning around to see Cocteau introducing himself to me. Cocteau was one of my first French friends, and in my first years in Paris we were often together. His conversation was always a highly diverting performance, though like a feuilletonist his careerism was too obvious. I soon learned to appreciate his many excellent qualities, and we have remained lifelong friends. In January 1913, just before my first London visit, I moved to the Crillon, where an electric sign in the lobby flashed Channel weather conditions, which Diaghilev watched in a perpetual state of alarm. Cocteau lived near by, and we began to dine together. We used to frequent a café at which stamps were sold, as well as drinks and food, and once when a waiter there said, '*Cognacs, messieurs?*' Cocteau replied, '*Non merci, je préfère les timbres.*' In 1914, Cocteau came to Leysin, Switzerland, with the painter Paul Thévenaz, to try to enlist my collaboration in a ballet he proposed to call *David*. Cocteau's letters to me afterwards were covered with attractive

sketches for the never-to-be-realized ballet. But Cocteau is a master designer whose quick eye and economical line can fix the character of any quarry in a few lines and loops. His best caricatures are as good as any but Picasso's, I think, and whereas Picasso's were sometimes much modified by erasure, Cocteau scrawled his with a photographer's speed. When Cocteau first discussed his costumes and masks for our 1952 *Oedipus Rex*, he ended each verbal description by scribbling the design on a piece of paper, in a few seconds. Each of these drawings – I kept them all – is a testament to his talent.

His true persona, by the way, is generous and disarmingly simple. A first-rate critic, brilliant writer, he is a theatrical and cinematographic innovator of a high order. Think of the angel Heurtebise in *Orphée*. This was the name of a well-known Parisian elevator company, hence the word suggested levitation. But Cocteau also made Heurtebise a glazier who carried wing-shaped slats of glass.

R.C. To what extent did you collaborate with Cocteau on *Oedipus Rex*? What was your purpose in translating the libretto into Latin? What were your first ideas for staging the work, and have they ever been realized? What do you mean by opera-oratorio?

I.S. I date the beginnings of *Oedipus Rex* from September 1925, but I had been aware of a desire to compose a large-scale dramatic work at least five years earlier, after composing chamber music only during the war. Returning from Venice to Nice at that time, I stopped in Genoa to renew my memories of the city in which I had spent my fifth wedding anniversary, in 1911. There, in a bookstall, I saw a life of Francis of Assisi which I bought and, that night, read.[9] To this book I owe the formulation of an idea that had occurred to me ever since I had become *déraciné*. The idea was that a text for music might be endowed with a monumental character by translation – backwards, so to speak – from a secular to a sacred language. 'Sacred' might mean no more than 'older', as one might say that the language of the King James Bible is more sacred than the

9 A French translation of Jorgensen's Danish biography. [R.C.]

language of the New English Bible, if only because of its greater age. But I thought that an older, even an imperfectly remembered, language must have an incantatory element that could be exploited in music. The confirming example from Francis of Assisi was the saint's hieratic use of Provençal, the poetic language of the Renaissance of the Rhône, in contrast to his quotidian Italian, or Brass Age Latin. Prior to that moment of illumination in Genoa, I was unable to resolve the language problem in my future vocal works. Russian, the exiled language of my heart, had become musically impracticable, and French, German and Italian were alien. When I work with words in music, my creative saliva is set in motion by the sounds and rhythms of the syllables. 'In the beginning was the word' is, for me, a literal, localized truth. But the problem was resolved, and the search for *'un pur langage sans office'* ended with my rediscovery of Ciceronian Latin.

The decision to compose a work on Sophocles' play followed quickly upon my return to Nice, but the choice was preordained. I wanted a universal plot or, at least, one so well known that I would not have to elaborate on its exposition. I wished to leave the play behind, thinking by this to distil the dramatic essence and to free myself for a greater degree of focus on a dramatization purely in music. Various Greek myths came to mind as I considered subjects, and then, in automatic succession, I thought of the play that I loved most in my youth. In a final moment of doubt I reconsidered the possibility of using a modern-language version of one of the myths, but only *Phèdre* fulfilled my conception of the statuesque, and which musician could breathe in that metre?

I invited Cocteau to collaborate with me on *Oedipus* because I admired his *Antigone*. I confided my ideas to him and explained that I did not want an action drama, but a 'still life'. I also said that my ideal was a conventional libretto with arias and recitatives, though I knew that the conventional was not his strong suit. He seemed enthusiastic about the project, except for the notion that his phrases were to be recast in Latin, but the first draft of his libretto was precisely what I did not want: a music drama in flamboyant prose.

'Music drama' and 'opera' have long since blurred together,

but they were firm categories in my mind, and I even used to uphold such extenuating notions as that the orchestra has a larger and more exterior interpretative role in 'music drama'. I would now replace these terms by 'verse opera' and 'prose opera', identifying the categories with such pure examples as *The Rake's Progress* for the type of the former and *Erwartung* for the type of the latter. No matter how factitious, divisions of this sort are necessary to me.

Cocteau was patient with my criticisms and rewrote the libretto twice, even submitting it to a final shearing after that. (I am a topiarist by nature, and love clipping things.) What is purely Cocteau's in the libretto? I am no longer able to say, but I should think less the shape of it than the gesticulation of the phrasing. I am not referring to the practice of repeating words, which is habitual with me. The device of the speaker was Cocteau's idea, and the notion that the speaker should wear a *frac* and comport himself like a *conférencier* (which has too often meant like a master of ceremonies). But music goes beyond words, and the music was inspired by the tragedy of Sophocles.

I visualized the staging as soon as I started to compose the music, seeing the chorus first, seated in a single row from end to end of the proscenium and in front of it. I thought the chorus should seem to read from scrolls, and that only these and the outlines of their bearers' cowled heads should be seen. The chorus, I thought, should not have a face.

My second idea was that the actors should wear *cothurni* and stand on pedestals behind the chorus, each character at a different height. But 'actors' is the wrong word. No one 'acts'. Only the narrator moves, and he simply to distance himself from the other stage figures. *Oedipus Rex* may or may not be an opera by virtue of its musical content, but it is not at all operatic in the sense of movement. The characters relate to each other not by gestures, but by words. They do not even turn to listen to each other's speeches, addressing themselves directly to the audience. I thought that they should stand rigidly. My first conception was that the people of the play should be revealed from behind small individual curtains, as in *The Soldier's Tale*, but I soon realized that the same effect might be accomplished more easily by lighting. Like the Commendatore, the singers should be illuminated during their arias, then recede into the shade as they became vocally galvanized statues. Oedipus himself should stand in full view throughout, until his '*Lux facta est*', after which he must change masks. (He could be recountenanced in the dark, or while turning away from the audience.) His self-violence is described, but not enacted: he should not move. Those directors who whisk him offstage and then bring him back realistically staggering have understood nothing of my idea.

I am often asked why I should have tried to compose a waxworks opera. My answer is that I abhor *verismo*, but a complete reply would be more positive and more complex. For one thing, I consider this static representation a more vital way to focus the tragedy not on Oedipus himself and the other individuals, but on the fatal development that, for me, is the meaning of the play. My audience should not be indifferent to the fate of the person, but far more concerned with the person of the fate and the delineation of it which can be expressed uniquely in music. But so far as visualization may give support, the stage figures are dramatically isolated and helpless precisely because they are plastically mute, and the portrait of the individual as the victim of circumstances is made more starkly effective by this static presentation. Crossroads are impersonal, geometrical. And what concerned me was the geometry of tragedy, the inevitable intersecting of lines.

I have been asked why I failed to go further and use puppets, as my friend Robert Edmond Jones once did for an *Oedipus* performance at the Metropolitan Opera. This notion did occur to me, in fact, and I had been impressed by Gordon Craig's puppets when he showed them to me in Rome in 1917. But I am also fond of masks, and while composing Oedipus' first aria, I imagined him wearing a roseate, ogival one, like that of a Chinese sun god.

My staging concepts were not realized because Diaghilev lacked time to mount the work at its première. Its existence was kept secret from him until the last moment, and I was late in finishing the score. But since the first performance was unstaged, most people have mistakenly assumed that I preferred the piece in concert form. *Oedipus Rex* was composed as an eighteenth-anniversary present for the Diaghilev Ballet – '*Un cadeau très macabre*' was his response. He was cool to it at the première, but I think this may have been because of Cocteau. To spite him, Diaghilev deliberately chose a handsome young man as the speaker, knowing that Cocteau had written the part for himself. The singers had scarcely learned the notes before the piano preview performance, which took place at the Princesse de Polignac's a few days before the public one. At this Polignac soirée I accompanied them on the piano. From the reactions of the guests, I could see that *Oedipus* was not likely to succeed with the ballet audience. But my austere vocal concert, following a 'romantic' and colourful ballet, *Firebird*, was a greater failure than I had anticipated. The audience was hardly more than polite, and the Sganarelles of the press were a lot less than that: '*Celui qui a composé Pétrouchka nous présente avec cette pastiche Handelienne . . . Un tas de gens mal habillés ont mal chanté . . . La musique de Créon est une marche Meyerbeerienne*',[10] . . . Performances were rare in the next two decades, but since then *Oedipus* has become almost popular.

I have participated as a conductor in only a few staged performances and have seen only a few other stagings. (Of recent ones, I should mention the Vienna Opera's, where the '*e peste*' sounded as though the singers really did have the plague, and the Washington Opera's, where the white faces of the chorus glistened like the craters in Emmental cheese.) The most pleasing visually was Cocteau's in the Théâtre des Champs-Elysées, in May 1952. His huge masks were very striking, and so was his use of symbolic mime, though it contradicted my idea. I wince when I recall the staged performances at the Kroll Oper, Berlin, though they were well prepared by Klemperer. The speaker wore a black Pierrot costume. I complained to the director that this did not seem relevant to the *Oedipus* story, but his answer permitted no further argument: 'Herr Professor Strawinsky, in our country only the *Kapellmeister* is allowed to wear a *Frack*.' Hindemith and Schoenberg were in the Berlin audience, the former *hingerissen* [spellbound], the latter *abgekühlt* [cool].

In what sense is the music religious? I do not know how to

10 'The composer of *Petrushka* offers us a Handelian pastiche . . . A gaggle of badly costumed people sang badly . . . Creon's music is a march that might have been written by Meyerbeer.' [R.C.]

answer because the word does not correspond in my mind to states of feeling or sentiments, but to dogmatic beliefs. I can testify that the music was composed during my strictest and most earnest period of Christian Orthodoxy. At the beginning of September 1925, with a suppurating abscess in my left fore-finger, I left Nice to perform my *Sonate* in Venice. I had prayed in a little church near Nice, before an old and 'miraculous' icon, but I expected that the concert would have to be cancelled. My finger was still festering when I walked on stage in Venice. I addressed the audience, apologizing in advance for what would inevitably be a poor performance, then sat down at the keyboard, removed the little bandage, felt that the pain had suddenly stopped, and discovered that the finger was – miraculously, it seemed to me – healed. I do, of course, believe in a system beyond Nature.

R.C. Did you choose Jean Daniélou to make the Latin translation?
I.S. Daniélou was a friend of Cocteau. I did not know him, and in fact we never met. He was attached to a monastic order in India then, or so I think, but I may be confusing him with his brother Alain, the orientalist and musicologist, who now lives in Venice. Jean Daniélou eventually became a high-ranking member of the College of Cardinals and an author of books on patristic typology.[11]

I chose Latin rather than Greek because I had no notion of how to treat Greek musically (or Latin, Latinists will say, but there I had *my* idea). I sometimes see in programme notes that the language of my *Oedipus* is 'medieval Latin', a rumour no doubt derived from the fact that the translator was a Catholic cleric. But judging by the sentence structure, the placement of modifiers, and the use of the historical infinitive, the Latin is Ciceronian. I have found only one 'ecclesiastical' word in the whole libretto, and that – the *omniskius pastor* – can be called such only by association. Unusual grammatical constructions can be found – for example, the ablative form *'Laudibus Regina'* –

11 See especially the *Sacramentum Futuri* (Paris, 1950), which contains an absorbing study of Philo and Alexandrian Judaism. His only work in English that I know is an essay on Gregory of Nyssa, my wife Catherine's most beloved saint.

which Daniélou may have borrowed from an old text – but they are rare. Idiomatically, the language is all pre-Boetian. (Say 'Boeeotian', as Harold Nicolson tells us.) But Latinists are already horrified by the first letter of my score, the 'K', which does not exist in the language they know. The purpose of this barbarian orthography was to secure hard, or at least non-Italianized, sounds instead of the usual potpourri of classic and ecclesiastic.

'Stravinsky's scansion of the Latin syllables is sometimes rather unorthodox' is a much quoted criticism but, in fact, my scansion is entirely unorthodox. It breaks every rule, if only because Latin is a language of fixed accents, and I accentuate freely according to my musical dictates. Even the shift from 'OEdipus' (which should be pronounced 'OYdipus' by the singers and 'EEdipus' by the speaker[12]) to 'OeDi'pus' is unthinkable from the point of view of speech, which, of course, is *not* my point of view.

*

R.C. What do you recall of the genesis of your *Apollo*, the circumstances of its commission, the choice of subject, the career of the work in performance? Was it your first idea to imitate Alexandrines melodically – you have referred to *Apollo* as an exercise in musical iambics? Your own recorded performance differs from the printed score on the question of double-dotting.

I.S. *Apollo* was commissioned by Elizabeth Sprague Coolidge for performance in the Library of Congress. Or, more precisely, Mrs Coolidge asked for a work of thirty minutes' duration, a condition that I satisfied with the exactitude of a film composer, and an instrumentation appropriate to a small hall. The choice of subject was my own.

Diaghilev was irate when learned that I had composed a ballet for someone else, and though he acquired it gratis after the Washington première, he never forgave my 'disloyalty', and attributed my motive to money. Financial discussions with Diaghilev were always the same and always unresolvable,

12 The '*pus*' must rhyme with 'moose'; 'Tiresias' must be pronounced 'Tyreesias', and Jocasta in three syllables – 'Io-kas-te'.

but the cachet this time was only $1,000, and what he called stinginess I called economy. To be sure, I was never a spend-thrift, but neither was the promise of numismatic bliss my only inspiration. (Diaghilev always pretended that the '*or*' in Igor meant gold.) But Diaghilev disliked the music so much that he cut the Terpsichore variation when his company was on tour, and would have done so in Paris if I had not conducted all twelve performances there myself.

I tried to discover a melodism free of folklore in *Apollo*. The choice of another classical subject was natural after *Oedipus Rex*, but Apollo and the Muses suggested to me not so much a plot as a signature, or what I have already called a manner. The Muses do not instruct Apollo; as a god he is a master beyond instruction. They exhibit their arts to him for his approval.

The success of *Apollo* as a ballet must be attributed to the dancing of Serge Lifar and to the beauty of Balanchine's choreography, especially to constructions such as the 'troika' in the coda and the 'wheelbarrow' at the beginning, in which two girls support a third carrying Apollo's lute.

*

The Fairy's Kiss probably began as far back as the 1890s, during my first visit to Switzerland, which I remember because of the English tourists who came to look at the Jungfrau through public telescopes. In 1928 Ida Rubinstein commissioned me to compose a full-length ballet. The year was the thirty-fifth anniversary of Tchaikovsky's death – the actual day was observed in Paris's Russian churches – therefore I conceived my compatriotic homage as an anniversary piece. I chose Andersen's *The Snow Maiden* because it suggested an allegory with Tchaikovsky himself. The fairy's kiss on the heel of the child is also the muse marking Tchaikovsky at his birth – though the muse did not claim Tchaikovsky at his wedding, as she did the young man in the ballet, but at the height of his powers. *The Kiss* was composed in Talloires, between April and September 1928. My precept in selecting the music was that none of the pieces had been orchestrated by Tchaikovsky. My selection would have to come from piano music and songs. I was already familiar with most of the music I used, but the other pieces were happy discoveries. At this date I do not remember which music is Tchaikovsky's and which mine.

The Fairy's Kiss was responsible for the final breakdown of my friendship with Diaghilev. He would not forgive me for having accepted Ida Rubinstein's commission, and he was loud, both privately and in print, in denunciations of the ballet and of me.[13] But Diaghilev was vexed with me about another matter as well. He had wanted me to acclaim the genius of his newest prodigy, Igor Markevitch, but I could not oblige for the reason that the prodigy did not have any. In consequence, communications between us were severed, and our last meeting was so strange that I sometimes think it did not happen to me, that I must have read about it in a novel. One day in May 1929 I entered the Gare du Nord *en route* to London, where I had taken an apartment in Albemarle Street. On the train I saw Diaghilev, his new prodigy, and Boris Kochno. Seeing that he could not avoid me, Diaghilev spoke to me with embarrassed kindness, and we went separately to our compartments on the train. He did not leave his, and I never saw him again.

Diaghilev was diabetic, but he refused insulin injections and preferred to risk the consequences of the disease. I do not know the exact medical explanation of his death, but the event was a terrible shock to me, the more so because of the break over *The Fairy's Kiss*, and because we were not reconciled when he died.

I have recently uncovered a packet of letters and other documents addressed to me at the time of his death. One of these was a German newspaper describing Diaghilev as '*ein berühmter Tanzer*' ['a famous dancer']. One of the letters is from Manuel de Falla:

Antequeruela Alta 11
Granada
22nd August 1929

Bien cher Igor,

    I am profoundly moved by the death of Diaghilev and it is my wish to write to you before I speak to anyone else. What a terrible loss for you. Of all the admirable things he did, the first was his revelation of you. We owe him that above all. And without you, besides, the Ballets Russes couldn't have existed . . . However, it is a consolation that our

---

13 '*Notre Igor aime seulement l'argent.*' Mme Ida Rubinstein had paid me $7,500 for *The Kiss*, in fact, and she would pay me the same sum later for *Perséphone*.

poor friend died without surviving his work. I always remember his fears during the war that someone might come and take his place. Later we understood how useless were such fears, for, of course, no one could ever take his place. And now I beg one favour of you: please give my most passionate condolences to the head of the Diaghilev Ballet, whoever that is now. I ask you to do this because I do not know anyone there now who could receive them.

I embrace you with all my old and true affection,

MANUEL DE FALLA

During the *Petrushka* period, at Cipa Godebski's [Paris], I was introduced to a man of my own height, very shy, modest, and withdrawn. He was Manuel de Falla. I liked him immediately and increasingly as I came to know him. He had an unpityingly religious nature and a concomitant insensibility to all manifestations of humour. During a party in his honour following a performance of his puppet opera *El Retablo de Maese Pedro* at the home of the Princesse de Polignac, it was suddenly noticed that Falla and I were sitting alone in a corner engrossed in conversation, not, as one would expect, about the music, but about the merits of our respective neckties.[14]

I was always surprised that a man of such reclusive habits could bring himself to appear on a stage. But he conducted and even played the harpsichord in his Concerto – a piece I admire and have conducted myself. In fact, the last time I saw him was at a performance of this Concerto in London in the 1930s.

Falla was always very attentive to me and my work. After the première of his *Tricorne*, I told him that the best music in the score was not necessarily the most 'Spanish', and I knew that my remark impressed him. He did develop, I should add, though his material was limited. I thought of him as the most devoted of my musical friends. Whereas, for instance, Ravel turned his back on me after *Mavra* – indeed, the only later works of mine he ever noticed at all were *Oedipus* and the *Symphony of Psalms* – Falla followed me in all my later music. His ear was very fine and his appreciation genuine.

*

14 This corrects the original published text, but the story about the cravat contest was in Stravinsky's repertory, and it comes from other sources as well, most importantly Vera Sudeykina. [R.C.]

My first religious works, the 1926 *Pater Noster*, the *Credo* (1932), the *Ave Maria* (1934), and the unfinished prayer, *And The Cherubim* (1934), were inspired out of antipathy to the bad music and worse singing in the Russian Church at Nice, where I became a communicant in 1925, the year before composing the *Pater Noster*. I knew very little about Russian Church music at that time, or now, but I had hoped to find deeper roots than those of the Russian Church composers who had merely tried to continue the Venetian style from Bortniansky by way of Galuppi. Whether my choruses recapture anything of an older Russian tradition I cannot say; but perhaps some early memories of church singing survive in the simple harmonic style that was my aim. *All* traditions of Russian Church singing are in decay now, in any case, for which reason I rewrote the *Credo* in June 1964, spelling out the *faux bourdon*.

As I said earlier, at fourteen or fifteen I began to criticize and rebel against the Church, and before leaving the gymnasium I had abandoned it completely, a rupture that was left unrepaired for almost three decades. I cannot evaluate the events that, at the end of thirty years, made me discover the necessity of religious belief. Though I admire the structured thought of theology, Anselm's ontological proof of the existence of God in the *Proslogion*, chapter 2,[15] is to religion what counterpoint exercises are to music. I can say that some years before my actual 'conversion', a mood of acceptance had been bred in me by a reading of the Gospels. When I moved from Biarritz to Nice, a certain Father Nicolas of the Russian Church came into my life, and even into my home; he was a member of our household for five years. But intellectual and priestly influences were not of primary importance to me. Incidentally, Diaghilev's last letter to me should be read with my new-found religion in mind. Before taking Communion I had written to tell him of my intention to re-enter the Church.

The *Credo* and *Pater Noster* are liturgical pieces, whereas the *Ave Maria*, though sung in several services, is a concert piece. I composed it on a Wednesday in Lent (4 April 1934), but do not

15 Stravinsky is actually referring to K. Barth's *Fides quarens intellectum, Anselm's Beneis der Existenz Götter* (Munich, 1931). [R.C.]

recall the first time I heard it. I do remember the *Pater Noster* sung by the Afonsky Choir at the Requiem for my sister-in-law, Lyudmila Beliankina, in the spring of 1937, forty days after her death, according to Russian custom.

This ceremony took place in the Alexander Nevsky Church in the rue Daru, which played an important role in my life in the 1930s. Built in the period and style of Alexander II, it was an island of Russian colour in its drab Parisian neighbourhood, and not one island only, but a whole archipelago of Russian shops, bookstores, restaurants, cafés, *bijouteries*, *antiquaires*. On feast days the neighbourhood would resemble an oriental fairground, both in décor and in mayhem. I can remember gathering birch twigs in a forest near Paris to help deck the church at the Feast of the Trinity. I also remember the wedding there between the American heiress, Barbara Hutton, and the disinherited Russian Prince Mdivani, for which the sidewalks were strewn with flowers.

In the Paris of the 1920s, this church, with the cafés and restaurants near by, was a focus of Russian life, for believers and non-believers alike. Then in the mid-1930s came the Rome *versus* Constantinople split. Some of the congregation decided to recognize the Soviet Metropolitan in Moscow over his opposite number in Paris. I remained loyal to the Nevsky Church myself, which became the centre of the anti-Soviet church-in-exile. Dissenting churches, some of them portable and pocket-sized, sprouted up all over Paris, housed in apartments and studios. I remember one, in the rue d'Odessa, that was located over a night-club, owing to which money had to be raised to buy a half-hour of quiet during the Saturday-night Easter service. Then at midnight, immediately after the proclamation '*Christos Voskreseh*', business resumed below with a bam, a boom, and a crash.

R.C. Do you recall what determined your choice of texts in the *Symphony of Psalms*? What were the circumstances of the commission?

I.S. The commissioning began with the publisher's routine suggestion that I write something popular. I took the word, not in the publisher's meaning of 'adapting to the understanding of the people', but in the sense of 'something universally admired', and I even chose Psalm 150 in part for its popularity, though another and equally compelling reason was my eagerness to counter the many composers who had abused these magisterial verses as pegs for their own lyrico-sentimental 'feelings'. The Psalms are poems of exaltation, but also of anger, judgement, and even curses. Although I regarded Psalm 150 as a song to be danced, as David danced before the Ark, I knew that I would have to treat it in an imperative way. My publisher had requested an orchestral piece without chorus, but I had had the psalm symphony idea in mind for some time, and that is what I insisted on composing. The music was written in Nice and in my summer home at Echarvines. I began with Psalm 150; my first notation was the figure that bears such a close resemblance to Iocasta's 'Oracula, oracula'.

*

R.C. Would you say something about your Violin Concerto, the background, the genre, the later career of the piece as a ballet? I.S. The Concerto was commissioned for Samuel Dushkin by his patron, the American Blair Fairchild, who had discovered Dushkin and his talent for the violin at an early age, and had sponsored his education and career thereafter. The Schott publisher, Willy Strecker, a longtime friend of Dushkin, persuaded me to accept the commission. The first two movements and part of the third were composed in Nice, but the score was completed at La Vironnière, a château near Voreppe which I rented from a country lawyer who looked like Flaubert. I was very fond of this house, and especially of my attic workroom, which had a view of the Val d'Isère, but the inconveniences of country life and the need to drive to Grenoble for provisions were too much for us and we eventually moved to Paris.

Balustrade (1941), the ballet that George Balanchine and Pavel Tchelichev made of the Violin Concerto, was one of the most satisfactory visualizations of any of my works. Balanchine composed the choreography as he listened to my recording, and I could observe him conceiving gesture, movement, combination, composition. The result was a series of dialogues co-ordinated with the dialogues of the music. The corps de ballet was small, and the second Aria was a solo piece for Tamara Toumanova.

The ballet was produced by Sol Hurok, that *savant* of the box office, in which sense it may have been his first misjudgement. The set exposed a white balustrade on a dark stage, and the costumes were sinuous patterns in black and white.

*

R.C. What do you recall of your association with Hindemith?
I.S. I met him for the first time in Amsterdam in 1924, at a concert by the Amar Quartet, of which he was the violist. I remember him as short, stocky, and even at that time almost bald. He was already widely discussed as a composer, but I had not heard any of his music, and I am no longer certain which of his pieces I heard first, though I think it might have been the attractive unaccompanied Viola Sonata, opus 11, played by himself. I encountered him often in the late 1920s – I think I also met him in Brussels in 1924, when he was still the violist of the Amar Quartet – but I knew him well only after 1930, when we were both published by Schott's Willy Strecker. Strecker was extremely effective in promoting Hindemith's music, and he persuaded me to publish a favourable opinion about Hindemith's *Das Unaufhörliche*, a work I only thought very appropriately named, just as, years later, Strecker induced me to sign a squib recommending Henze's *Boulevard Solitude*, which I liked.

In Berlin, one day in 1931, I was invited to the Hindemiths' for lunch. When I arrived, the housekeeper said that the composer and his wife had not yet returned from their exercises. Just then they came running up the stairs, both in white linen shorts and both breathless. They had been trotting in the Grünewald with their athletic instructor and, judging from their panting, they must have run all the way home. I think of this incident every time I hear one of those setting-up-exercise concertos by Hindemith.

Hindemith and I travelled the same concert circuit in the 1930s, and our paths often crossed. We were neighbours for a time in Positano in the summer of 1937, and I recall with pleasure an excursion to Paestum taken together. I was composing my Concerto in E♭ at the time and he his ballet *St Francis*, which I heard later that year in Paris. Our friendship continued to develop in the United States during World War II, but after it we saw each other only rarely. I heard him play the viola d'amore in Bach's *St John Passion* in New York in April 1948, saw him in Munich in 1957 at the time of his opera *Harmonie der Welt*, and in Santa Fe in 1961, where he conducted his *Neues vom Tage*, while his wife protected him from the tourists.

Knowing next to nothing of Hindemith's music, I am hardly entitled to an opinion of it. I have seen none of his operas and heard only a few pieces of his concert music. I did not like *Das Marienleben*, but enjoyed *The Four Temperaments* in Balanchine's choreography, also his other ballet, *Hérodiade*. The *Schwanendreher* seemed pleasant when I heard him play it in 1935 or 1936. As for *Ludus Tonalis*, which he sent to me, I found it interesting to look at but arid and indigestible as cardboard and as little nourishing. But Hindemith was a loyal friend, always very elegant in behaviour, and with a delightful fund of humour. I shall never forget how he bravely excoriated the Berlin Radio Orchestra for its sloppy performance of my Violin Concerto in October 1931.

I remember playing a quarter-tone piano four-hands with him in the Berlin Hochschule in the 1920s, and how quickly our ears became accustomed to it. But a quarter-tone is a considerable differentiation, after all. Later, in 1930, I met Alois Hába at a concert that I conducted in Prague.[16] He struck me as a serious musician, and I listened to his talk and to his music – well, anyway, to his talk – with interest. Since then I have thought about quarter-tones but avoided writing them. After all, we hear unintentional quarter-tones all the time. The beautiful exception, the perfect exploitation of the quarter-tone is in Alban Berg's *Kammerkonzert*, where it is perfectly prepared by a phrase in whole tones, a diatonic phrase, and a phrase in chromatics: here the distinctions are clear, convincing and effective. But wasn't Ives interested in quarter-tone tuning long before any other composer, and didn't he write quarter-tone music before his European contemporaries?

I met Berg, with Webern, at a reception for me in Vienna after I had played my Piano Concerto there in 1926. The two of them

16 This concert occasioned one of the most enthusiastic receptions I have ever received. Throughout my stay in Prague, I was very kindly treated by M. Beneš and by President Masaryk, the latter a tall, Slav intellectual–*littérateur*. He could speak Russian with the assistance of his daughter, who was always there to help translate.

must have been mystified by my motoric music, particularly Berg, who only a year before had changed music history with *Wozzeck*. I saw him next in Venice, in September 1934, at a rehearsal in La Fenice, where I conducted my *Capriccio* in a Biennale concert shared half and half with him. Hermann Scherchen conducted his *Der Wein*. After hearing the *Capriccio*, Berg told me that he wished he could write 'such happy music', but when he came to me in the artists' room after the concert his manner was slightly cool. In Hollywood years later I learned from the woman who had sung his piece that he felt I had taken too much rehearsal time and left too little for him.

R.C. Did you know Bartók personally?
I.S. I remember meeting him once in Paris and once in London, both in the 1920s. Fritz Reiner could have brought us together in New York but never did, though one of his letters conveys kind words from him about my *Song of the Nightingale* after Reiner had conducted it at a Philharmonic concert. I respected Bartók's devotion to folklore, but could not share his lifelong gusto for it. His premature death, in circumstances of desperate need in the centre of wealthy New York, has always struck me as one of the least excusable tragedies of the affluent society.

R.C. Finally, what are your memories of George Gershwin?
I.S. I met him in New York in January 1925 at the Fifth Avenue home of Arthur Sachs, after my first concert with the New York Philharmonic. Since he knew a few words of Russian, but no French, we had to talk through someone. I remember him as a tall man, very nervously energetic. At that time I hardly knew who he was, and I was totally unacquainted with his music. I saw him again in Paris, when our mutual friend Paul Kochanski, the violinist, brought him to my apartment, and again in Hollywood shortly before his death, at a dinner given for me by Edward G. Robinson, with Chaplin, Paulette Goddard, Marlene Dietrich. Gershwin was very *à la page* then, but he had not been spoiled.

*

R.C. Your autobiography does not reveal the circumstances of your collaboration with André Gide. To what extent was *Perséphone* actually a collaboration? And, Gide having been one of your earliest acquaintances in Paris, would you describe him when you first met him?

I.S. Gide is a complicated subject in every respect, and as a social being, unforthcoming. If I were to hear someone else describe him, I think I could comment on the accuracy of the description, but for me to talk about him is difficult.

I think we met in Misia Sert's rooms at the Hotel Meurice, which would have been in 1911 or 1912. After that I saw him from time to time at ballet rehearsals, but whether he came to those of *The Rite of Spring* I do not know. In the summer of 1917 he visited me in Switzerland to discuss a project to provide incidental music for a staging by Ida Rubinstein of his translation of *Antony and Cleopatra*. I said that the musical style would depend on the style of the whole production, but he had no stylistic concept as yet. Later, he was shocked by my suggestion that the production be in modern dress, and deaf to my arguments that we would be nearer to Shakespeare by inventing something new. A verismo *Antony and Cleopatra* was out of the question, I made clear. I believe that the music in Shakespeare's plays should be Shakespearean period music. But modern music could be justified in modern-dress versions. My sketches for the proposed *Antony* were re-routed into the *Soldier* music.

Perséphone was a collaboration only in the children's choruses. I wished to repeat the music here and prevailed upon Gide to compose additional verses. I did not know his early *Perséphone* poem. Madame Ida Rubinstein had asked me to read it and to meet Gide to discuss the possibility of a collaboration based upon it. A dance-mime role would have to be created for her, but we both understood that this was the point of the commission. Ida Rubinstein was a beautiful woman, and an accomplished actress. She was also enormously wealthy. At age eighteen she had hired a private train to take her from St Petersburg to Moscow, and in Paris had commissioned Bakst to arrange the flowerbeds of her garden so that all the flowers were in trays and the layout could be changed every few weeks.

In January 1933 Gide came to see me in Wiesbaden, where we read his original *Perséphone* together, and decided on the device of the speaker and on the three-part form. He reconstructed and rewrote the original book in the weeks after this meeting.

There are at least two explanations for Gide disliking my *Perséphone* music. The principal one is that the accentuation of the music was a jolting surprise for him, though I had warned him that I would stretch, stress and otherwise 'treat' French as I had Russian, and though he understood that my ideal texts were syllable poems, haiku, in which the words do not impose strong tonic accentuation of their own. The other explanation is simply that he could not follow my musical language. When I first played the music to him at Mme Rubinstein's, he said only, '*C'est curieux, c'est très curieux*', and disappeared soon afterwards. He did not attend the rehearsals, and if he was present at any of the performances, *I* did not see him. A play of his was then being staged in the Petit Théâtre des Champs-Elysées, but this shouldn't have prevented him from hearing at least one of the three performances of *Perséphone*. Shortly after the première he sent a copy of the newly published libretto with the dedication 'in communion'. I answered that 'communion' was exactly what we did not have. We never met again after *Perséphone*, but I do not think we were really angry with each other. Indeed, how could anyone be angry for long with a man of so much probity?

If I could distinguish between Gide's talent and his writing, it would be to proclaim a preference for the latter, though the writing, too, is very often like *eau distillée*. I thought *Voyage au Congo* the best of his books, but did not care for either the spirit or the approach in his fiction. He was not grand enough as a creator to make us forget the sins of his nature, as Tolstoy makes us forget the sins of *his* nature.

Gide was not a conspicuously loving critic, but he was at least inside the art he criticized. And his criticism could and did illuminate. His limitation, I thought, was his 'reason': all he did or said had to be reasoned, with the result that he lacked enthusiasm and could find no sympathy for the bottomless unreasonableness in man and art. 'It is better to reason', he would say, 'than to make an enthusiastic mistake.' I am not convinced of that. He had wit, as is evident from his reply when asked to name the greatest French poet: '*Hélas*, Victor Hugo', and verbal precision such as his is always enviable. But he was at his best in company, with Valéry, or Claudel, Martin du Gard, or Ramuz, for then the conversation would always revert to the

French language, and on this subject he was on his strongest ground.

Fascinated by Pushkin, Gide would sometimes call on me in my Paris apartment to talk to me about the poet, and indeed about everything Russian. He also called on me in Berlin in October 1931. Apart from Pushkin and Russia, his favourite conversational subject was religion. I had returned to the Orthodox Church in 1925 and was not a likely quarry for proselytizing Protestantism, but I have more respect for him and his views than for some of the Catholic Pharisees who ridiculed him.

I do not know how to describe him in appearance. He was quite undistinguished and must have wished to become even more so by deliberately dressing like a *petit bourgeois*. The one physical characteristic of his I can remember is that when he spoke only his lips and mouth moved: his body and the rest of his face remained perfectly immobile and expressionless. He also wore a little smile which I thought ironic but which may not have been. If I had not known so much *about* Gide, wouldn't I have been more open with him myself?

R.C. What do you recall of the original staging of *Perséphone*, and what are your present ideas for staged presentations of the work?
I.S. The unstaged preview performance at the Polignacs' is clearer in my recollection than the actual première, which I conducted. I can still see the Princess's salon, myself groaning at the piano, Souvtchinsky, loud and abrasive, singing Eumolpus, Claudel glaring at me from the other side of the keyboard, Gide bridling more noticeably with each phrase.

The actual performance was visually unsatisfactory, which must be why my memory is so discreet about it, but my failure to remember the staging surprises me because the music was composed and timed to a tightly fixed plan of stage action. The form is so specifically theatrical that two episodes make little sense in concert performances: Pluto's mute march-aria for oboe and basses, and the sarabande interlude that precedes the appearance of Mercury.

Described in the score as a melodrama, which C. S. Lewis defines as 'the tragic in exile', *Perséphone* is, in fact, a masque or dance-pantomime co-ordinated with a sung and spoken text.

Mme Rubinstein declaimed the text at the première, but did not dance, which was as it should be. The mime should not speak, the speaker should not mime, and the part should be shared by two performers. I say this because few mimes, and even fewer dancers, are trained speakers as well, and because the division of labour allows greater freedom for movement. This is important for the reason that Perséphone's longest soliloquies are musically motionless, but also because in retrospect I think it is stylistically wrong to grant powers of speech to only one figure.

Perséphone should stand at a point antipodal to Eumolpus, and an illusion of motion should be established between them. The chorus should stand apart from and remain outside the action. The resulting separation of text and movement would mean that the staging could be worked out entirely in choreographic terms. Balanchine would have been the ideal choreographer, Tchelichev the ideal decorator. At the première, Eumolpus stood deep downstage on a tall pedestal, just out of sight of my beat and just out of hearing. The chorus did not move, not in accordance with any aesthetic precept, but because their labour union wouldn't let them. In the original production Pluto and Mercury did not appear, though they should have, and Tryptolemus and Demeter as well, if only because their embodiments would help to dramatize the static narrative. Both by costume and stage position Demeter must be related to Eumolpus, who is her priest. But narcissi and pomegranates are better kept in the cupboard of comic props now associated with the Gide–Wilde age.

Whether *Perséphone* is the dramatically flaccid patchwork and the bonbon that its critics claim is not for me to say, nor will time tell more than a circumstantial truth. So far no one has cited the section that I grafted whole from a 1932 sketchbook (the G minor flute and harp music in Eumolpus' second aria in Part II) as stylistically discordant.

The music in 3/8 metre near the end of *Perséphone* is too long, and the melodramas beget long stretches of *ostinato*. But I still love the music, especially Eumolpus' aria with trumpet obbligato, the flutes in Perséphone's final speech (this needs a dancer), and the final chorus (when it is played and sung in tempo, quietly, without a general *crescendo*). I love the chord before the C minor Russian Easter music, and I love the lullaby,

'*Sur ce lit elle repose*'. I composed this *berceuse* during a separation from Vera Sudeykina, who was suffering from a heat wave in Paris, and I wrote it originally to my own Russian words.

*

R.C. Your long friendship and admiration for Paul Valéry are well known. How do you remember him?

I.S. I think I met him for the first time in 1921 or 1922 at a reception by the Princesse de Polignac. He was small – about my own height, in fact – quick, quiet (he spoke in very rapid, *sotto voce* mumbles), and gentle. His monocle and *boutonnière* made him seem a dandy, but that impression dissolved as soon as he began to talk. Everything he said was instinct with wit and intelligence.

Valéry was a deep source of intellectual and moral support to me on two important occasions. One of these concerned my Harvard lectures, *The Poetics of Music*. I had asked him to read and criticize the manuscript, but ended up reading it to him at Nadia Boulanger's country house at Gargenville, in September 1939. He suggested various changes in phrasing and word order, but endorsed the argument of the lectures without reservation.

My other 'professional' call on him came at the time of the first performance of *Perséphone*. From my conversations with him, I felt he had understood my views on that tiresome subject of 'music and words'. Not that these views were difficult, or obscure, or original; Beethoven had already expressed them in a letter to his publisher: 'Music and words are one and the same thing.' Combined with music, words lose rhythmic and sonorous relationships that obtain when they were words only; or, rather, they exchange these relationships for new ones, a new 'music'. They mean the same things, no doubt, but they become magical as well as meaningful. I do not say that a composer may not try to preserve or imitate effects of purely verbal relationships in music. I have done that myself, in instances where the verse form is strict or where the verse metre has suggested a musical construction (in the sonnet *Musick to Heare*). But this approach implies something of what is meant by the phrase 'setting words to music', a limited, pejorative description that is certainly as far from Beethoven's meaning as it is from mine.

Gide understood little or nothing of all this, or, if he

understood, demurred. (That Gide understood nothing about music in general is apparent to anyone who has read his *Notes on Chopin*.) He had expected the *Perséphone* text to be sung with exactly the same stresses that he would use reciting it. He believed my musical purpose should be to imitate or underline the verbal pattern: I would simply have to find pitches for the syllables, since he considered that he had already composed the rhythm. The history of *poesia per musica* meant nothing to him. And, not understanding that a poet and musician collaborate to produce *one* music, he was only horrified by the discrepancies between my music and his.

When *Perséphone* was premièred at the end of April 1934, Valéry continued to support me, attending all of the performances, a fact I much appreciated, especially since his *Semiramis*, first produced only a week after *Perséphone*, must have taken a good deal of his time. Shortly before my première, I composed a manifesto[17] of my views on the relations of text and music and on the musical syllabification of a text. As published in the Paris *Excelsior*, I concluded with the words: '. . . a nose is not manufactured: a nose just *is*, thus, too, my art.' After the première I received the following letter from Valéry:

The French Academy
2nd May 1934

My dear Stravinsky, I could not get to you Monday evening to tell you of the extraordinary impression the *Perséphone* music made on me. I am only a 'profane listener', but the divine *detachment* of your work touched me. It seems to me that what I have sometimes searched for in the ways of poetry, you pursue and join in your art. The point is to attain purity through will. You expressed it marvellously well in the article yesterday, which I immensely enjoyed. LONG LIVE YOUR NOSE.

Valéry may not have been one of the great innovators of his age. The processes of creation absorbed him too much, and he worshipped intellect to the point of valuing himself more as an intelligence than as a poet. *Monsieur Teste* stopped at *epistamenos*, with 'knowing how'. His brilliant writings about poetry may have kept him from writing more of it.

I have never *seen* a Valéry play, and am therefore inclined to

17 With C.-A. Cingria. [R.C.]

regard them as dialogues to be read. (The didactic dialogue on mind in *The Only One* is certainly 'to be read'.) Reading the plays now [1968], I hear all of the characters speaking in Valéry's voice. I read, and heard, *Mon Faust* this way in the last spring of the war, not knowing that I would never again hear his living voice. I grieved for him. I felt his loss as a personal one.

*

R.C. More surprising to most readers is your enthusiasm for Louis-Ferdinand Céline.

I.S. I enjoyed and was stimulated by *Journey to the End of the Night* and *Death on the Instalment Plan*. Céline sent his books to me, and we corresponded. He proposed a theatre collaboration, which came to nothing. After the disgrace in which he became involved during and after the war, I quite naturally do not mention him now. But he was a gifted, original writer.

*

R.C. Returning to your own compositions, please say a few words about your Concerto for Two Pianos.

I.S. I began the composition in Voreppe immediately after finishing the Violin Concerto in 1931, but stopped composing because I could not hear the second piano. All my life I have tried out my music as I have composed it, orchestral as well as any other kind, four hands at one keyboard. That way I am able to test it, as I cannot when the other player is seated at another piano. When I took up the Concerto again, after finishing the Duo Concertant and *Perséphone,* I asked the Pleyel company to build a double piano for me, in the form of a small box of two tightly wedged triangles. I then completed the Concerto in my Pleyel studio, test-hearing it bar by bar with my son Soulima at the other keyboard.

The Concerto is symphonic in both volumes and proportions, and I think I could have composed it as an orchestral work, especially the variation movement. But my purpose was otherwise. I needed a solo work for myself and my son, and I wished both to incorporate the orchestra and to do away with it. The Concerto was intended as a vehicle for concert tours in cities without orchestras.

The variations – originally the second movement – were separated from the *Con moto* movement by three years and much change of musical focus. I started composing them as soon as *Perséphone* was finished, but was interrupted again, this time by an appendectomy. My son Theodore had had a burst appendix, and an emergency removal. Since the operation fascinated me, I decided to have my own appendix removed, however unlikely the danger of peritonitis in my case. I forced the operation on my other children, on Vera Sudeykina, and some of my friends – or, rather, to put myself in a better light, I recommended it highly. This surgical spree took place shortly after the première of *Perséphone* and just before I became a French citizen on 10 June 1934. I was still wobbly when I went to London at the end of that month to record *The Wedding*.

I had steeped myself in the variations of Beethoven and Brahms while composing the Concerto, and in Beethoven's fugues. I am very fond of my fugue, and especially of the after-fugue or fugue-consequent. But, then, the Concerto is my 'favourite' among my purely instrumental pieces. The second movement, the *Notturno*, is not so much night music as after-dinner music, in fact a *digestif* for the larger movements.

The first performance of the Concerto was sponsored by L'Université des Annales, a literary lecture society. I introduced the music with a fifteen-minute talk (which I would not like to see reprinted), and I read this little discourse before many of my later performances of the work as well. The concert, in the Salle Gaveau, was a matinée, which we repeated that same evening for a different audience. I performed the Concerto many times with my son in Europe and in South America (Buenos Aires, Rosario, Montevideo), sometimes preceding it with Mozart's C minor Fugue for two pianos. After playing my double concerto in Baden-Baden in 1936, we made a commercial recording (French Columbia).

*

R.C. You travelled in the Axis countries – Germany, Italy – during the 1930s.
I.S. Yes, I am ashamed to admit. One day in Munich, at the end of January 1933, only days before Hitler came to power, I saw

a squad of Brownshirts enter the street below the balcony of my room in the Bayerische Hof and assault a group of civilians, who tried to protect themselves behind sidewalk benches, but were soon crushed beneath these clumsy shields. The police arrived, eventually, but by then the attackers had dispersed. That same night I dined with Vera Sudeykina and the photographer Erik Schaal in a small Allee restaurant. Three men wearing swastika armbands entered the room, and one of them began to talk insultingly about Jews, and to aim his remarks in my direction. With the afternoon street fight still in our eyes, we hurried to leave, but the now shouting Nazi and his myrmidons followed, cursing and threatening us. Schaal protested, and at that they began to kick and hit him. Vera Sudeykina fled the restaurant and ran for help. She found a policeman and told him that a man was being killed, but this failed to stir him to any action. A timely taxi rescued us, and though Schaal was battered and bloody, we went directly to a police court, where the magistrate was as little perturbed with our story as the policeman had been. 'In Germany today, such things happen every minute,' he said.

R.C. Why did you go to Germany in 1936?
I.S. Willy Strecker, who had commissioned the Double Concerto, implored me to do it, saying that no publicity would be attached, that I would not be associated with a German orchestra, and that Baden-Baden was a small provincial town full of foreign tourists. Furthermore, I would be there for only a few hours. I know now that I shouldn't have gone, and also not have recorded in Berlin in February 1938, except that Telefunken was the only company recording at the time, that no one except the orchestra knew I was in the studio, and I wanted to record *The Card Game*.

The fortunes of my music in the Third Reich are unaccountable. It was banned entirely at first, then defended for the wrong reasons, by, of all people, Richard Strauss.[18] In May 1938, I was the chief butt, with Schoenberg, Berg, Hindemith and Weill, of the scurrilous *Entartete Musik* ('Degenerate Music') exhibition

18 See the *Fränkischer Kurier*, 28 November 1934.

in Düsseldorf. Several rooms there were devoted to a display of 'decadent', 'Jewish', 'cultural Bolshevist' music, the visitor being confronted with viciously defamatory photographs and documents, while his and her ears were entertained with a recording of *Pierrot Lunaire,* described on a poster as '*Hexensabbat*' music. A reproduction of one of Jacques-Émile Blanche's portraits of me adorned one of the walls, with an accompanying placard saying, 'Judge from this whether or not Stravinsky is a Jew.' When photographs of the exhibition and clippings from German newspapers reached me in Paris, I protested through the French Ambassador in Berlin, M. François-Poncet, but of course nothing came of it. Some of my music was performed in Germany up to 1939, when Schmidt-Isserstedt recorded my *Dumbarton Oaks* Concerto. Then with the war it fell under a total ban, except in German Occupied countries. (Charles Munch conducted a performance of *The Rite of Spring* at the Paris Conservatoire in 1942.) But then, Berg's *Wozzeck,* the most anti-Nazi music drama imaginable, was presented in Rome during the war.

*

R.C. Do you recall the circumstances in which you performed Debussy's *Nuages* and *Fêtes* in Rome?

I.S. That was on 23 February 1933. The host organization asked me to play 'something French', which, of course, could only mean Debussy. What I remember most clearly about the visit was that Mussolini sent for me and that I had to go to him. I was taken to his office in the Palazzo Venezia, a long hall with a single large desk flanked by ugly modern lamps. A square-built, bald man stood in attendance. As I approached, Mussolini looked up and said, 'Bonjour, Stravinsky, aswye-ez vous [*asseyez-vous*]' – the words of his French were correct, but the accent was Italian. He was wearing a dark business suit. We chatted briefly about music, and he said that he played the violin. He was quiet and sober, but not very polite. His last remark was: 'You will come and see me the next time you are in Rome, *and I will receive you.*' Afterwards I remembered that he had cruel eyes. In fact, I avoided Rome again for that very reason – until 1936. In that year I was rehearsing at the Santa Cecilia when Count

Ciano appeared and invited me to visit his father-in-law. I remember talking to Ciano about an exhibition of Italian masterpieces then in Paris, and expressing concern for their safety during travels abroad. Ciano grunted at this and said, 'Oh, we have kilometres of such things.' Mussolini was surrounded by absurd grandeur this time. He was in uniform, and a path of military personages came and went the whole time. He was gayer and bouncier than on my first visit, and his gestures were even more ridiculously theatrical. He had read, and mumbled something about, my autobiography. He promised to come to my concert, too, but mercifully did not.

*

R.C. What was your first idea for *The Card Game*?
I.S. More than a decade before composing it, I thought of a ballet with playing-card costumes and a green-baize gaming-table backdrop. I have always enjoyed card games, and from time to time have been interested in cartomancy. I have been a card player ever since I learned *durachki* as a child. Poker was a favourite pastime during the composition of *The Card Game*, as was Chinese checkers during the composition of the *Rake*.

The origins of the ballet, in the sense of the attraction of the subject, go back to a childhood holiday with my parents at a German spa, and my first impressions of a casino there, the low rows of tables at which people played baccarat and bezique, roulca and faro, as now, in the bowels of ocean liners, they play bingo. In fact the trombone theme with which each of the ballet's three 'Deals' begins imitates the voice of the master of ceremonies at that first casino. '*Ein neues Spiel, ein neues Glück*,' he would trumpet – or, rather, trombone – and the timbre, character, and pomposity of the announcement are echoed and caricatured in my music.

The period and setting of *The Card Game*, if I had been asked to fix them, would have been in a German spa such as Baden-Baden in the Romantic Age; and it is as part of that picture that the marches, and the tunes by Rossini, Messager, Johann Strauss, and from my own Symphony in E♭, might be imagined drifting in from the Municipal Opera, or the concert by the Kursaal Band. The score was not designed for any particular audience. But it has been especially popular in Germany and was performed there in all of the larger cities, and by eminent conductors, in 1937 and 1938. But if spirit of place exerted any influence, the spirit of the music would have been Parisian. Only one segment, the passage from 189 to 192, which resembles the beginning of the Limoges piece in Ravel's instrumentation of *Pictures at an Exhibition*, was written on German territory, aboard the SS *Kap Arcona*, on which I sailed from Boulogne to Buenos Aires in 1936; this passage is rare in my music, too, in that it was not composed at the piano. The remainder of the score was completed in my Paris apartment.

I began *The Card Game* on 2 December 1935 with, besides the trombone theme, some of the music in the coda of the second 'Deal'; by the end of the month most of the first 'Deal' had been sketched, and parts of the third. I began the second 'Deal' with the *Marcia*, then the *Variations*, composed in that order. The second variation was completed on 8 September 1936, the third on 18 September. The *Waltz* in the third 'Deal' was completed next, followed by the last bars of the ballet on 19 October. The intervening music of the third 'Deal' was composed in November.

At one point during the early stages of the composition I invited Cocteau to collaborate with me, thinking that he might devise a more interesting plot than the one I had worked out by myself. But he was embroiled with his bicephalous eagles and bleeding bards by then and declined. My own scheme called for a three-part division, each with a deal of poker as its argument, and with the Joker as the principal dancer. In the first 'Deal', one of the three players is defeated and the other two remain with even straights. In the second, the Joker wins by becoming the fourth ace, which defeats four Queens. And in the third, the Joker is beaten by three flushes. I no longer remember the details of the choreographic action I must have had in mind as I composed. But I did not provide Balanchine with an explicit programme, being confident that the choreographic character of each episode was unmistakable in the music.

Playing-cards are ideal ballet material because of the rich possibilities in combining and grouping the four suits with the solo-dancer royalty. The latter divided into sexes, moreover;

...ember 1925: on a train from Nice to Venice, photographed by Vera Sudeykina.

...ember 1939, Hollywood: with Walt Disney, discussing *The Rite of Spring* in *Fantasia*.

Sonorous Paris
Television française most
make to Stravinsky *direct an*
money offer for each of their
three propositions you mention

Sincerely
Robert Craft
Avn 20/66

December 27, 1949

Mr Ralph Hawkes
30 W. 57 St. NYC

Dear Mr Hawkes,

Mr Stravinsky is confined to bed with a cold and has asked me to
write to you concerning a letter he has just received from Mr Stein.
In preparing to print the SYMPHONIES OF WIND INSTRUMENTS Mr Stein
had sent Mr Stravinsky the "calques" of the old 1921 version. He is
apparently unaware of the new 1947 version which is of course the
one which must be printed as the old version is completely impracticable.
As Mr Stein does not have this score would you kindly send him the
copy in your N.Y. office.

Happy New Year.

Sincerely,

Bul Croft

August 24, 1949

Mr Erwin Stein
Boosey and Hawkes
34 Regent St
London, England

Dear Mr Stein,

I enclose an errata sheet for the full score of the new edition
of SACRE DU PRINTEMPS. Mr Stravinsky has checked these, and hopes
it will be added to the score. He also would like to know if there
will be a new set of parts to conform to the new score.

Sincerely,

R. Croft

19 1949: three letters by Stravinsky on which he has written the signature
'Robert Craft'.

mber 1951, La Scala, Milan: with W. H. Auden during a rehearsal of *The Rake's*

21 February 1953, Columbia Records' 30th Street studio, New York: the composer is
listening to playbacks during a recording session of *The Rake's Progress*.

gust 1957: in Salisbury Cathedral.

23 1959: on the porch of the Stravinsky home at 1260 N. Wetherly Drive, Hollywood. The composer, his wife, and the editor have just received a copy of *Conversations with Stravinsky*. Stravinsky captioned the picture 'Trio con Brio'.

24 December 18, 1969, New York: Stravinsky is at the head of the table opposite W. H. Auden (head on table). Vera Stravinsky is at the poet's left. George Balanchine, the editor, and Lincoln Kirstein are seated at the composer's left.

saying "there is nothing after death, death is the end, period." I then had the temerity ~~to say~~ to suggest that perhaps ~~nothing×after×death~~ this was also merely one point of view, but was made to feel for some time thereafter that I should have kept my ~~place~~ peace.

I thought I had found friends in Rimsky's sons, three young gentlemen who at least in provincial St. Petersburg were beacons of enlightenment. Andrei, a man three years my ~~number~~ senior and a 'cellist of some ability was especially kind to me, though this kindness lasted only while his father was alive; when I had gone to Paris in 1910 and my name had come back to Russia he, and in fact the entire Rimsky-Korsakov family ~~suddenly~~ turned against me. He reviewed Petroushka for a Russian newspaper dismissing it as "Russian vodka with French perfumes." Vladimir, his brother, was a competent violinist, I owe to him my first knowledge of violin fingering ~~problems~~. ~~Rimsky's daughters did not appeal to me at all, however, and I especially disliked Sophie. Incidentally,~~ My last contact with the Rimsky-Korsakov family was through her husband Maximilian Steinberg who had come to Paris in 1924 ~~to hear~~ and heard me play my Piano Concerto (you may imagine his response to that work when I tell you that the best he could do even for my Fireworks was to shrug his shoulders) After hearing the Concerto he wanted to lecture me on my whole mistaken career, ~~and~~ He returned to Russia thoroughly annoyed when I refused to see him. ~~I was not fond of Mme. Rimsky-Korsakov either, as I have said elsewhere. She was an avowed enemy of Diaghilev too, but while she attacked his production of Sheherazade she was delighted at the same time to receive very handsome royalties from it.~~

s first draft of one of Stravinsky's 'Conversations' reveals more of his true feelings
he Rimsky-Korsakov family than the published text. The typescript was dictated by
sky; the emendations in red ink were made by the editor.

[Facsimile of handwritten manuscript]

URGENT
you can not ampli[te]
IStr
Oct 3/6

Orpheus

1. The subject was whose idea?   Balanchine
   " commission came when?   1946
   When did you start to compose?   1946

2. When did Balanchine come to Los A. to discuss it (1946
   How did you plan the action together?   Together
   Is the ordering of the plot jointly yours + Balanchine
   whose version of the myth did you follow (the titles
   were composed by whom?) (Ovid?) I used Ov
   by myself

3. Did you have any mural conceptions for the staging
   any costumes ideas? Not when What about the masks?
   Noguchi was Kirstein's idea? I think so
   How did you find the staging in comparison to your
   conception? Ideal, when I saw at Noguchi's stu
   his small theatre maquette (theatrical sketch)

4. Did Balanchine offer any precisions as to lengths of
   the individual scenes? more or less, but
   decided it ourselves when

5. What music by other composers most attracted you
   at the time and were there any "influences"?
   nobody's   I didn't and don't
                                for it

6. Orpheus is what I may to prefer of all my,
   so called, neo-classical period.

26 October 1964: the questions concerning *Orpheus* were prompted by a request from
Columbia Records for programme notes, but the result was included in the original
'Conversations'.

male and female are to ballet composers what *forte* and *piano* were to eighteenth-century *concerto grosso* composers. The Joker is a bonus, an element of chance, and an escape from these very combinations. He interrupts the music as well as the choreography, wins all the battles, and loses the war. The contest results in his defeat, where he enters at the head of a sequence of spades. But, like Petrushka, he reappears at the end. His return is represented by the final seventh-chord, which, together with the return of the master-of-ceremonies music, signifies that the game is perpetual, as all games are.

I did not reveal even this sketchy programme to Balanchine, and in fact hardly discussed the choreography with him. But I did send the piano score from Paris and, on my arrival in New York for a concert tour two months before the performance, I rehearsed *tempi* with him. In fact, I participated in the staging only to criticize the costume designs, which were inspired by Tarot and medieval playing cards, handsome in themselves but too sumptuous for my 'brittle' and 'heartless' music. I asked the artist to copy some ordinary playing cards.

The Card Game was my first commission from Lincoln Kirstein, a young giant then, a bellicose champion of the beautiful, and a fierce enemy of the sham. His career as a patron had only just begun. A few days after the première I received news of the death of Lyudmila Beliankina, my wife's sister and my own close friend since childhood, and I returned to Europe with a heavy heart. The Paris première occurred at the time of another sad event, the death of Ravel. And it was the last work I conducted in Europe before the war, at a concert in La Scala in May 1939.

*

Immediately on my return to France after *The Card Game*, I began my *Dumbarton Oaks* Concerto. The name is that of the District of Columbia estate of the late Robert Woods Bliss, who commissioned the music, sponsored its first performance there in 1938, and in April 1950 purchased the principal manuscripts for the Dumbarton Oaks Museum. I started work on this composition in the Château de Montoux, near Annemasse in the Haute Savoie, where I had moved for the sake of my daughter

Mika, who had been confined to a tuberculosis sanitarium near by. Not long before, Mika had married Yuri Mandelstam, a Russian writer and cousin of the great poet Osip Mandelstam, working in Paris for the émigré newspaper *Sovremenniya Zapiski* and unable to leave his position there and stay with her.[19] Annemasse is near Geneva, and my good friend Charles-Albert Cingria often came to visit me from there during this difficult period.

I played Bach regularly in Annemasse, and then, as always, was greatly attracted to the Brandenburg Concertos. The first theme of my own Concerto resembles that of the Third Brandenburg (which I have conducted), and, like the Bach, it uses three violins and three violas, both groups sometimes *divisi a tre*. I have been much censured for these resemblances, but since Bach frequently borrowed in this way himself, I do not think he would have begrudged me the use of his example.

My last composition in Europe, the first two movements of the Symphony in C, date from the most tragic year of my life. Most of the first movement was written in my rue Faubourg St-Honoré (Paris) apartment in the autumn of 1938, although the last section was not finished until 17 April 1939. On 22 November 1938 I left Nice for the Excelsior Hotel in Rome, and a concert in that city. On the 29th, before leaving Rome for a concert in Turin, I called Paris and heard that Mika's condition had become grave. On my arrival at the Turin railway station, I called again and learned that she had died at five o'clock that morning. It is no exaggeration to say that in the following weeks I was able to continue my life only by working on the Symphony, which is *not* to say that the music exploits my grief. Three months later, 2 March 1939, a haemorrhage ended my wife Yekaterina's fifty-year struggle with the same disease. Unable to remain in the apartment after that, and having been further warned about my own condition, I moved to the same sanitarium in Sancellemoz where Yekaterina and Mika had spent so much time, and where I was an outpatient for the next five months. One of my infrequent absences was to attend the funeral of my

19 Mandelstam remarried a year after Mika's death; then soon after the occupation of Paris he was deported to Poland and never heard from again.

mother, who died on 7 June. For the third time in half a year I heard the Requiem service chanted for one of my own family, and for the third time walked through the fields to the cemetery of Saint-Geneviève-des-Bois, Montlhéry, on the road to Orléans, and dropped a handful of dirt in an open grave. Once again I was able to go on only by composing, though no more than before do the parts of the Symphony written in these dark days represent an expression of my anguished feelings. The pastoral second movement was begun 27 March and completed 19 July.

My visitors in Sancellemoz included Pierre Souvtchinsky and Roland-Manuel. Souvtchinsky knew me more closely than perhaps anyone else in Paris at that time. He had always fed books to me, and I remember that at Sancellemoz he brought the novel *La Nausée* by the new writer of the moment, Jean-Paul Sartre. Having agreed to give the Charles Eliot Norton lectures at Harvard in the winter of 1939–40, I sought Souvtchinsky's assistance to help draft my texts in Russian, and Roland-Manuel's to revise and polish the French.

Back in Paris, Souvtchinsky reported that the score of Tchaikovsky's First Symphony was on my piano, and this information, together with the discovery of a similarity of first themes in my Symphony and Tchaikovsky's, was responsible for the rumour that was soon crediting the latter with model status. (If Souvtchinsky had reported which Haydn and Beethoven scores were on my piano, no one would have paid any attention, of course, yet both of those composers stand behind at least the first two movements far more profoundly than any music by my much-too-lonely compatriot.) At the same time, a rapport would naturally exist between the two works, given the Russian sentiment in the E♭ minor episode in my first movement, as well as in the introduction to my last movement; but Tchaikovskian antecedents have been discovered elsewhere as well: my eighteenth century and Tchaikovsky's share Russian family likenesses.

To turn to the chronicle of the later movements, the world events of 1939–40 did not bear tragically on my personal life, but they did disrupt the composition of the Symphony. The third movement was written in Boston (completed at the beginning of April), and the finale in California (completed 17 August), where I had gone to escape New England, whose only seasons, so it seemed to a Mediterraneanized European, were winter and the Fourth of July. The American movements are said to be different in spirit and design from the European, and it has been claimed that they divide the Symphony down the middle. But I am no judge of that. Perhaps the two bars before $\boxed{104}$ would not have come to my ears in Europe; and the passage beginning at $\boxed{145}$ might not have occurred to me before I knew the neon glitter of Los Angeles's boulevards from a speeding automobile. Perhaps. But I do not agree that the metrical irregularity and tempo changes in the third movement, the most extreme in the whole of my work, as it happens, constitute a schism, simply because they follow a second movement with a steady *ductus*, and a first movement without any variation of metre.

Alas, ill-fated personal associations of the Symphony were not at an end. I was conducting it in Berlin, 2 October 1956, when, near the end of the first movement, I felt a paralysing pain in my right side, and an eclipsing blackness. After the concert, orchestra members said that I failed to beat the final bars of the movement and paused an unconscionable time before beginning the second one. I *did* continue, nevertheless, and brought the Symphony to an end, though in my dressing room I was unable to write my name and had only partial control of my speech. Two days later, in Munich, where I had flown for another concert, a doctor told me I had suffered a cerebral thrombosis. I spent the next seven weeks there in the Red Cross hospital.

But enough of autobiography. And of musical biography, too, for what can one say about music that is so unmysterious, and so easy to follow at every level and in all relationships? The answer, of course, is that reviewers (who must earn their livelihood) will find a great deal of nothing to say.

How do I evaluate the Symphony thirty years afterward? The answer is that I don't. It may be too episodic, the key centres may be overemphasized, and certainly there *are* a great many *ostinati*.

The score, like that of the *Symphony of Psalms*, is inscribed 'à la gloire de Dieu'.

STRAVINSKY IN ALBION

Robert Craft

The original *Conversations* contain little about Stravinsky in England. True, before World War I he visited the country only twice, very briefly, and only once in the decade following World War II, years before the first 'Conversations' books were compiled. Moreover, his career as a performer in the UK was confined to 1927–37 and, after a long hiatus, to a few concerts in the late 1950s and early 1960s. But English readers deserve to be told more of their country's role in Stravinsky's life from his perspective.

In July 1933 Stravinsky wrote to his London concert agent in connection with a tour in England the following winter, 'In my entire life as a performer, the Liverpool honorarium of 47 guineas is the lowest I have ever been offered. I accept it simply to establish a record.' In fact, he pocketed the fee because he had agreed to conduct the Manchester Hallé Orchestra the day before the Liverpool date.[1] Further, he would accept much lower fees after Liverpool for recitals with Samuel Dushkin: eight guineas from Cambridge, and, two days later, twelve from Oxford. Since the Oxbridge excursions began and ended in London, where Stravinsky, Dushkin, and the clarinettist Reginald Kell performed the

1 The *Liverpool Post*, 24 February 1934, reported that Stravinsky, *en route* to a luncheon in his honour, was informed of the death of Elgar: 'Stravinsky paid a warm tribute to Elgar, asking the guests to stand for a moment in silence as a mark of respect for him. Stravinsky said he knew many of Elgar's works and had attended concerts at which he conducted. Stravinsky had heard Elgar's *Cockaigne* Overture in St Petersburg.'

five-movement trio version of *The Soldier's Tale*[2] in Queen's Hall, the engagements were certainly not profitable. One wonders what the rock bottom really was, how many shillings and pence.

In terms of audience and press reception, Stravinsky's first two visits to London, in January 1913 and June 1914, were among the most bountiful of his life. The first occasion was in compliance with an invitation by Diaghilev to attend the London première of *Petrushka*, and to teach the last part of *The Rite of Spring* to Nijinsky and the Ballets Russes dancers. *Petrushka* was an instant success. Stravinsky was invited to the Royal Box to meet Queen Alexandra, and lionized everywhere. His scrapbook for the month is heaped with newspaper cuttings of interviews, reviews and invitations to dinner parties and receptions by Lady Cunard, the Marchioness of Ripon, and others of the beautiful people of the period.

The June visit, again at Diaghilev's request and expense, was to attend the London première of *The Nightingale*, which took place on the composer's thirty-second birthday at the Theatre Royal, Drury Lane. Richard Strauss was in the audience, and the stripling composer Serge Prokofiev, who complained about Stravinsky's 'many deliberate dissonances'. Osbert Sitwell has left a description of Stravinsky acknowledging the applause:

I was excited to see the great Russian composer, the master of the epoch, walk before the curtain. Slight of frame, pale, in his early thirties, with an air both worldly and abstracted and a little angry, he bowed with solemnity to an audience that little comprehended the nature of the great musician to whom they were doing an honour.

The anger in Stravinsky's expression was his characteristic bow-taking demeanour until late in life. In this instance it may be attributed to his displeasure with the staging, as he described it in a letter to a friend in Russia. After the première, he and Artur Rubinstein, who came backstage and introduced himself without telling Stravinsky that he was a pianist, attended one of

---

2 The second performance anywhere of the complete *Soldier's Tale* music took place in London in July 1920, conducted by Ernest Ansermet. For this occasion Stravinsky substantially expanded the final dance of the Devil from the version used at the première in Lausanne in 1918, hence the London performance was the first of the music as we now know it.

Richard Strauss's rehearsals of his ballet *Josephslegende*. Rubinstein's memoirs describe Stravinsky's comments on the music as unprintable. After the rehearsal, Rubinstein took his new friend to lunch with two fellow Polish musicians, the composer Karol Szymanowski and the violinist Paul Kochanski, for whom, a decade later, Stravinsky would arrange a suite from *Pulcinella* and two excerpts from *The Firebird*. During the 1914 trip, Stravinsky made notations of the bells of St Paul's.

Thomas Beecham was also a member of that June 1914 *Nightingale* audience. At the beginning of the 1914–18 war, Beecham sent 500 Swiss francs to Stravinsky in Switzerland, in the event that his income from Russia might be cut off. Stravinsky recalled that 'the money came like manna on the very day I had to pay my mother's passage from Morges back to Russia – on a Brindisi-to-Odessa boat, the only route still open'. Many years later (in the summer of 1940), the composer saw Beecham from time to time in Mexico City, and later still, in New York in 1941, together with Percy Grainger.

Stravinsky was also on good terms with two other English conductors, Edward Clark and Eugene Goossens. Clark, who became a BBC 'music programme builder', was the first English musician closely associated with Schoenberg, and he conducted the world première of the Monn–Schoenberg Cello Concerto with Feuermann as soloist. Goossens, born into a family of musicians, was an early champion of Stravinsky's music. He had attended all of Monteux's rehearsals for the 1913 London performances of *The Rite of Spring*, and conducted the piece himself in London, at the Queen's Hall, on 7 June 1921.

In July 1913, between *Petrushka* and *The Nightingale*, London had heard and seen *The Rite of Spring*, and, in contrast to Paris, taken it in its stride. The only troubles were internecine. Pierre Monteux, faithful to the absent composer, refused to make a cut, whereupon Diaghilev replaced him with Rhené Baton. And, on the other side of the curtain, Diaghilev's spokesman, Edwin Evans, was heckled off the stage during an allocution apparently thought to be condescending.

As it happened, Evans would become Stravinsky's first English friend. Three years later he arranged for the commission of the Etude for Pianola. His future association with the composer as programme and player-piano roll-annotator was not always smooth, and came to an end with his notes for the British première of *The Card Game*. Notwithstanding, he ranks with Berners, Beecham, Goossens, Adrian Boult, Clark and his wife Elisabeth Lutyens as one of the handful of Stravinsky's long-term British musician friends. Beecham resolved to, and did, conduct the *The Nightingale* himself after World War I, but Stravinsky was working in Switzerland and could not attend. Sir Adrian Boult was another ('Bold' in Stravinsky's captions on photographs taken of him in Paris in September 1939 as the composer was departing for America with Katherine Wolff[3]). Boult had conducted *The Rite of Spring* with the BBC Symphony in Paris in April 1936 to great acclaim, though Stravinsky, in South America, was not told about the performance until his return. During World War II Boult gave the English première of the Symphony in C.

Stravinsky's third trip to London, in June 1921, was to attend the première of his *Symphonies of Wind Instruments*, conducted by Serge Koussevitzky. The fourth trip, in November, was for Diaghilev's revival of *The Sleeping Beauty*, in which Vera Sudeykina played the role of the Queen. His fifth trip, in 1925, was by aeroplane, to attend the British première of *The Wedding*.[4] The nearly unanimously scathing press reception of this masterpiece inspired H. G. Wells's brilliant philippic in its defence. Stravinsky's next London visit was from the 17th to the 29th of June 1927, for an hour-long matinée broadcast concert sponsored by the BBC. He and Mme Sudeykina stayed at the Felix Hotel in Jermyn Street, leading a busy social life culminating in a festival of Stravinsky's music attended by the King of Spain. Again that year, between the 2nd and 15th of October, the couple returned to London (by way of Ostend–Dover) for concertizing. And they returned in May 1928, Calais to Dover,

---

3 A musician friend of Stravinsky through Nadia Boulanger, Mlle Wolff was a teacher at the Curtis Institute in Philadelphia.

4 He flew from Le Bourget to Croydon, where he was met by Diaghilev, and attended the première on 19 June.

together with Andrés Segovia, who became a lifelong friend, to conduct *Oedipus* for the BBC on the 12th and 13th of the month. Stravinsky recorded *Petrushka* in London on 27 and 28 June 1928, his first recording of a major work.

Between 15 and 18 May 1929, Stravinsky recorded at Aeolian Studios. A month later, on 19 June, he and Mme Sudeykina returned on the night train from Dunkirk to Tilbury to play his Piano Concerto at a matinée concert in Queen's Hall, London, under Eugene Goossens, after only one rehearsal. (Four days later, in Berlin, Stravinsky was the soloist in the Concerto under Klemperer. A few days after that, *Apollo* and *The Rite of Spring*, conducted by Ansermet, brought ovations for the Ballets Russes at Charlottenburg, but by this time both Stravinsky and Diaghilev had returned, separately, to Paris.) On 23 June Stravinsky and Mme Sudeykina boarded the night train to London, discovering to their dismay that Diaghilev was on the same train. As aforesaid, this was to be the last glimpse the impresario and the composer had of each other. In London, Stravinsky rehearsed the BBC Orchestra three times on the 25th and once on the 26th, after which he visited Hampton Court with his friend Willy Strecker. Another rehearsal took place on the 27th in Kingsway Hall, and in the evening Stravinsky conducted the concert (*Apollo* and *The Fairy's Kiss*). He and Mme Sudeykina returned to Paris the next day, but the Ballets Russes performed *The Rite of Spring* in London in mid-July. Two weeks later Diaghilev was in Venice, where, on 19 August, he died, 'alone in a hotel, like a vagabond', as Ansermet wrote to Stravinsky.

In June 1930 Stravinsky conducted a concert in Queen's Hall and was Ansermet's piano soloist in another one. He was in London with Mme Sudeykina between 26 January and 2 February 1931, playing both the Piano Concerto and the *Capriccio* with the BBC Symphony under Ansermet (Queen's Hall) on 28 January. During this trip he listened to Jack Hylton's arrangement for his jazz band of the quartet from *Mavra*, assisted at a recording of it, and even conducted it himself at least once. Mme Sudeykina's diary mentions a visit with Stravinsky to the British Museum at this time, and notes that the two of them were house guests at Elizabeth Courtauld's Portman Square home and that Otto Klemperer was staying there as well. They also dined with Lord Berners, and, on 1 February, after tea with the wife of former Prime Minister Herbert Asquith, they attended a concert conducted by Willem Mengelberg, dining with him afterwards. Stravinsky was in London alone for a concert at the end of February, but when he returned in mid-November (the Langham Hotel) to conduct his Violin Concerto with Samuel Dushkin on the 16th and 17th, Mme Sudeykina was with him. Two years later, at the end of February 1933, Dushkin wrote to Stravinsky to say that Mrs Stephen Courtauld had invited them to stay at her London home during the period of their BBC recital on 13 March.

Stravinsky returned to London in July 1934 to record *The Wedding*, and in November to conduct a BBC concert of *Perséphone* on the 28th, and to play his *Capriccio* in the first half of the programme. Sir Victor Gollancz, who published an English-language translation of Stravinsky's autobiography in 1935, once told me that he dined twice with the composer at the time of the *Perséphone* performance, and that on each occasion the composer chose Scottish smoked salmon for both the hors d'œuvre and the entrée courses. By this time, evidently, the composer's tastes had become partly Anglicized. He had begun to wear Savile Row suits and Hilditch and Key shirts, and to purchase English silver – tableware, candlesticks, picture frames, étuis, flasks. His next engagements in England were on 24 March 1936, when he played his Two-Piano Concerto with his son Soulima in Brighton, a strange venue for that opus, and in November 1937, when he conducted the British première of *The Card Game*.

The principal publisher of Stravinsky's music worldwide is the British firm of Boosey & Hawkes. Among the family owners, I knew only Ralph Hawkes and Leslie Boosey, his less flamboyant successor. It seems that *en route* to a Stravinsky première in Venice, Mr Boosey shared a railway carriage from Milan with Nicolas Nabokov, who told Stravinsky that this travelling companion, in a moment of daring, had said to him, 'Mr Nabokov, I am only a businessman, but I believe in God.' Anthony Fell became director of the company only after Stravinsky's death, but he had sung in the chorus of *Symphony of Psalms* when the composer conducted it in Johannesburg in May 1962. I was deeply moved in September 1982 when Mr Fell came from London to attend Vera Stravinsky's funeral in Venice.

In view of the critical failure of *The Wedding* in London in 1925, it seems remarkable that Stravinsky's first recording of the work was made there, and sung in English. Part of the reason for this is that Ansermet had recently prepared and performed it with the same singers and instrumentalists. But a no less important consideration was that Stravinsky did not want to record it in C.-F. Ramuz's French, which, to accommodate the text, requires many changes in the rhythms of the vocal parts. On one occasion, Leonard Bernstein, who had been brought up on the London recording, sang bits of it to me out of the blue: 'You must always be of good cheer'; 'Increasing their homestead'. The quaint Brit translation *was* memorable.

The main reason for Stravinsky's switch from French to English, as his principal language after Russian, was my ignorance of any other, but the most important influence on the change was his collaboration on *The Rake's Progress* with W. H. Auden, which began in November 1947. The friendship grew steadily over the years, as can be seen in one of the conversations about him, from December 1969 in the Essex House, New York, recorded later in this volume. Fifteen months later, Auden was the last friend of the composer to visit him before his death.

In October 1952, Leslie Boosey visited Stravinsky in California to convey an invitation to conduct a concert with the Royal Philharmonic Orchestra, after which he would be invested with the organization's gold medal. On further thought, Stravinsky wrote to Boosey & Hawkes:

I am accepting the engagement more as a friendly gesture than as business because there is no money to be made in England with the outrageous tax situation. Though I love London, it is too much of a non-profitable proposition. I want to point out that 500 pounds is less than 1500 dollars, which is my minimum fee anywhere.

Shortly before the concert, on 27 May 1954, Stravinsky, in Geneva, had purchased what he believed was a mouthwash, but which had been mislabelled and proved to be formaldehyde.

Gargling with it and suffering scorching pain, he also lost his voice and had to cancel an interim concert in Cologne. Meanwhile, his son-in-law, who was to have accompanied him to London, fell ill with bronchitis, and his wife, Stravinsky's daughter, though she had never escorted her father before, came in her husband's place. Thrice unlucky, Stravinsky was detained at London Airport by Immigration authorities, who had found some irregularity in his or his daughter's papers. He managed to call Boosey & Hawkes, who, just as a furious Stravinsky was about to return to Switzerland, provided a lawyer who obtained the admittance.

The concert was a gala event and, in addition to the medal, Stravinsky was given a rosewood baton with a silver handle and tip that belonged to the orchestra in the early nineteenth century and was said to have been used before that by Joseph Haydn. The medal was lost or stolen during the Stravinskys' move from California to New York in 1969, but the baton is intact.

In December 1956 Stravinsky came to London by train, via Rome and Paris, for a concert introducing his *Canticum Sacrum* in St Martin-in-the-Fields. As it happened, Stravinsky did not conduct the performance, but I did, while the composer sat in a pew in the first row beyond the orchestra, next to Ralph Vaughan Williams. The performance was at least accurate, with one of those superb English choirs and good solo singers and instrumentalists. After it we went to a late dinner party at 14 South Audley Street hosted by William Glock. The other guests were Michael Tippett, Mr and Mrs Stephen Spender, Peter Heyworth, Edward Clark and Elisabeth Lutyens.

In the summer of 1957, the Stravinskys spent two weeks at Dartington. Glock had invited me to conduct there, and the Stravinskys, eager to see more of England, came with me. They fell in love with the Devon landscape, with the cathedrals of Wells, Exeter, Salisbury, and with Bath. *Life* magazine's photographer Gjon Mili photographed Stravinsky in Salisbury – he had always been a great admirer of Constable – and at Stonehenge, following which he became obsessed with related questions of astronomy and archaeology.

In 1959 Stephen and Natasha Spender drove the Stravinskys and me to Stratford-upon-Avon to see Laurence Olivier as

Coriolanus, and two days later accompanied us on a visit to Edinburgh. Four years after that, again escorted by the Spenders, the Stravinskys visited Canterbury and Saltwood Castle, where they spent a day with Sir Kenneth and Lady Clark. In the mid-1960s, Lina Lalandi, founder of the English Bach Festival, entered Stravinsky's life. He conducted at Oxford for her, and in 1966 she arranged an open-air concert for him with the London Symphony Orchestra in the Herod Atticus amphitheatre in Athens. She also visited him at the Dolders Hotel in Zurich in 1968.

Increasingly vexed by air pollution and by the violence of life in Los Angeles, which included murder and robbery, the Stravinskys seriously thought at one point of moving to England. But this, ironically, would have deprived them of such close friends as Aldous Huxley, Christopher Isherwood, Christopher Wood, Gerald Heard and Edward James, all Englishmen living in Hollywood. His other closest English friends were Sir Isaiah and Lady Berlin.[5]

5 See *An Improbable Life* (Vanderbilt University Press, 2002) for an account of Isaiah Berlin's role in Stravinsky's life.

THE AMERICAN YEARS

1939–1971

Introduction

Robert Craft

Stravinsky's American period was the longest in his active life
as a composer, longer than the Russian (1900–1913), and than
the Swiss and French combined (1910–1939). The *Conversations* reveal little about the first decade in California, however,
and even less about the background of his World War II
experience in the United States. A brief review of this should be
helpful to an understanding of the composer's later years.

The forty-two-year-old Stravinsky arrived in Manhattan for
the first time on 4 January 1925, after a stormy crossing from
Le Havre on the SS *Paris*. Four days later he conducted the New
York Philharmonic in a programme of his music in Carnegie
Hall. This first US concert appearance received an ovation that
clearly acknowledged his stature as the pre-eminent figure of
musical modernism. His name had been known in the city since
June 1910, when the *Herald Tribune* reported the première of
The Firebird at the Paris Opéra as a front-page news event. Six
years later his genius was made evident to New Yorkers when
this ballet and *Petrushka*, with Vaslav Nijinsky in the title role
of the latter, were presented by Sergey Diaghilev's Ballets Russes
at the Metropolitan Opera. Thenceforth, music publications
kept theatre- and concertgoers informed of Stravinsky's latest
creations, of which at least five were performed locally: the
Three Pieces and the *Concertino for String Quartet*, the latter,
23 November 1920, for the first time anywhere. Soon after,
Leopold Stokowski and his Philadelphians gave the New York
premières of *The Rite of Spring*, *Renard*, and the *Symphonies of
Wind Instruments*.

What interests us today is the reception of the unknown new pieces in Stravinsky's 1925 concerts, particularly those in his chamber music programme in Aeolian Hall on 25 January, and the Piano Concerto, played by him under Willem Mengelberg with the Philharmonic on 5 and 6 February. The little *Ragtime* was generally regarded as a corny imitation of the idiom. More surprisingly and consequentially, the Octet, the first example of Stravinsky's neo-classicism to be heard locally, seems to have baffled everyone. The influential critic Lawrence Gilman found nothing to like in this joyous, witty and entirely original opus, now recognized as the most inventive for an ensemble of eight wind instruments since Mozart; the critic even failed to notice the jazz element in the syncopated coda. The Piano Concerto, a less consistently interesting piece, fared better, no doubt because of the liveliness and excitement of the outer movements and the contrasting Romantic clichés of the middle one.

This first visit to New York must have been extremely difficult and demanding. Stravinsky was not a professional conductor, after all, and did not speak English. He had retained a bilingual Russian to translate for him as well as to serve as his valet, but this person proved inadequate to convey Stravinsky's thoughts in interviews and rehearsals. Apart from his performances as conductor and pianist, Stravinsky's main musical curiosity in New York was in the new Duo-Art system of producing pianola rolls, by which the paper was perforated directly as the pianist played. He recorded the first movement of the Piano Concerto using this technology, and also made 78-rpm discs of some of his short piano pieces using improved American methods.

The composer's 'leisure time' was fully occupied with social commitments. Thus the 8 January concert was followed by a dinner party at the home of his friend Arthur Sachs, the banker (Goldman Sachs) and Philharmonic patron who had journeyed to Biarritz two years earlier and persuaded him to undertake the stateside tour. Among the fellow guests that evening were the twenty-six-year-old George Gershwin, the violinist Leopold Auer (Stravinsky's St Petersburg friend and the teacher of Jascha Heifetz), and Wilhelm Furtwängler. In the previous month, Stravinsky had performed his Piano Concerto with Furtwängler in the Gewandhaus in Leipzig, and in Berlin, and Furtwängler would conduct *The Rite of Spring* with the New York Philharmonic later in the month.

More strenuous, surely, was the afternoon musicale a few days later in the Astor mansion at 840 Fifth Avenue, since Stravinsky was required to play the piano. But to judge from photographs of the dinner in the composer's honour at Steinway Hall on 11 January, the day after his third Philharmonic concert, this occasion would appear to have been the most trying of his social obligations. He is seated in the front row, arms folded, eyes glowering with anger and boredom, a reaction, perhaps, to the testimonials of his Steinway hosts and of other speakers. Also prominent in the photo are Rakhmaninov, Furtwängler, Fritz Kreisler, and Josef Hofmann.

A curious encounter was in store for Stravinsky on the day before his return to Europe. He attended a performance of *Petrushka* at the Metropolitan Opera – on a double bill with *Pagliacci*! – and at the end had to bow from the stage. Entering from the wings, he looked up and saw the ballet's set and costume designer, Sergei Sudeykin, approaching from the opposite side. Having dreaded just such a confrontation since his arrival in the city, Stravinsky turned on his heel and fled. In 1922, Mme Sudeykina had left her artist husband for the composer.

On Stravinsky's next voyages, in 1935 and 1937, New York was the focal point for transcontinental recital tours with the violinist Samuel Dushkin, his close friend and collaborator in arranging excerpts for their two instruments from *The Firebird*, *The Nightingale*, *Pulcinella* and *The Fairy's Kiss*. In New York in 1935 Stravinsky also conducted the Radio City Symphony in a national NBC broadcast, and in 1937 he led six concerts with the Philharmonic. In the latter year his programmes included works by other composers as well, a Glinka overture, Rimsky-Korsakov's little-known tone-poem, *Sadko*, a Mozart concerto, Tchaikovsky's Second Symphony and the *Nutcracker* Suite. As a measure of the lack of musical sophistication in mid-1930s America, it should be noted that the press berated Stravinsky for choosing Mozart's great G major Piano Concerto. Reviewers thought he should have offered a more popular example, citing the D minor and the 'Coronation'.

During the 1935 visit, Stravinsky heard, and abominated,

Shostakovich's *Lady Macbeth of Mtsensk*, performed by Artur Rodzinsky and the Cleveland Orchestra. In 1937 he sat through another new opera, the young Gian Carlo Menotti's *Amelia Goes to the Ball*. His companion that evening, Dagmar Godowski, daughter of the pianist Leopold and the ex-movie partner of Rudolf Valentino, remembered that Stravinsky was 'patronizing' about the work. He also spent time with his young Parisian friend Boris Kochno, without being aware that he was living with Sergei Sudeykin. Stravinsky's primary interest in New York in 1937 was in the triple bill of his ballets, *Apollo*, *The Fairy's Kiss* and the world première of *The Card Game*, all three choreographed by George Balanchine and performed at the Metropolitan Opera, the composer conducting.

World War II had broken out in Europe when Stravinsky next entered New York harbour in September 1939 on a ship overcrowded with refugees. The steamer, the SS *Manhattan*, sailing from Bordeaux, was so thronged that he was obliged to share a cabin with six others, even though all seven had paid for private accommodation. Toscanini was on board, too, but they did not meet. The fiery Italian had refused to enter his cabin, since it also bunked six other passengers. Apparently he slept in the lounge. (More than thirty years later, one of Stravinsky's cabin mates, from Cleveland, returned a shirt that the composer had loaned to him during the voyage.)

Unaware that Stravinsky was not seeking asylum in the country – he had a return ticket in his valise – the Immigration official who interviewed him asked the most startling question of his life: 'Do you want to change your name?' When Stravinsky laughed, the official said, 'Well, most of them do.' Stravinsky himself, of course, had not remotely supposed that his intended stay of a few months would last until 1951.

On arrival, Stravinsky immediately departed for Boston, which at that time was his home territory in the United States. Between 1935 and 1949 he guest-conducted there more frequently than anywhere else in the country, taught composition students there in 1939–40, as he had done previously only in Nadia Boulanger's classes in Paris in 1935, and, uniquely in his career, gave a book-length series of lectures at Harvard. The third movement of his Symphony in C was composed there in

1939–40, and in the latter year he married near by and lived in Boston for two months following. He also had more friends in Boston from the mid-1920s through the early 1940s than in any other US city, and partly because one of them, Serge Koussevitzky, was both the conductor of the local orchestra and Stravinsky's publisher, more of Stravinsky's music was performed there than in any other American musical metropolis.

'With Koussevitzky's Boston Symphony', Stravinsky wrote to Nadia Boulanger, 'I have always been considered a member of the family.' An important factor in this relationship was that he could speak Russian, French, Italian, and German with the orchestra and be understood. After the Russian Revolution, many of its string players followed Koussevitzky from Russia to Paris, where he founded 'Les Concerts Koussevitzky'. When he became Music Director of the Boston Symphony in 1924, after Pierre Monteux, the best Russian string players, together with some of the finest French wind instrumentalists, came with him to the United States. Stravinsky respected and was on friendly terms with several of these artists, and in the case of some of the Russians on a first-name-plus-patronymic basis. The concertmaster Richard Burgin was one, Louis Speyer, the English horn player, another; both men alternated as guests and hosts of the composer at dinners.

The contrabassoonist Boaz Piller was the closest to Stravinsky of all. They had been introduced in the composer's Paris studio by Pierre Monteux on 10 June 1922, as Piller reminded Stravinsky in a seventy-fifth birthday letter to him, adding, 'You made your appearance in a *robe-de-chambre*, like Liszt.' On his arrival in Boston in October 1939, Stravinsky extended a standing invitation to Piller for afternoon tea. He was also the only one to whom the composer confided the news of his forthcoming marriage, and it was Piller who found an apartment for the couple in the Hemenway Hotel, which was within walking distance of Symphony Hall. Piller helped the Stravinskys organize their domestic life as well as cope with Immigration officials, tax collectors and the like, and he arranged dental appointments for Stravinsky with a Dr Fink, who, on 6 May 1940, took 'home movies' of the composer that I, for one, would like to see.

I should add that Stravinsky was on good terms not only with Boston's virtuoso musicians but also with its music critics, pre-eminently Moses Smith, who later wrote a scathing biography of Koussevitzky that Boston, famous for banning books, promptly banned.

The first Stravinsky world première to take place in Boston was of a suite from *Pulcinella*, not to be confused with the one we know today. This took place on 22 December 1922, under Monteux, who had been conductor of the orchestra since 1919. With the mercenary motive of collecting two performance fees instead of one, Stravinsky had formed two suites from the ballet. The first one ended, unsuitably, with the comic duet for trombone and contrabass, and the second began with the G minor *alla breve* dance, which, for its new purpose, he titled *Preludio*. Although the first suite could have lasted no longer than ten minutes, it was warmly received, as Monteux reported to the composer, adding that some listeners thought it did not have enough Stravinsky, while others objected that it had too little unspiked Pergolesi. The 'second suite' would have been performed as well, but the parts had not been extracted, and when Monteux asked permission to postpone it to the following season, Stravinsky insisted that both suites be played five times in 1922, according to his contract, and refused to extend the time limit.

Throughout his first twenty-five years as Director of the Boston Symphony, Serge Koussevitzky regularly invited Stravinsky to guest-conduct. His music had been introduced to Boston audiences before, of course, and not only orchestral works – the *Three Pieces for String Quartet*, played by the Flonzaleys, had shocked the American public as early as 1915, and inspired, if that is the word, some verses by the poet Amy Lowell. More important, in 1916 *Firebird* and *Petrushka* were staged in Boston by Sergey Diaghilev's Ballets Russes, with Nijinsky dancing the title role of the latter. Stravinsky's own first appearances in Boston, in January 1925, were as soloist (twice) in his Piano Concerto, which he and Koussevitzky had first performed in Paris the year before. In 1935 Stravinsky gave the American première of *Perséphone* at his Boston Symphony concerts. But on his next transatlantic tour, two years later, he came no closer to the city than Worcester, Massachusetts, where he gave a recital with Dushkin on 8 January 1937.

The most important monument to Stravinsky's association with Boston is the *Symphony of Psalms*, commissioned by Koussevitzky to commemorate the orchestra's fiftieth anniversary. (Stravinsky first conducted it with the orchestra, and others of his works, on 28 November 1939.) The other Stravinsky opus commissioned and first performed in the city is the 1943 *Ode*, in memory of the conductor's wife, Natalie, a woman for whom Stravinsky had the highest regard, and whose tea fortune had underwritten Koussevitzky's career. On 26 February 1947, Stravinsky's young Harvard friend, Irving Fine, conducted an arrangement by Claudio Spies for chorus and two pianos of the *Kyrie* and *Gloria* from his *Mass*, the only completed movements at that date. I should mention, too, that the *Greeting Prelude*, dedicated to Monteux, was first performed in Boston in 1955, conducted by Charles Munch.

Less well known is that, starting in 1945, Stravinsky revised *Petrushka*, tableau by tableau, with the Boston Symphony in mind, and performed parts of it with the orchestra. Evidence of this is in a surviving major error in the published score of the 1947 version: the trumpet parts at the end of the first tableau mistakenly indicate that 'trumpets in C' are required. Stravinsky had forgotten to change this to 'trumpets in B♭' and most recordings of the work still preserve the passage in the wrong key.

Stravinsky and Vera Sudeykina were married at the Pickman country home near Bedford, Massachusetts, on 9 March 1940, in a civil ceremony performed by Justice of the Peace Arthur Carson. Hester Pickman was the daughter of Margaret Chanler, 'doyenne', as Lincoln Kirstein describes her, 'of an ancestral domain in the Genesee Valley in Upper New York State'. Hester's brother, Theodore Chanler, a composer (Boulanger pupil), had succeeded Edward Hale as music critic of the *Boston Herald*. The witnesses to the wedding were Dr Alexis Kall and Dr Timothy Teracuzio, the former a friend of Stravinsky from their days as fellow law students at the University of St Petersburg, the latter a Russian-born member of Harvard's

Slavic Languages Department. Kall was Stravinsky's translator throughout his months in Boston in 1939–40, as well as the composer's secretary, though, as Vera Stravinsky noted in her diary, 'This charming companion with interesting memories of another life in St Petersburg should not be allowed to come near any business matters.'

On 10 March, Koussevitzky gave a lavish lunch for the newly-weds at his home, but the only other guests, partly because it was so widely known that the bride and groom had been living together for nineteen years, were Teracuzio and Gregor Piatigorsky, the latter a long-time friend of the Stravinskys and Koussevitzkys in Europe. The Stravinskys spent their honeymoon and next two months at the Hemenway.

On 13 March, Stravinsky read one of his Charles Eliot Norton lectures at Harvard, then departed on the night train to New York. There, on the following afternoon, in Town Hall, he conducted an ensemble of Boston Symphony players in his *Dumbarton Oaks* Concerto, *The Soldier's Tale*, the Octet, and played his *Concerto per due pianoforte soli* with Adele Marcus. This concert was sponsored by Mildred Bliss (Mrs Robert Woods Bliss) and the French Embassy to raise money for French war relief and musicians in France. Stravinsky returned to Boston on the night train and resumed work on the Symphony in C in the morning. On 17 March, he, his wife, and Adele Marcus entrained for Exeter, New Hampshire, where the Two-Piano Concerto was performed again, this time with Stravinsky reading his newly written programme note about it. On the 20th he delivered his Norton Lecture on Russian music, for which he displayed maps of Europe on the wall. On the 26th he began rehearsals for a concert of *Apollo* and *Oedipus Rex* with the Boston Symphony. At the last minute the Jocasta cancelled because of illness, and Stravinsky spent his pre-concert hours coaching a substitute.

At the end of the month an interviewer for the Boston *Daily Globe* reported that

He does not like this winter weather – he has a cold in the head – and it gives him headaches, but he is happier than he has been in a long time. For two weeks now the diminutive, moody Master musician has been happy . . . He talks animatedly to his friends in fluent, sparkling

French. He is like a man in love. He *is* a man in love . . . Next week he will go to New York to conduct the Philharmonic Orchestra.

At the first Philharmonic rehearsal, on 1 April, Stravinsky discovered that the orchestra parts did not conform to his revised score, and he had to correct them himself between and during the next two rehearsals. On the 8th the Stravinskys were in Washington trying to sort out their Immigration status with the French Ambassador. Back in Boston, Stravinsky gave another Norton Lecture on 11 April, after which he entered the first notations in his sketchbook for the final movement of the Symphony in C.

From the time of his arrival in Boston in early October 1939, Stravinsky lived on the top floor at Gerry's Landing, the Cambridge home of Edward Waldo Forbes, Director of Harvard's Fogg Museum, whose fame now rests on his refusal to allow Pietro Francavilla's marble group of Venus, nymphs, satyrs and two dolphins (1600) to be exhibited 'in the middle of a Harvard building'. (It is now in the Hartford Connecticut Athenaeum.) Against board-member opposition, Forbes had arranged for Stravinsky to read his lectures at the college in French. The inaugural one had taken place on 18 October 1939, at 7.30 in the evening. Frederick Jacobi's description of the occasion appeared in the next issue of *Modern Music* (New York):

Ushers in black ties lined the walls of the Harvard music department . . . Then sleek limousines began to drive up with Beacon Hill dowagers radiating white hair, evening dresses, diamonds, and dignity . . . No sooner had we settled down to Beacon Hill than the New Lecture Hall rustled again. This time it was for Koussevitzky.

Eager, tense, the audience waited for Stravinsky . . . He made a sweeping entrance in tails, and, then, after a low, courtly, athletic bow . . . began his *Prise de Contacte*. Reading a manuscript of beautifully written French, he spoke slowly, distinctly, with a soft Russian accent. He looked up from his paper infrequently and then rather jerkily . . . Wild applause greeted [him] as he concluded . . . He bowed . . . shook Dr Forbes warmly by the hand and breezed out, his tails flying behind.

The language barrier helps to account for each lecture being progressively less well attended. People came to see, rather than to hear Stravinsky, and the presence, what with his concerts and appearances on campus, was becoming familiar. Vera Stravinsky's diary remarks that even the Russian- and French-speaking audience found the substance too abstruse.

Stravinsky's stay with the Forbes family, October 1939 to February 1940, was, in aggregate, the longest in his life as a guest in a private home. I do not know if he composed at the Forbes piano, but he did meet there with one of his private composition students, Robert Stevenson, whose lessons continued in the Hemenway. Stravinsky's classes with his dozen or so students took place on Tuesdays and Fridays at Eliot House. The composer Vladimir Ussachevsky was one of the pupils.

Stravinsky's limited teaching experience made him leery of presiding over composition classes in English. He had accepted Mlle Boulanger's invitation in 1935 to supervise her course in analysis at the Ecole Normale de Musique with a monetary motive. Maurice Perrin, one of her twelve students (Elliott Carter was another), recalled, 'He said little but his every remark was a horizon. He told us that at the first rehearsal of *Perséphone* the chorus sang "*Reste avec nous*" sentimentally. When he asked why, they said that "the music seems particularly expressive". "Then why do you want to *make* what already is?"'

On 21 November 1939, the *Christian Science Monitor* published an account of one of Stravinsky's classes at Eliot House:

Seated at the piano, Mr Stravinsky grouped about him would-be Stravinskys of the future. Professor Merritt announces the purpose of the session, and Mr Stravinsky invites a volunteer to play for him . . . After some urging, a Mr Jan La Rue of Ann Arbor . . . produces a clarinet and a manuscript. As he begins to play, Mr Stravinsky comes and stands beside him . . . Stravinsky's face is devoid of expression. Then, sitting beside his pupil, Stravinsky proceeds to analyse the work in detail. 'The musical thought is a little difficult to follow in places. This motif should be developed, restated, that idea should be repeated, not verbatim but with interesting variations.' [Another student], William Austin, plays two piano preludes. Sitting beside [him] and turning the pages, Mr Stravinsky occasionally inserts a note in the bass . . . He saves comment until the end. Then, rather harshly, he points out a mixture of styles, a lack of form . . . 'Square-cut' is his word for some of the phrases . . . Then, always punctual, methodical, practical, Mr Stravinsky notes the time and suggests that the meeting should close for the day.

In an interview shortly before leaving Boston, Stravinsky said that his

... meetings with students were the good things that filled me with the best impressions and interest ... No effort is required to listen to the radio. One turns a knob. One can listen without hearing, as we can look without seeing ... The secrets of creation are perhaps in the artist – the secrets of nature. But it is no difficult matter to see how music is made. That can and should be learned.

Here I should add that the third sentence from the end derives from Immanuel Kant and is at the root of Stravinsky's philosophy of art. In the margin of a book by the Russian philosopher Nesmielov, Stravinsky quotes Kant: 'Genius is the innate disposition of the mind (*ingenium*) through which nature gives its rules to art.' A corollary of this is that the artist is himself the source of his gifts and, Stravinsky would have added, is under a sacred obligation to develop them.

The Stravinskys' social acquaintanceship in Cambridge included the sociologist Pitorim Sorokin, the astronomer Harlow Shapley, and the architect Walter Gropius, who had been married to Alma Mahler, widow of Gustav. Otto Klemperer called on the Stravinskys there during a crisis in his manic-depressive illness. 'A very moving encounter,' Vera Stravinsky's diary describes his visit. 'He looks ill but elegant, and he brings a rose.' George Balanchine was a frequent visitor, and the dinners with Koussevitzky became a ritual. The conductor faithfully continued to escort the composer to his lectures.

The Forbes were hosts to the Stravinskys on many occasions after their marriage, and photos show that Nadia Boulanger was often present, helping Stravinsky to correct the score and parts of his Symphony in C. The third movement was finished in the Hemenway Hotel on 27 April 1940.

Only a dwindling few will remember Stravinsky from his year of lecturing, teaching and conducting in Boston, but more will recall his visits as conductor in 1941, 1944, and later years, when he would fulfil two- and three-week stints. Koussevitzky engaged him partly because a composer–conductor was not a competitor, and partly because he found Stravinsky's irregular metres difficult to conduct, and, by the 1940s, the Boston Symphony was expected to programme Stravinsky's music.

On 13 January 1944, Stravinsky opened his Boston Symphony programme with his arrangement of the US National Anthem. After the concert he was detained in his green room by members of the Boston Police Department, who charged him with desecrating national property. A 'mug-shot' was taken of the criminal with a numbered board hanging around his neck: henceforth the composer had a police record. Needless to say, nothing in the version that Stravinsky performed, except the sprawling tune itself, could have offended any listener, and the pity is that Stravinsky never heard his beautiful six-part male-chorus arrangement of the work.

Stravinsky did not conduct the Boston Symphony again after Koussevitzky's death in 1951. I do not know the reasons for this. Henriette Hirshman, the daughter of a wealthy Moscow banker and patron of music, Vladimir Osipovich Hirshman, whom Vera Sudeykina had known in Moscow, was Koussevitzky's and his successor Charles Munch's secretary. She had been a close friend of Igor Stravinsky since 1905 in St Petersburg, and of Vera Stravinsky since 1921 in Paris. Henriette Hirshman was the sister of Paul Léon, James Joyce's legal representative and close friend in his last years in France. During the Stravinskys' visits to New York in the 1950s she called on them regularly. (I met her there in 1955, and at Stravinsky's 1957 New York Philharmonic performance of *Perséphone*.[1]) She told Stravinsky that Maître Munch, with whom he was on good terms and who had conducted the *Canticum Sacrum* in Boston, wished to invite him to conduct the Boston Symphony again. But this did not happen.

Stravinsky's later association with Boston began in 1953

1 She talked constantly, affectionately and perceptively about Joyce, and helped me to persuade the Stravinskys to read him and to visit the Martello tower (first scene of *Ulysses*). Alexis Léon, her nephew, sold the Joyce cache of two hundred manuscript pages to the National Library of Ireland for $11.7m (see the front page of the *New York Times*, 31 May 2002). The collection was retrieved from Joyce's apartment by Paul Léon (he also used the first name 'Noel') when the landlord was threatening to confiscate it for Joyce's unpaid rent. Shortly before Paul Léon was arrested by the Gestapo in 1941 – he died in Auschwitz in April 1942 – he gave the manuscript for safekeeping to Count O'Kelly, the Irish Diplomatic Representative in Paris.

when he conducted *The Rake's Progress* with Sarah Caldwell's Boston University Opera School. At that time Ms Caldwell was not yet conducting orchestras, for which reason I preceded Stravinsky by several days, rehearsing the singers and instrumentalists for him. Ms Caldwell's talents had long been recognized, but this presentation of Stravinsky conducting his opera, the only time he conducted it after the Venice première, except for the two recordings, was a major *coup* for her.

I regret to say that all did not end well, for the reason that when the performance quickly sold out, a repeat matinée was scheduled for the following day with an understudy cast that had not rehearsed with Stravinsky. The exhausted composer failed to give cues to the singers and the performance ended up as a stop-and-start read-through. After it, Max Reinkel, Stravinsky's doctor from MIT since 1949 – I had met him with Stravinsky at that time at a Gerry's Landing party – confined him to bed for two weeks and ordered him to cancel a concert in Chicago. (Reinkel examined me during this period and told Stravinsky that my autonomic nervous system, tension and reflexes were exactly the same as his.)

Another event in Boston, on 22 May 1953, was the meeting between Stravinsky and Dylan Thomas that Sarah Caldwell had arranged in the hope of commissioning an opera from them for Boston University. As we know, Stravinsky was enthusiastic about the project and deeply grieved by the poet's death, as can be heard in his *In Memoriam: Dylan Thomas*.

Stravinsky paid a final visit to Boston, round-trip from New York by automobile, in December 1964, to conduct *Pulcinella*, *Elegy for J.F.K.*, and some other short pieces in Symphony Hall. (I conducted *Abraham and Isaac* and Richard Strauss's *Bourgeois Gentilhomme* Suite on the first half of the programme.) Since Stravinsky's portion of the concert was televised, one hopes that the video still exists and can be seen by future generations.

The story of Stravinsky's American orientation is thus largely an East Coast one, and even in the war years his life as a performer, a conductor of concerts and ballets, brought him to that side of the country more frequently than to the hinterland, which also had fewer top-quality orchestras. While composing *The Rake's*

Progress, he lived in his California home virtually in retreat. The opera was followed by a metamorphosis in his musical–compositional attitudes, with a concomitant reduction in concertizing. The crisis of this development, with the première of *Agon* on his seventy-fifth birthday, coincides with the beginning of the *Conversations*.

The California Years
1940–1969

Symphony in Three Movements, Orpheus, Mass,
The Rake's Progress, Canticum Sacrum, Threni,
Movements for Piano and Orchestra, The Flood,
Abraham and Isaac, Variations, Requiem Canticles

R.C. You were in California in December 1939, before moving there with your wife.

I.S. In December 1939 I travelled to San Francisco for concerts and on to Los Angeles to see what Walt Disney had done to *The Rite of Spring* in *Fantasia*. I returned to New York via Washington, where I spent a few days at Dumbarton Oaks, and, on 13 January 1940, met my bride-to-be, Vera de Bosset Sudeykina, arriving from Genoa on the SS *Rex*. At the end of the spring semester at Harvard, where I was teaching, we sailed from Boston to New York, and from there to Galveston, continuing to Los Angeles by train. I had thought of living somewhere in the hideous but lively Los Angeles conurbation since my first trip, in 1935, mainly for reasons of health, but also because so many of my fellow refugee friends had settled there. It seemed a good place to begin a new, clean-slate life.

Shortly after our arrival, we went to Mexico City for concerts, but primarily because we could re-enter the United States from there and apply for naturalization papers on the Mexican quota, the Russian quota being closed to us. We became United States citizens on 28 December 1945. Edward G. Robinson was my witness – I had known him for several years – but during the proceedings he was discovered to be an illegal resident himself, having 'jumped ship' in New York during World War I. I completed the Symphony in C in a rented house at 124 South Swall Drive, Beverly Hills, where we lived until December. We then moved to the Chateau Marmont, on Sunset Boulevard, for

March and April 1941, going from there to 1260 North Wetherly Drive in Hollywood.

*

R.C. Your *Symphony in Three Movements* was commissioned by the New York Philharmonic as a 'Victory Symphony'. In what ways is the music marked by world events?

I.S. Since it was written under their sign, it must express my reactions to them. Certain specific events excited my musical imagination. Each episode is linked in my mind with a concrete impression of the war, almost always cinematographic in origin. For instance, the beginning of the third movement is partly a musical reaction to newsreels I had seen of goose-stepping soldiers. The square march beat, the brass-band instrumentation, the grotesque crescendo in the tuba – all these are related to those repellent pictures. In spite of contrasting musical episodes, such as the canon for bassoons, the march music predominates until the fugue, the beginning of which marks the stasis and the turning point. The immobility here seems to me comic, and so, to me, was the overturned arrogance of the Germans when their machine failed at Stalingrad. The fugal exposition and the end of the Symphony are associated with the rise of the Allies, and the final, albeit too commercial, D♭ chord – instead of the expected C – is a token of my extra exuberance in the triumph. The rumba in the finale, developed from the timpani part in the introduction to the first movement, was also associated in my imagination with the movements of war machines, while the first movement was inspired by a war film, a documentary of scorched-earth tactics in China. The middle part of the movement – the music for piano, strings and a few winds, which mounts in intensity and volume until the explosion of the three chords at 69 in the rhythm of the *Eroica* – was conceived as a series of instrumental conversations to accompany a cinematographic scene showing the Chinese people scratching and digging in their fields.

The formal substance of the Symphony – perhaps 'Three Symphonic Movements' would be a more exact title – exploits the idea of counter-play among several types of contrasting elements. The most obvious of these is that of harp and piano, the principal instrumental proponants. Each has a large obbligato role and a whole movement to itself. Only at the turning-point fugue, the *queue de poisson* of the Nazi machine, are the two heard together and alone.

But enough of this. In spite of what I have admitted, the Symphony is not programmatic. Composers combine notes. That is all. How and in what form the things of this world are impressed upon their music is not for them to say.

*

R.C. Why did you write a Roman Catholic Mass when you yourself are a member of the Russian Orthodox Church?
I.S. I wanted my *Mass* to be used liturgically, and this was impossible so far as the Russian Church was concerned, since it proscribes musical instruments in its services, and I can endure unaccompanied singing in only the most harmonically primitive music. My *Mass* has been used in Catholic churches rarely, as yet, but used nevertheless. It was partly inspired by some Mozart Masses that I found in a secondhand music store in Los Angeles in 1942 or 1943. As I played through these rococo operatic sweets-of-sin, I knew that I had to write a Mass of my own, but a real one. The Slavonic language of the Russian liturgy has always been the language of prayer for me, in my childhood as now. I was a regular communicant of the Orthodox Church from 1926 to 1939, and again, later, here in America. Though I have lapsed in the last decade – more because of laziness than of intellectual scruple – I still consider myself a Russian Ortho-doxist. Incidentally, I first heard Machaut's *Mass* a year after mine was composed, and I was not influenced in mine by any 'old' music whatever, or guided by any example.

R.C. Your *Psalms* [1930], *Mass* [1948], *Cantata* [1952], *Canticum Sacrum* [1955], and *Threni* [1958] are surely the twentieth century's strongest contributions to church music.
I.S. I hope you are right. Whether or not the Church was the wisest patron – though I think it was; composers commit fewer musical sins in church – it was rich in musical forms. How much poorer we are without the sacred musical services, without the Passions, the round-the-calendar cantatas of the Protestants,

the Masses, the motets, sacred concerts, the Lamentations and the Vespers of the Catholics. These are not defunct forms but parts of the musical spirit in disuse.

The Church knew what the Psalmist knew: music praises God. Music is as well or better able to praise Him than the church building and all its decoration; it is the Church's greatest ornament. Glory, glory, glory; the music of Orlando di Lasso's motet praises God, and this particular 'glory' does not exist in secular music. And not only glory, though I think of it first because the glory of the *Laudate*, the joy of the doxology, is all but extinct. The spirit disappears with the form. I am not comparing 'emotional range' or 'variety' in sacred and secular music. The music of the nineteenth and twentieth centuries is all secular, is 'expressively' and 'emotionally' beyond anything in the music of the earlier centuries: the *Angst* in *Lulu*, for instance – gory, gory, gory – or the tension, the perpetuation of the moment of *epitasis*, in Schoenberg's music. What I am saying is simply that without the Church, 'left to our own devices', we are poorer by many musical forms.

R.C. Did you have an old-masters model for *Threni*, as you had de Lauze's *Apologie de la danse* and Mersenne's musical examples in some of the dances in *Agon*?
I.S. I had studied the *Lamentations* of Tallis and Byrd, but I don't think any 'influence' of these masters can be found in my music.

R.C. Why did you dispense with bar lines in the *Diphonas* and *Elegias* of your *Lamentations*?
I.S. Because the voices are not always in rhythmic unison. Therefore bar lines would cut at least one line arbitrarily. There are rhythmic unison strong beats in these canons, but not always, hence the singer must count out the music as he counts out a motet by Josquin. For the same reasons I have also written half-notes [minims] rather than tying quarter-notes [crotchets] over bars. My notation is more difficult to read, but it is truer.

When I call the nineteenth century 'secular', I mean to distinguish between religious religious music and secular religious music. The latter is inspired by humanity in general, by art, by *Übermensch*, by goodness, and by goodness knows what. Religious music without religion is always vulgar. It can also be dull. There is dull church music from Hucbald to Haydn, but not vulgar church music. Of course, there is vulgar church music now, but it is not really of or for the church. My sacred music is a protest against the Platonic tradition, which has been the Church's tradition through Plotinus and Erigena, of music as anti-moral. Of course Lucifer had music. Ezekiel refers to his 'tabrets and pipes' and Isaiah to the 'noise of his viols'. But Lucifer took his music with him from Paradise, and even in Hell, as Bosch shows, music is able to represent Paradise and become the 'bride of the cosmos'.[1]

The Church's answer is that the corruption comes from musicians, and, indeed, the musical history of the Church is a series of attacks against polyphony, the true musical expression of Western Christendom, until music retired from it in the nineteenth century, or confounded it with the theatre. The corrupting musicians Bosch means are probably Josquin and Ockeghem, the corrupting artefacts the polyphonic marvels of Josquin, Ockeghem, Compère, Brumel.

R.C. Must one be a believer to compose in these forms?

I.S. Certainly, and not merely a believer in 'symbolic figures', but in the Person of the Lord, the Person of the Devil, and the Miracles of the Church.

In 1944, while composing the *Kyrie* and *Gloria*, I was often with Franz Werfel. As early as the spring of 1943, the distinguished poet and dramatist tried to encourage me to write music for his *Song of Bernadette* film. I was attracted by the idea and by his script, and if the conditions, business and artistic, had not been so entirely in favour of the film producer, I might have accepted. I actually did compose music for the 'Apparition of the Virgin' scene; it became the second movement of my *Symphony in Three Movements*. Werfel was a person of acute musical judgement. I remember that when showing him my newly composed *Ode*,[2] he quickly remarked that the first movement was 'a

---

[1] Stravinsky is referring to the right panel of the triptych in the Prado, *The Garden of Earthly Delights*, in which a nude human body is crucified on the strings of a harp. [R.C.]

[2] The middle movement of the *Ode* was originally intended for film use. Orson Welles had urged me to compose the music for his *Jane Eyre*. I read the

kind of fugue with accompaniment'. I respected and admired him for other qualities, of course, and above all for his courage and sense of humour. Werfel was an attractive person, with large, lucid, magnetic eyes. We were regular guests in each other's homes during the war. I recall seeing him for the last time in his house one evening when we were together with Thomas Mann. Soon after I stood in a mortuary grieving for him.

R.C. Thomas Mann mentions an evening at Werfel's during which he says you talked about Schoenberg. Do you remember this?

I.S. Yes, and I seem to remember having expressed the opinion that *Pierrot Lunaire* should be recorded without voice so that the record buyer could add the ululations himself, a 'do-it-yourself' record. But I associate Werfel less with Schoenberg than with Berg and Kafka (Werfel had known both men well), and I recall some of Werfel's talk about them. Mann was interested in musical discussions, and his own favourite theme was that music is the art most remote from life, the art that needs no experience. Mann was a professorial figure, with an erect, stiff-necked, military posture, characteristically, and with his left hand often in his coat pocket. The portrait he draws of himself in *A Sketch of Myself*, and the personality that emerges from his *Letters to Paul Amann* are not – to me – very sympathetic. But never mind. He was personally courageous and intellectually persistent. I had known him since early Diaghilev days in Munich, where he came to the performances of our Ballet, and I saw him again there in January 1933, and in the 1920s in Zurich. I like his description of my wife in the following account of an evening together in Hollywood:

A conversation with Stravinsky at a party in our house sticks in my memory with remarkable clarity. We talked about Gide – Stravinsky expressed his ideas in German, French and English – then about literary 'confessions' as a product of the different culture spheres, the Greek-Orthodox, the Latin-Catholic, and the Protestant. In Stravinsky's opinion, Tolstoy was essentially German and Protestant . . .

———

book and, charmed by it, composed this piece for one of the hunting scenes. All of my aborted film music – the *Norwegian Moods*, the *Eclogue* [*Ode*], the middle movement of the 1945 Symphony, and the *Scherzo à la Russe* – belongs to the years 1942–44.

Stravinsky's wife is a *'belle Russe'*, beautiful through and through, a specifically Russian type of beauty in which the sympathetic human quality is at its very height.[3]

(My wife *is* beautiful, but she has not a single pinprick of Russian blood.)

*

R.C. Did Mann ever mention his son-in-law, Auden, and do you think he had read Auden?

I.S. No to both. The family connection never came up, though when Mann was in Chicago for his cancer operation, Auden and Isherwood stayed in his Pacific Palisades house. Unlike Auden, Mann was stiff and formal. But I loved Auden in every sense, as human being and artist, and he fascinated me more the longer I knew him. In November 1947, when we were working on the *Rake* libretto, he would explain verse forms to me, and compose examples almost as quickly as he could write. I still have a specimen sestina and some light verse that he scribbled for my wife. Any technical question of versification put him in a passion about which he could be eloquent. The making of poetry he seemed to regard as a game, albeit to be played in a magic circle. The latter had already been drawn, and the poet's task, as he considered it, was to redefine and be the custodian of its rules. All his conversation about art was, so to speak, *sub specie ludi*. I still remember some of the things he said on that first visit – though not his exact words. He was forever putting forth little scholastic or psychoanalytic propositions: 'Angels are pure intellect'; 'Tristan and Isolde were unloved only children'; Pelléas suffered from 'alarming trichomaniac tendencies'; 'The sign of a man's loss of power is when he ceases to care about punctuality' (Auden himself lived by the clock – 'I am hungry only if the clock says it is time to eat'); 'A woman has lost her power when she stops caring about dress.'

At first I was puzzled by what I mistook to be contradictions in his personality. He would sail on steady rudders of reason and logic, yet profess to superstitious beliefs – in graphology, for

3 In *Die Entstehung des Doktor Faustus*, under the date August 1943.

instance (I have a graphologist's chart with an analysis of his and
my writing, the souvenir of an evening in Venice), in astrology
in the telepathic powers of cats, in black magic (as described in
Charles Williams's novels), in categories of temperament (I was
a 'Dionysian' if I happened to work at night), in preordination
in Fate. Another, though more apparent than real, contradiction
in him was his display of good citizenship. However lofty his
criticism of society, he was almost too conscientious in fulfilling
his everyday democratic duties. He would even serve on juries
(I remember him having stalled one for two weeks [in February
1949]: 'Not for Justice, of course – I quite understood the point
of that – but because the housewife jurists were motivated purely
by revenge against the taxi driver.') He was properly outraged
by our failure to vote.

I recall only two events of his 1947 visit, apart from our
work. One day he complained of pressure in his ears. We took
him to a doctor, who removed large globes of wax from each
one. Auden was intrigued by this and kept referring to the
'extraordinary little creatures' that had been harbouring in his
auditory canals. We also attended a two-piano performance of
Così fan tutte together – an omen, perhaps, for the Rake is
deeply involved in Così.

But I have strayed.

The following letter came from Auden after his return to
New York:

7 Cornelia Street
New York 14, N.Y.

Dear Mrs. Stravinsky:

First, an account of my stewardship, I have

(a) Posted the letter to the Guggenheim Foundation.

(b) Called Miss Bean.

(c) Called Mr. Heinsheimer

The journey was a nightmare. The flight was cancelled; I was trans
ferred to an American Airlines local, which left at 7:00 A.M., stopped
everywhere, and reached New York at 4 A.M. this morning. The meals
as usual, would have tried the patience of a stage curate, so you can
imagine what I felt, after a week of your luxurious cuisine. And finally
of course, I got back here to a pile of silly letters to answer – a job I
loathe. The only consolation is the pleasure of my writing to you this
bread-and-butter letter (how do you say that in Russian?). I loved every

minute of my stay, thanks to you both, and shall look forward with impatience to the next time we meet.

Greetings to Vassily, *Das krankheitliebendes Fräulein*, Popka, Mme Sokolov, *La Baroness des Chats*, etc.[4]

Yours ever,

WYSTAN AUDEN

P.S. Could you give the enclosed note to the maestro?

Du Syllabiste – Au compositeur
Cher Igor Stravinsky,
Memo. Act I, Sc. 1,

Je crois que ça sera mieux si c'est un oncle inconnu du héros au lieu de son père qui meurt, parce que comme cà, la richesse est tout à fait imprévue, et la note pastorale n'est pas interrompue par le douleur, seulement par la présence sinister du villain. En ce cas, la girl possèdera pas un oncle, pas un père.

Êtes-vous d'accord? Je tiendrai silence pour oui,

WYSTAN AUDEN

P.S. I can't tell you what a pleasure it is to collaborate with you. I was so frightened that you might be a *prima donna*.

Salut au 'making'.

*

R.C. What about Mann and Schoenberg? Did you read *Dr Faustus*?

I.S. No, and neither did Schoenberg. I saw his copy of it in his studio after his death.

R.C. Can you add to what you have said about Schoenberg?

I.S. I had heard his name as early as 1907, but *Pierrot Lunaire* was the first contact with his music that I remember, although Prokofiev played two of his opus 11 pieces in a St Petersburg concert whose date I do not recall. I had not seen any score by him before *Pierrot Lunaire* either. I do not know how the Berlin

---

4 Vassily was our cat, the 'illness-loving Fräulein' was our housekeeper, Evgenia Petrovna, and Popka was our parrot. We had forty parrots and love-birds at that time, Popka being the special favourite of Evgenia Petrovna; a relationship alarmingly like that in Flaubert's *Félicité* obtained between them. Mme Sokolov was the wife of the actor Vladimir and our dear friend and neighbour. The Baroness Catherine d'Erlanger, another friend and neighbour, was overly devoted to two Persian cats.

meeting with him came about, but it must have been initiated by Diaghilev, who hoped to commission a work by Schoenberg. I remember sitting with Schoenberg, his wife Mathilde, and Diaghilev at a performance of *Petrushka*, and I have a clear memory of Schoenberg in his green room after he had conducted the fourth performance of *Pierrot Lunaire* in the Choralion-Saal, 4 Bellevuestrasse, Sunday, 8 December 1912, at twelve noon. I still have my cancelled ticket. Albertine Zehme, the *Sprechstimme* artist, wore a 'Pierrot' costume and accompanied her epiglottal sounds with a small amount of pantomime. I remember that the musicians were seated behind a curtain, but I was concentrating too closely on the copy of a score Schoenberg had given me to notice anything else. I also remember that the audience was quiet and attentive, and that I wanted Frau Zehme to be quiet too, so that I could hear the *music*. Diaghilev and I were greatly impressed with *Pierrot*, though he classified it as *Jugendstil*.

I encountered Schoenberg several times during my short stay in Berlin, and I was in his home at least once. (I arrived at the Adlon Hotel from Switzerland on 20 November 1912; I remember that I had been working on the orchestra score of *The Rite of Spring* on the train.) Schoenberg was small in stature. I am 5 feet and 3 inches and weigh 120 pounds. These measurements were exactly the same fifty years ago, but I remember Schoenberg as slightly shorter than I was. He was bald, too, with a wreath of black hair around the rim of his white cranium, like a Japanese actor's mask. He had large ears and a soft, deep voice – not as *basso* as mine – with a mellow, Viennese accent. His eyes were protuberant and explosive, and the whole force of the man was in them. I did not know then what I know now, which is that in the three years prior to *Pierrot*, Schoenberg had written the *Five Pieces for Orchestra*, *Erwartung*, and *Die glückliche Hand*, a body of works that we now recognize as the centre of the development of our musical language in 1909–10. (By 'we' I mean a small group still, for most composers are still bumping into each other in the dark.) The real wealth of *Pierrot* – sound and substance, for *Pierrot* is the solar plexus as well as the mind of early twentieth-century music – was beyond me as it was beyond all of us at that time. I was aware, nevertheless, that this was the most prescient meeting in my life, though the future is never an idea in one's mind, is never part of one's thoughts at such moments. Time does not pass but only *we* pass, and I do not know *more* than I did then, for the quality of my knowledge is different, but I did know and recognize the power of the man and his music at that meeting half a century ago.

Shortly after the performance of *Pierrot*, Schoenberg left for St Petersburg to conduct his *Pelleas und Melisande*. We were on good terms at parting, but we never met again. In Morges, in 1919, I received a cordial letter from him asking for pieces of my chamber music to include in his Vienna concerts, 'The Society for Private Performances'. I wrote and he wrote again. Then, in 1920, I heard *Pierrot* in Paris, conducted by Darius Milhaud and quasi-sung by Marya Freund. After that, incredibly, I did not hear another note by Schoenberg until the *Suite*, op. 29, in Venice in 1937 and the *Prelude to Genesis* in Hollywood in November 1945.[5] At the later occasion we might well have met, since we were in the recording studio at the same time, but sitting on opposite sides of the room. We were also both in the Wilshire Ebell Theater for the première of the *Genesis Suite*.

Schoenberg conducted his *Serenade* in Venice in September 1925, and I played my Piano Sonata there the next day. I did not hear his piece, but he heard mine, and back in Vienna reported that I had turned in a mistaken direction. When I came to Los Angeles in 1935, Klemperer brought Schoenberg to one of my concerts with the Los Angeles Philharmonic,[6] but we did not meet. I saw Schoenberg for the last time in 1949, when he appeared on stage and read a delicately ironic speech acknowledging the honour of the freedom of the city of Vienna just conferred on him by the Austrian consul. I remember that he repeatedly addressed the consul as 'Excellency', and that he read from large sheets of paper extracted one by one from his pocket, his eyesight being very poor, and each page containing only a few words. Even on such an occasion, instead of an all-Schoenberg programme, only the early *Kammersymphonie* was played.

5 Stravinsky heard the première of Schoenberg's *Music to Accompany an Imaginary Film Scene*, in Berlin in 1930, conducted by Klemperer. [R.C.]
6 The correct date is 11 March 1937. [R.C.]

Two days after Schoenberg's death, during a visit to Mrs Mahler-Werfel, I happened to see Schoenberg's not-yet-dry death mask, unwrapped for me by her sculptress daughter, Annie Mahler. Less than a year later, his *Erwartung* and my *Oedipus Rex* – an unthinkable juxtaposition just a few years before – were performed together in Paris by Hans Rosbaud, as a double bill.

*

R.C. You were on friendly terms with Sergey Rakhmaninov in California during the last years of his life. What are your memories of him there?

I.S. To think of Rakhmaninov is to think of a scowl. He was a six-and-a-half-foot scowl. I do not mean that he was dour or unfriendly, but he was by no means outgoing, and to sustain social relations with him required perseverance. In fact, my meetings with him during our mutual California period were rather with his wife, for he remained silent. Late one night in the summer of 1941 he came to my house in Hollywood bearing the gift of a pot of honey, which he left on my doorstep, one of our mutual Russian friends having told him that I was fond of it. The lateness of the hour was because he wanted to avoid me. For some reason he was frightened of me, or perhaps of *The Rite of Spring*, although he told mutual Russian refugee friends that he thought *Firebird* the greatest creation in all Russian music. People had told him that I did not like his music, and it is true that we composed very differently at the time. Nevertheless, I was moved by the thought of him climbing the steep steps to my door. After all, I had often heard him perform in Russia in my youth, and had admired his music when I was composing my first sonata.

The conversation during one of our dinners together was concerned with my matutinals:

MME RAKHMANINOV: What is the first thing you do when you rise in the morning, Igor Fyodorovich?

MYSELF: For fifteen minutes I do exercises learned from a Hungarian gymnast and Kneipp Kur maniac called Siposs. Or rather, I did them until I learned that he had died very young and very suddenly. Then I stand on my head against a wall, then take a shower.

MME RAKHMANINOV: You see, Sergey, *Stravinsky* takes showers. How extraordinary. Do you still say you are afraid of them? And you heard Stravinsky say that he exercises? What do you think of that? Shame on you who will hardly take a walk.

RAKHMANINOV: (*Silence.*)

I remember Rakhmaninov's earliest compositions. They were 'watercolours', songs and piano pieces freshly influenced by Tchaikovsky. Then at twenty-five he turned to 'oils' and became a very old composer. But do not expect me to denigrate him for that. In fact he was an awesome man, and there are too many others to be denigrated long before him. As I think about him, his silence looms as a noble contrast to the self-approbations that are the only conversation of most musicians. Besides, he was the only pianist I have ever seen who did not grimace when he played. That says a great deal.

*

R.C. Which conductor in America do you admire the most?

I.S. Dimitri Mitropoulos had conducted *Petrushka* and *The Soldier's Tale*, but as a missionary of Mahler and a specialist in the *Alpine Symphony*, he could not have had any serious interest in my music. This explains my surprise when he came to call on me in Hollywood one summer evening in 1945. He spoke French, mixed with Slav and German words, which, together with his wobbly movements, was somehow endearing. We talked about the Orthodox Church and examined my collection of icons. The next day I attended his rehearsal of Prokofiev's Third Piano Concerto in Hollywood Bowl and was amazed by the virtuosity of his performance, playing the solo part and conducting at the same time. But Mitropoulos was not only a freakishly gifted man, he was also gentle, humble, generous and very kind. His premature death in Milan in 1960 shocked and saddened me. I had last seen him conduct Schoenberg's *A Survivor from Warsaw* in Carnegie Hall and was greatly impressed by the music and by him.

*

R.C. Did you have a narrative or choreographic scheme in mind when composing the *Scènes de Ballet*?

1.s. When Billy Rose telephoned one spring day in 1944 with an offer of $5,000 for a fifteen-minute ballet suite, he said that my solo dancers would be Alicia Markova and Anton Dolin, and that Dolin would compose the choreography. But in fact the choreography was my own, in the sense that I conceived the sequence, character and proportions of the individual pieces and visualized the dance construction of this plotless, 'abstract' ballet as I composed. In fact, no other score of mine prescribes a choreographic plan so closely.

The orchestral introduction exposes two identifying devices, the blues chord, and the melodic-pull idea, meaning the oboe melody in the *Apotheosis*. The curtain opens on the corps de ballet dancing in groups. A melody in 5/8 time is played by four violas and danced by four ballerinas. The idea of the *Pantomime* was that different groups of dancers should enter from different positions, each group in co-ordination with one of the arpeggiated figures in the music. The *Andantino* is a solo dance for the ballerina. When I first played it to Markova and Dolin, in my Hollywood home, they said the flute cascades suggested falling stars, but I am unaware whether any such pictorial business was realized in the performance, or even whether this part of the piece was performed at all. My only scenic idea was that the ballerina should wear a black tutu with diamond sequins, her partner a classical gilet.

The *Pas de deux* trumpet solo is associated with the male dancer, the horn solo with the female, but the shapes of the instruments, yin–yang, tell you that. The frilled phrase-endings in the ballerina's *Allegretto* were conceived as possibilities for pirouettes. The recapitulation of the *Pas de deux* with the full orchestra now sounds to me like movie music: the happy homesteaders, having massacred the Indians, begin to plant their corn. In the last two bars of this number, the solo dancers disappear at opposite sides of the stage. The orchestral *tutti* that follows is the male dancer's solo variation, the cello duet is the ballerina's solo. The final *Pantomime* unites the solo dancers, and the remainder of the score, from the 3/8 jazz movement to the *Apotheosis*, assembles the whole company. For the finale, I envisaged a stage full of groups twirling in a mounting '*delirando*'.

The story of the first performance of *Scènes de Ballet* is all too worldly. Page by page, as I completed the orchestra score, my friend Ingolf Dahl arranged it for piano. Mr Rose professed to like the music in this piano version, or so I was told, but not my orchestral cellophane. When *The Seven Lively Arts*, the show for which it was composed, opened in New York, my music had to be drastically cut since the orchestra could not play in 5/8 time. After the Philadelphia preview, I received a telegram from Rose: YOUR MUSIC GREAT SUCCESS STOP COULD BE SENSATIONAL SUCCESS IF YOU WOULD AUTHORIZE ROBERT RUSSELL BENNETT RETOUCH ORCHESTRATION STOP BENNETT ORCHESTRATES EVEN THE WORKS OF COLE PORTER. I telegraphed back: SATISFIED GREAT SUCCESS.

Scènes de Ballet is a period piece, a portrait of Broadway in the last year of the war, and the mood is upbeat. It is featherweight and sugared, my sweet tooth not yet being carious, but I will not deprecate it, not even the second *Pantomime*, and all of it is at least well made. I still like the *Apotheosis*, especially the voicing of the chords at the beginning, with the repetition of the upper line in canon and in different harmonic contexts. The *Apotheosis* was composed on the day of the liberation of Paris. I remember that I interrupted my work every few minutes to listen to the radio reports. I think my jubilation is in the music.

*

I began the four-hands Sonata before, and completed it after, *Scènes de Ballet*. At first I thought of it as a piece for one performer. Then, when I saw that four hands were required to voice the four lines clearly, I redesigned it for two pianos. I have played it publicly only once, at a Mills College students' concert with Nadia Boulanger as my partner. I was staying with Darius Milhaud then, and the Sonata reminds me of an incident concerning the Milhauds' plumbing. One morning the drains stopped functioning. A plumber came, but we soon found that an archaeologist would have been more appropriate. Trenches had to be dug. The Milhauds had been emptying coffee grounds down the sink for years, and the pipe from their house to the street was silted solid with them.

*

R.C. What prompted your arrangement of *The Star-Spangled Banner*?

I.S. A patriotic feeling and a desire to improve the orchestrations then in use. I wrote it on 4 July 1940, and it was first performed in Hollywood Bowl,[7] 27 August 1940, conducted by me, at the beginning of a staged performance of *Firebird* that was repeated on the 30th. Afterward I sent the manuscript to Mrs Roosevelt for a War Fund auction, but one of my chords in the second strain of the piece, the part patriotic ladies like best, must have distressed some official, since the manuscript was returned to me with an apology. I then gave it to Klaus Mann, who auctioned it for war relief. When I performed it with the Boston Symphony, 14 January 1944, I stood with my back to the orchestra and conducted the audience, which was supposed to sing, but didn't. No one seemed to notice that my arrangement differed from the standard version. The following year I arranged the piece for *a cappella* male chorus with a far superior harmonization, but I have never heard it.

*

R.C. What were the origins of your pieces for so-called jazz and other popular band ensembles – the *Circus Polka*, *Scherzo à la Russe*, *Ebony Concerto* – and how do you regard this music today?

I.S. These pieces were journeyman jobs, commissions I was forced to accept because the war in Europe had so suddenly reduced the income from my compositions. The idea of the *Circus Polka* was George Balanchine's. He wanted a short piece for a ballet of elephants, one of whom was to carry Vera Zorina, his actress wife. The quotation from the *Marche militaire* came to me naturally, and I resent the characterization of my use of it as a parody. The music was first performed by the Ringling Brothers' Circus Band in David Raksin's arrangement for wind

7 A letter from Mrs Stravinsky to Ira Belline in Paris describes the occasion: 'A concert in the Bowl entails many difficulties. Try to imagine 20,000 people all with their own automobiles . . . it takes a half-hour to park and as long again to walk uphill, after which you must walk a considerable distance to find your seat. Most women sit in fur coats, for no matter how hot in the daytime, the Bowl is always very cool at night.' [R.C.]

band and organ. Once, after conducting a broadcast of my orchestral version, I received a congratulatory telegram from Bessie, the young pachyderm who had borne the belle ballerina and who had heard the broadcast in the circus's winter quarters at Sarasota. I never saw the ballet, but I met Bessie in Los Angeles and shook her paw.

The *Scherzo à la Russe* was commissioned by Paul Whiteman for a special radio broadcast. I originally wrote it to the specifications of his ensemble, then rewrote it for standard orchestra – which gave me some trouble, since the volume of harp and guitar in the trio canon was so much lighter than that of harp and piano. Whiteman conducted the first performance himself, much too rapidly. He and others professed to hear reminiscences of *Petrushka* in it.

The *Ebony Concerto* was also written for a prescribed instrumentation, to which I added a French horn. Mr Woody Herman wanted the piece for a concert already scheduled, and I had to compose it in a few weeks. My plan was to write a jazz *concerto grosso* with a blues slow movement. I studied recordings of the Herman band and enlisted a saxophonist to teach me fingerings. 'Ebony' does not mean 'clarinet', incidentally, but 'African'. The only jazz I had heard in the United States was in Harlem, and by bands in Chicago and New Orleans, and the jazz performers I most admired at that time were Art Tatum, Charlie Parker and the guitarist Charles Christian. To me, 'blues' meant African culture.

I conducted the recording in Los Angeles some weeks after the première performed by Walter Hendl and the New York Philharmonic. All that I remember of my recording session was the smoke in the studio. When the musicians did not blow horns they blew smoke, and of such tangibility that the atmosphere looked like Pernod clouded by water. Their instrumental mastery was astonishing, but so was their lack of *solfeggio*. Of the four pieces you name, I like *Ebony Concerto* best, though it is remote from me now, like the work of a sympathetic colleague I once knew well.

*

[At the time of the Boston Opera production of *The Rake's Progress* in 1953, Mrs Stravinsky was asked to contribute a memoir of the première in Venice, 11 September 1951, for the programme booklet. She called the piece 'La Prima Assoluta':]

It was a night of stifling heat and sirocco. The alleys near the theatre were roped off to keep the Fourth Estate at bay during the arrival procession, although most of those in Estates 1–3 did not arrive on foot but were deposited directly at the side canal entrance to the theatre by gondolas and motor launches. Our own (pedestrian) party included Nadia Boulanger, who carried Igor's valise, Wystan Auden and Chester Kallman (both nervous in spite of liquid fortifications – a moat of Martinis, in fact), Dr David Protetch, Auden's physician friend.

Among the immediately familiar faces in the foyer, one remotely familiar one veered toward me with an expression of great excitement. It was Zinovy Peshkov, Maxim Gorky's adopted son, last seen in the Caucasus during the Russian Revolution. But General Peshkov[8] was soon crowded out by other old friends who came to criticize and otherwise 'assist' at the performance.

The Fenice glittered that night in honour of the début, with bouquets of roses, like débutantes' corsages, garnishing each loge. But the beauty of these stalls on the inside was even less than 'skin deep', the plush seemingly having suffered from moth-pox. They were also in need of deodorants, which may have been part of the reason for the roses. The seats were uncomfortable, and they faced each other, as they do in European railroad compartments, so that the occupants on the stage side (i.e. the men, if polite) face toward the rear of the theatre, an arrangement more suited to grasshoppers, whose ears are said to be encased in their abdomens and legs. The audience glittered, except for the man from the *New York Times*,[9] whose jobbery on the event proved to be consistent not only with his apparel but with his lifelong devotion to the commonplace.

In Italy, nothing respectable begins on time. During the long

8 See Harold Macmillan's memoirs for a view of 'Colonel Pechkoff' of the Gaullist mission in North Africa during World War II. [R.C.]
9 Harold Taubman.

delay before the curtain my thoughts drifted back through the weeks of preparation to the first conferences with stage directors and conductors. These took place in Naples, where I spent my own mornings in the aquarium, as Paul Klee once did, drawing an old *jolie laide* crustacean, a 'liquid prisoner pent in walls of glass'. I thought, too, during the wait, about some of the echoes in the opera from Igor's so-called private life: the card game, for example; the harpsichord arpeggios imitating Igor's way of shuffling cards; and the *staccato* of that instrument recalling his way of snapping them on a table. Auden had seen Igor playing solitaire and he may have heard him vent some Russian *gros mots* when the wrong card appeared, which in turn may have suggested the idea for 'The Deuce!' I thought, too, how the pointing to the audience in the Epilogue – 'you and you' – was inspired by Walter Huston in *The Devil and Daniel Webster*, a film Igor liked.

At 21:35, a prompt thirty-five minutes late, Igor entered the pit and bowed low to the audience, which, though ultra *demi-mondaine*, seemed to applaud him with a core of genuine appreciation. He then turned to the orchestra so that only his extraordinary occipital bumps and small, vital beat were visible, and began. The singers were Robert Rounseville, who had not quite fully emerged from a career on Broadway, but who was aptly cast as Tom Rakewell; Elisabeth Schwarzkopf, who was a cool and perfect Anne; Hugues Cuenod, a subtle Sellem; and Jennie Tourel, who as the diva Baba could have managed her grand exit on an elephant without risking a snigger. At first-act intermission we retired to the Campo San Fantin to drink *caffè espresso*, avoid impertinent judgements, and revel in the memory of Frl. Schwarzkopf's high C. But a literary friend of Auden's joined us here and noted that the phrase 'and small birds twitter' (in the brothel chorus) occurs in Wordsworth's poems (1807).

Igor used to claim no more for the music than that it was conventional. But what beautiful *in*ventions are in it, too: the harmonic progressions at the end of the first half of the *cavatina*, the modulation to 'O wilful powers', the transformation of the ballad tune in the final scenes, and the style-embalmed representations of Tom's fear in the graveyard (the double *appoggiaturas*), and their reappearance during his mad scene. It seemed that Igor had saved his most beautiful inspirations for the ending, in 'Venus, mount thy throne', in the 'foolish dream' duet, and in 'Where art thou, Venus?', which, to me, is some of the most touching music he ever wrote.

The *'prima assoluta'* was a tentative performance in many ways, at times almost falling apart, in fact, and everywhere showing 'might' more as the preterite of 'may' than in the sense of power. Nevertheless, it conveyed much of the opera's true feeling, and I think everyone except the unglittering New Yorker was moved. We went afterward to a post-mortem party at the Taverna Fenice that did not break up until the bleary dawn.

*

I.S. If the greatest crisis in my life as a composer was the loss of Russia, the second greatest followed *The Rake's Progress*, though I was not aware of it as such at the time, continuing as I did to move from work to work. The 'period of adjustment' was even longer, and looking back on it now I am surprised myself at how long I continued to straddle tonality and atonality. Was it because at seventy unlearning is as difficult as learning? In any case, I now see the *Movements for Piano and Orchestra* [1959] as the turn of the corner in my later music.

*

R.C. Would you say something about the *Movements*?
I.S. I have discovered new serial combinations in them, and in the process realized that I am becoming not less but more of a serial composer. The *Movements* are the most 'advanced' music from the point of view of construction of anything I have composed. No theorist could determine the spelling of the note order in, for example, the flute solo near the beginning, or the derivation of the three Fs announcing the last movement simply by knowing the original order, however unique the combinatorial properties of this particular series. Every aspect of the composition was guided by serial forms, the sixes, quadrilaterals, triangles, etc. The fifth movement, for instance (which cost me much effort – I rewrote it twice), uses a construction of twelve verticals. Five orders are rotated instead of four, with six

alternates for each of the five, while, at the same time, the six 'work' in all directions, as though through a crystal.

Now that I have mentioned my new work I should say, too, that its rhythmic language is also the most 'advanced' I have so far employed; perhaps some listeners might even detect a hint of serialism in it too. My polyrhythmic combinations are meant to be heard vertically, however, unlike those of some of my colleagues. Though parallels are not equivalents, look at Josquin for a parallel, that marvellous second *Agnus Dei* (the three-voice one) in the *Missa l'homme armé*, or at Baude's *Pour le default du dieu Bacchus*, or, for even more remarkable examples, at the Cyprus Codex.

Each section of the piece is confined to a certain range of instrumental timbre (another suggestion of serialism), but the movements are related more by tempo than by contrasts of such things as timbre, mood, character; in a span of only twelve minutes, the contrast of an *andante* with an *allegro* would make little sense. Perhaps the most significant development in the *Movements* is in their tendency towards anti-tonality – in spite of long pedal-point passages such as the C of the first ending, the clarinet trill at the end of the third movement, and the string harmonies in the fourth movement. I am amazed at this myself, in view of the fact that in *Threni* simple triadic references occur so frequently.

*

R.C. Would you analyse your own composing process in any part of one of your more recent pieces – in, for example, the little *Epitaphium*?

I.S. I began the *Epitaphium* with the flute–clarinet duet, which I had originally thought of as a duet for two flutes, and which can be played by two flutes; the piece was written to be performed in a programme with Webern's songs, op. 15, which use the flute–clarinet combination. I heard and composed a melodic– harmonic phrase. I certainly did not, and never do, begin with a purely serial idea, and in fact when I began, I did not know, or care, whether all twelve notes would be used. But after I had written about half of the first phrase, I saw its serial pattern and began to work towards it. The constructive problem that first attracted me in the two-part counterpoint of the first phrase was the harmonic one of minor seconds. The flute–clarinet responses are mostly seconds, and so are the harp responses, though the harp part is sometimes complicated by the addition of third, fourth and fifth harmonic voices. The harp in this piece, as in all my music, must be pinched *près de la table* to produce the sound I want. The deep bass notes of the harp are, I think, the instrument's most beautiful range.

Only after I had written this little twelve-note duet did I conceive the idea of a series of funeral responses between bass and treble instruments, and as I wanted the whole piece to be muted, I decided that the bass instrument should be a harp. The first bar of the harp part was written last. As I worked the music out, it became a kind of hymn, like Purcell's *Funeral Music for Queen Mary*. There are four short antiphonal strophes for the harp, and four for the wind duet, and each strophe employs a complete order of the series – harp: O, I, R, RI; winds: O, RI, R, I.

*

R.C. What was the subject of the 'opera' you had planned to write with Dylan Thomas?

I.S. I don't think you can say that the project ever got as far as having a subject, but Dylan had an intriguing idea.

Curiously, I first heard of Thomas from Auden, in New York, in February or March of 1950. Coming late to an appointment one day, Auden excused himself by saying he had been busy helping to extricate an English poet from some sort of difficulty. He then told me about Dylan Thomas. I read him after that, and in Urbana, also in early 1950, my wife went to hear him read. Two years later, in January 1952, an English film producer, Michael Powell, came to see me in Hollywood with a project I found very attractive. He proposed to make a short film of a scene from the *Odyssey*; two or three arias as well as pieces of pure instrumental music and recitations of poetry would be required. Saying that Thomas had agreed to write the verse, he asked me to compose the music. Where were the angels, even the Broadway kind, and why are the world's commissions, grants, funds, foundations never available to the Dylan Thomases? I regret that this project was not realized. *The Doctor and the Devils* film script proves, I think, that the poet's talent could have created the medium.

Then in May 1953 Boston University proposed to commission me to write an opera with him. I was in Boston at the time, and Dylan came to see me. I was confined to bed on doctors' orders, exhausted from conducting an under-rehearsed *Rake* the day before. As soon as I saw the poet, from my bed, I knew that the only thing to do was to love him. He was nervous, chain-smoking the whole time, and he complained of severe gout pains . . . 'But I prefer the gout to the cure; I'm not going to let a doctor shove those bayonets into me.'

He was a shorter man than I expected from his portraits, about five feet five, with a large protuberant behind and belly. His face and skin had the colour and swelling of too much drinking, his nose was a red bulb, and his eyes were glazed. He drank a glass of whisky with me, which put him more at ease, though he kept worrying about his wife, saying he had to hurry home to Wales 'or it would be too late'. He talked to me about *The Rake's Progress*. He had heard the first broadcast from Venice, knew the libretto well, and admired it: 'Auden is the most skilful of us all.' I don't know how much he knew about music, but he talked about the operas he knew and loved, and about what he wanted to do. His opera was to be about the rediscovery of our planet following an atomic disaster. There would be a re-creation of language, and the new one would have no abstractions: there would be only people, objects and words. He promised to avoid poetic indulgences: 'No conceits, I'll knock them all on the head.' He talked to me about Yeats, 'the greatest lyric poet since Shakespeare', and recited from memory the poem with the refrain 'Daybreak and a candle-end'. He agreed to come to me in Hollywood as soon as he could. Returning there, I had an extension from our dining room built for him, since we have no guest room. I received two letters from him. I wrote to him in New York on 25 October, asking him for word of his arrival plans. I expected a telegram from him announcing the hour of his airplane. On 9 November the telegram came. It said he was dead. All I could do was cry.[10]

*

10 That evening Stravinsky drew a heart-wrenching cross over Thomas's name in his address book. [R.C.]

R.C. A word about Ortega y Gasset.

I.S. I saw him in Madrid, in March 1955, but felt I knew him from his work long before. He came to my hotel with Mme La Marquise de Slauzol, and we drank a bottle of whisky together and became *exalté*. He was charming and very kind. I have often thought that he must have known at the time that he had cancer, since he was dead only a few months later. He was not tall, but I remember him as a large man because of his great head, which was that of a Roman statesman or philosopher, and I tried all evening to recall just which one he most resembled. He spoke vivid r-rolling French in a strong, slightly husky voice. Everything he said was vivid. The Tagus at Toledo was 'arterio-sclerotic'; Cordoba was 'a rosebush but with the flowers in the ground, the roots in the air'. The art of the Portuguese 'is their memory of China, of pagodas'. Of his philosopher contempo-raries, he spoke reverently of Scheler, of Husserl, of his master Cohen, of Heidegger. As for the Wittgenstein school: 'Philosophy calling itself logical positivism now claims to be a science, but this is only a brief attack of modesty.' He talked about Spain (I regret his *Castles in Castile* does not exist in English) and laughed at tourists' sympathy for 'the poor people living in caves', which he said they do not do out of poverty but because it is an ancient tradition. He was interested in and intel-ligent about the United States when we talked of it – the unique European 'intellectual' I encountered that trip who knew some-thing beyond what he had read in Melville and the magazines. He proudly showed me a photograph, taken from his wallet, of himself and Gary Cooper in Aspen in 1949. He said that Thornton Wilder had translated for him there, but that his audiences had understood before the translations came, 'because of my extravagant gestures'.

*

R.C. What are your personal recollections of Evelyn Waugh, Gerald Heard, Christopher Isherwood, Aldous Huxley?

I.S. When I met Mr Waugh, in New York in February 1949, his popping blue eyes looked askance at me, and I soon found that the cutting edge in the books was even sharper in the per-son: he was not an endearing character. I admired his talent for dialogue and the naming of characters (Dr Kakaphilos, Father Rothschild SJ), and in person I admired, even while suffering from, the agility with which he caused my remarks to boomerang. But whether Mr Waugh was disagreeable, or only preposterously arch, I cannot say. I addressed him in French at first, and he replied that he did not speak the language. His wife contradicted him charmingly, and was harshly rebuked. I asked whether he would care for a whisky and was told, 'I do not drink whisky before meals', stated as a universal fact I should have known. I made an admiring remark about the Constitution of the United States and was reminded that Mr Waugh is a Tory. I used the word 'music' and was told that music is physical torment to him. We talked at length only about US burial customs, and here his impressive technical knowledge suggested that he was gathering material for a doctorate on mausoleums. (After reading *The Loved One*, I visited Forest Lawn and the Hollywood Pet Cemetery.) At dinner I recommended the chicken, but this was a new *gaffe*. 'It's Friday.' But by the time the meatless meal was over and he had peeled, sucked and blown a cigar, the clipped conversation was succeeded by some almost amiable sentences.

Gerald, Christopher and Aldous are dear and intimate friends – loved ones, in fact, though not in Mr Waugh's sense.

Gerald is a virtuoso talker, and he *likes* to talk, just as Artur Rubinstein *likes* to play the piano. Wystan Auden, by comparison, fishes, though profoundly, between words, and Aldous is too serenely high in tessitura, and in volume too suavely soft.

I was frightened of Gerald when we first met, and when we dined together after his talks I scarcely spoke. At that time I would unkindly think that, though the guru regarded his listeners intently in the short intervals allowed for reply ('yes', 'no'), he was in fact preparing new paragraphs that were not contingent on their answers. Later, when Gerald discovered that I had no idea what his talk was *about* – he used to lead off with questions like 'Have you seen Semov's latest work on the engram complex?' and then go on about the thalamus, which, for all I knew, could have been a vegetable – we relaxed and became the closest friends.

I first heard the name Christopher Isherwood from André

Maurois and read the Berlin stories on his recommendation. Later, when I knew Isherwood, I was astonished by how exactly like the 'Chris' of the stories he was. The question of (1) 'my art' and (2) 'my life' did not exist for him. His books were himself, and he stepped in and out of them without so much as unzipping a zipper.

Everything about Isherwood is boyish: his looks, his laugh, his candour, even the Americanisms – 'gee', 'gosh' – in his speech. His eyes are his most striking feature; they look through you and beyond – all the way up to Karma, in fact. But one also remembers the sharply notched nose, the side-of-the-mouth smile that quickly gives way to full-faced grins, and the high, resonant voice, more resonant after whiskey and accompanied then by a marked decline in diction, a peculiar wagging of the knees, and a protrusion of the tongue as if he were being garrotted. We have often been alcoholically elevated together, as often as once a week in the early 1950s.

On Christopher's first visit to my home, he fell asleep when someone started to play a recording of my music. My affection for him began with that incident. I soon discovered that conversation with him may appear to be relaxed, but is actually full of undertow. 'Serious' conversation, that is; Christopher has a weakness for movieland Hollywood, and about that he can talk without undercurrent trouble. But he is not now, nor ever could have been, a camera. His reflective processes are too agonizingly acute, and however natural his gifts, writing can only be a torture to a self-awareness of his kind, though, of course, a commensurate satisfaction, as well. Christopher's intelligence can clear a path of lucidity through even the fuzziest of subjects, and his merciless eye can pierce every disguise of hypocrisy and cant. This much I know from his journals, that Domesday Book in which, I fear, my own sins lie bared. But Christopher is a loyal friend, and I feel very close to him.

Aldous Huxley is the most aristocratic man I have ever known, and I do not mean in the sense of birth, though few people since J. S. Mill can have been so intellectually well-bred. Aldous is an aristocrat of behaviour. He is gentle, humble, courageous, intellectually charitable. Of the learned people I know, he is the most delectable conversationalist, and of that breed he is one of the few who are continually droll. True conversation requires a matching of participants, and though I myself am far from a match for him,[11] I have attended him with equals – his brother Julian, for one – and come away uplifted from Olympian hours of learning and wit. Julian is a good friend, too, though I have not seen him since 1957 – in Totnes, where we listened to Bach's *Aus der Tiefe* together with Arthur Waley – but Julian's is the Other Culture, and though I enjoy hearing him on the joys of eutelegenesis – artificial insemination by an admired donor – he is too recondite for me.

I met Aldous in London in 1934 through our mutual friend Victoria Ocampo. I remember only his spectacles and the thickness of the lenses, through which his eyes were like the magnified eyes of fish in an aquarium. The next time I saw him, in Hollywood a dozen years later, the spectacles had disappeared, but by then he was able to see only by force of mind, I think, yet somehow he could identify desert flowers from a speeding car, and I know that he discovered an unknown and unsigned Catherwood painting in a flea market from a distance of twenty feet. The fact of his weak eyesight undoubtedly accounts for certain of his feats of memory, as well as his ability to add large sums and solve complex numerical problems in his head, operations he performed with as much velocity and considerably less noise than a Univac robot.

I encountered him only rarely in my first years in California, the period of *The Perennial Philosophy*, when he lived in the desert, but we exchanged letters. Then, beginning in the summer of 1949, we lunched together at the Farmer's Market as often as three times a week, attended concerts, plays and film previews, and explored Southern California's museums, zoological gardens, and architectural oddities. I remember him in an art gallery diagnosing through a magnifying glass the pituitary disease of a stoatish, school-of-Bruegel peasant, and in the San Diego Zoo referring to each caged creature by its Latin name, while revealing fascinating facts about its sexual habits and IQ.

Aldous's 'point of view' is more nearly synoptic than that of anyone else I know, and he is my only friend equally at home in both of the Two Cultures. In his home I have met hypnotists, economists, parasitologists, speleologists, industrialists, physicists, occultists, a Lebanese magician (Tara Bey), holy men from India, actors, anthropologists, educators (Robert Hutchins), astronomers (Edwin Hubble), and even an occasional literary gent.

What is Aldous 'like'? He is willowy, like Beerbohm's drawing of him, especially the long, ever-folding and unfolding legs. He is passionate about music. He is morbidly shy. He cannot resist new gadgets, whether 'spiritual' ones like LSD, or physical, such as the vibrating chair in his study, which relaxes me about as much as would a raft ride in the English Channel. Other Aldine characteristics are the tendency to lip-smack over the short, black future of the human race, and the little expressions of shock at each day's discovery of each new example of human genius and/or bestiality ('One doesn't know what to think . . . The mind boggles . . . Absolutely extraordinary . . .'). Aldous addresses everyone with the same gentleness, and he assumes that other people possess his knowledge and intelligence; whether considering the history of the Baptist Church in Burma or Stendhal's recipe for *zabaglione*, Aldous assumes that you know all this but have momentarily forgotten. In spite of twenty-five years in Southern California, he remains an English gentleman. The scientist's habit of examining everything from every side and of turning everything upside down and inside out is also characteristic of Aldous. I remember him leafing through a copy of *Transition*, reading a poem in it, looking again at the title of the magazine, reflecting for a moment, then saying, 'Backwards it spells NO IT ISN(T) ART.'

A decade ago Aldous's friendship was a great comfort to me. And more: he is a healer: he cured me of insomnia by hypnosis. Since then he has suffered the tragic loss of his wife, Maria, and suffered from a fire that destroyed his home and all its contents, including his journal about D. H. Lawrence, that more emotionally combustible man who was the one human being Aldous completely admired. But Aldous is an aristocrat, and therefore a stoic, and stoicism takes an inward toll. The day after the conflagration, his only comment was: 'Well, it *is* inconvenient.'

Aldous once introduced a catalogue of my wife's paintings. I quote it both out of family pride and because it contains his finest qualities:

Fantasy in painting is of many kinds and runs the whole gamut, from dramatic and symbolic imagination at one end of the scale to purely formal imagination at the other. The imagination which animates Vera de Bosset's work lies somewhere between the two extremes and partakes, in some measure, of both. At the formal end of the scale, she possesses a wonderful gift for inventing coloured patterns; but this gift is combined with another, the gift of transforming her formal inventions into an amused and amusing commentary on the realities around her – an oilfield, for example, a fish bowl, a boulevard at night with all its headlamps and neons. She sees the heavenly oddity in things, she is touched by their absurd and pathetic loveliness; and she proceeds to render these aspects of reality, not directly, not in terms of impressions caught on the wing and recorded in calligraphic shorthand, but at one remove, through what may be called their visionary equivalent. This visionary equivalent of the world's preposterous beauties is a specially created universe of flat houses, depthless landscapes, two-dimensional aquariums – a private universe, where the colours glow with preternatural brilliance, where the darks are like lacquer and the lights like so many small apocalypses from another world of angelic gaiety and paradisal enjoyments. Here is a happy art, and as Jeffrey once ventured to tell Carlyle, 'You have no mission on earth (whatever you may fancy) half so important as to be innocently happy.' In these paintings Vera de Bosset has certainly done her duty and fulfilled her mission.

With much interest I have been reading the new volume of Aldous's letters. Humour was a larger element of his make-up than the letters suggest, and they also show him as more academic-minded. Another discrepancy is the puritan streak, so pronounced in the letters. Aldous tended to translate or reduce all moral categories to 'intelligent' or 'unintelligent' behaviour. He would regard an addiction to alcohol, for instance, not as a vice but as a lapse of the intellect.

Some of his defects – the credulity about 'authorities', the tendency to exaggerate, as in the letter to Frieda Lawrence on the decay of England in the later years of World War II, are even more apparent in the letters than in the essays (not that some of the *letters* aren't essays). But so are the far more important and more abundant virtues. The critical remarks about Valéry and Broch, for example, are more shrewd and candid than anything of the kind in his other books. Thus in 1947, when our own acquaintance was still young,[12] he notes that 'Stravinsky has something of the elephant's memory for real or fancied slights.'

R.C. And Wystan Auden?

I.S. My dear friend Wystan Auden has visited me more than once of late. On 18 December 1969, I did not provoke the great poet into saying anything momentous, anything that one would want to put in a locket and carry away, but, as always, his talk was diamantiferous. Let me add that perhaps not quite all of the sparkle depends on what he says, some minute amount just possibly being due to patterns of behaviour. Only one of these is exotic, the pasha-like felt carpet slippers that he favours in contrast to the boots and overshoes preferred by other people in this season. What I find most remarkable are the invisible clocks. Wystan's day is so strictly scheduled, his punctuality so tyrannical, that he will depart at some exactly predetermined hour – 9.15, say – even if this deadline should find him in mid-thesis and only halfway through the consommé. Moreover, his virtue is so firm and his habits are so fixed – if *I* had them, I would look like the Dong with the Luminous Nose – that he forbears even to glance toward the gin-containing refrigerator before sunset. And speaking of gin, both of us, at that first, pre-Christmas, reunion party, let our hair down – the more he, for reasons of supply – except that in his case the consequences were noticeable only by difficulties in marksmanship as he attempted to reoccupy the sleeves of his overcoat.

Wystan is troubled by the generation gap. He said that whereas the twenty-five-year age difference between the two of us hardly counted, the distance between himself and the very young was unbridgeable. 'The reason is that you and I are makers of objects. A poem is an object, just as a table is an object, one that, like a table, must be able to stand up.' He also said that we shared a sense of the continuity of the past, and he contrasted our state of affairs in this regard with that of the

---

12 The book wrongly gives 1947 as the date of our first meeting. I might add that the meagreness of the correspondence to his California friends is to be blamed on the advent of Alexander Graham Bell: Aldous actually enjoyed chatting on the telephone.

young, 'for whom, as for anyone else mad enough to suppose that it is possible to write or paint or compose independently of the past. One finds things in a certain way, and one goes on from there,' he said, and with that he went on to repeat his creed of 'work, *carnevale*, and prayer'. Wystan goes to early-morning Mass and gives money to Dorothy Day.

Seeing the two purple tomes of *Blake and Tradition* on one of our tables, he confessed that he had not read them because 'I can't "take" the Prophetic Books.' Then, finding a copy of his own *City Without Walls* in the same pile, he set about correcting misprints: capitalizing the pronoun for the Deity in 'Song of Unconditional Surrender'; correcting a German spelling in the 'Elegy'; deleting a gratuitous introductory 'b' on 'oggle': 'The proofreader, poor dear, had never heard of the word and what else *was* there but boggle?'

At one point he switched to German, wishing to say something personal and probably finding it easier that way. What he said was how much I had meant in his life, from as far back as his sixteenth year when he first played my *Eight Easy Pieces*. I was moved by his remarks, and by the unspoken thought behind them, though that came out, too, when he noted, near the end of the evening, that 'to record an obituary for someone and then have him die a month later – which happened to me in the case of T. S. Eliot – makes you feel as if you were in some way responsible'.

Wystan also talked about the Soviet poets, saying he had recently introduced an anthology of their work for Penguin, and that he considered Brodsky to be the best of them. 'Brodsky was to have been invited with Akhmadulina to a poetry conference in London last summer, but the Soviet official who had been approached to extend the invitation dampened the idea by advising us that "they will probably be ill at that time".'

Somehow Wystan got on to Goethe, simply because we had been speaking German, but possibly because a thought had crossed his mind about the drawing in of his own *Wanderjahre*; he said that he might soon cease to be a part-time or any-time New Yorker. With this, it became clear that the connection was a remark of mine about my dread of being recognized in public. 'Goethe', he said, not altogether pertinently, 'was the first intellectual pin-up, the first culture figure at whom people came to stare in the movie-star sense; and in consequence he may also have been the most conceited writer before Vladimir Nabokov.' On the question, still debated in Weimar in my own time, of whether Goethe 'did or didn't' with Frau von Stein, Wystan sided with the 'didn'ts'. The Stein woman was 'Hell', he said, and he gallantly defended Goethe's wife.

Part of our second evening together was spent looking at my manuscript sketches of *The Rake's Progress* – in which he seemed especially interested in my habit of translating syllables to note values before the pitches of the notes were composed. When we put the *Rake* aside, he gave me his new libretto, *Love's Labour's Lost*. When he began to quote from it, reading the following exchange, so like the catechism in the *Rake*: 'What is the end of study, let me know / To know what else we should not know,' I became envious and wanted to compose the music myself.

*

R.C. What were the origins of the *Requiem Canticles*?
I.S. Intervallic designs which I expanded into contrapuntal forms and from which, in turn, I conceived the larger shape of the work. The twofold series was also discovered early on, in fact while I was completing the first musical sentence. And so was the work's instrumental bias an early idea; my original title was *Sinfonia da Requiem*, which I did not use only because I seem to have shared too many titles and subjects with Benjamin Britten. The idea of the triangulate instrumental frame – string prelude, wind-instrument interlude, percussion postlude – came quickly after. I composed the interlude first, the formal lament. Then came the prelude, which initially puzzled the audience. Some thought it too 'light'. Others said it was 'like Bartók'; still others compared it to the beginning of Mozart's *Dissonance* Quartet. I think, myself, that its 'preluding' manner is just right.

R.C. May I ask if the music sounded exactly as you expected it to sound?
I.S. It did, instrumental changes implemented during rehearsals notwithstanding: two passages for trumpets were rescored for

trombones, the mallet parts were adjusted slightly, and a harmonium part was eliminated, its music being distributed at different times to horns, a string bass, bassoons. What I did not expect, as I said, were the echoes other people professed to hear in it: *Oedipus Rex* in the *Tuba Mirum*, *The Wedding* in the *Postlude*, the noises of the inmates in *Marat/Sade* in the mumbled congregational prayer in *Libera Me*. Still, most listeners seem to find it the easiest to take home of my late-period music.

R.C. What were the origins of *The Owl and the Pussy-Cat*?
I.S. I composed it for my wife. It was the first poem she memorized in English, back in 1940. It should be thought of, following the *Requiem*, as a musical sigh of relief. The origins were in the trimetre rhythms of the title. Rhythm first, in this instance, and in contrast to the *Requiem*. The rhythmic cell suggested a group of pitches, which I expanded into a twelve-note series in correspondence to the stanzaic shape of the poem. The piano octaves form a syncopated canonic voice as well as a double mirror, the vocal movement being reflected between both the upper and lower notes. Octaves are peculiarly pianistic. No other instrument produces them so well.

*

R.C. *Abraham and Isaac* is one of my own favourite pieces. Would you say a few words about it?
I.S. I call it a sacred ballad for high baritone and small orchestra. It is composed on the Masoretic text, *Genesis* (*'reshit*) XXII. Both as accentuation and timbre, the Hebrew syllables are a fixed element of the music, hence the work cannot be sung in translation. I did not attempt to follow Hebrew cantillation, which would have imposed crippling restrictions, but the verbal and musical accentuations are identical (I think), and that *is* a rarity in my music. Words are repeated – no rarity with me – but never accompanied by exact musical repetitions. The most often reiterated word is 'Abraham', and as a special mark it is sung the first time without instruments. The vocal line is partly melismatic (*bel*-cantor), partly an interval-speech of single syllables.
    The six parts of the ballad, including one purely instrumental

movement, are performed without interruption; each part is distinguished by a change to a successively slower pulsation. The nineteen verses are comprised in ten musical units, but whereas the story is sometimes expressed in dialogue form in the Bible, it is entirely narrated in my setting, the change of speaker being indicated by, among more interesting devices, changes in dynamics.

A twelve-note series is employed, but hexachordal and smaller units are stressed, rather than full serial orders. Octaves are common, and fifths and doubled intervals; so, too, no doubt, gravitations of key will be found to exist. But these are merely the result of concordances – or, as I call them, serial verticals – and they do not contradict the serial basis of the composition.

Of the multiple origins of every work, the most important is the least easy to describe. The initial stimulus was in my discovery of Hebrew as sound. At the same time, I do not discount a strong extra-musical motivation, which is that I wished to leave a token of my gratitude and admiration for the people of Israel, to whom the score is dedicated.

I composed the music for the first line of the text in Venice, 8 September 1962, immediately after my first visit to Israel. On 29 January 1963, I had come as far as the '*Elohim*' (with trumpet and tuba), and two weeks later had completed the '*Et-Yi-Khid-Kha Mi-Me-Ni*'. The score is dated 3 March.

*

R.C. Did the succession of pitches on which your *Variations* were composed occur to you as a melody?

I.S. In fact, I do not have a 'melody'. *Veränderungen* – alterations or mutations – Bach's word for the *Goldberg Variations*, describes my *Variations* as well, except that I alter or diversify a series rather than a theme or subject. Bach's theme is an entire aria.

The role of rhythm seems to be larger today than ever before in music, partly because, in the absence of harmonic modulation, it must assume a larger part in the delineation of form. More than ever before, too, the composer must build rhythmic unity into his variety. In these *Variations,* tempo is a variable, pulsation a constant.

The twelve-part variations are the main novelty of the opus; and the one for *ponticello* violins, which sounds like a sprinkling of very fine broken glass, is probably the most difficult music to analyse aurally in its entirety that I have ever composed. The listener might think of these three variations as musical mobiles, in Calder's sense, whose patterns change perspective according to the different dynamic characteristics of each performance. These dense sections are set off by music of contrasting starkness, and in the first variation, a single unharmonized-line, by *Klangfarben*.

Length (duration) is separable from depth and/or height (content). But whether full, partly full, or empty, the musical statements are concise, rather than short. They are in radical contrast to the prolix speech of the music that provides the pabulum of our concert life; and herein lies a difficulty, mine with you no less than yours with me.

I can guide the listener only by urging him to listen not once but repeatedly. He should not be concerned about the boundary lines of each variation but should try instead to hear the form as a whole. The orchestra itself is a guide in its contrasts of families and individuals – flutes, bassoons, trombones play the leading solo roles. The orchestral *dramatis personae* is unusual in that four, rather than the standard five, string parts are required (only one group of violins), and in that all the parts must be equal in weight. No percussion instruments are used, but their function is filled by the piano and harp, which are treated as a couple. The trumpet and horn families have singularly little to do, and perhaps my economy is inconsistent in employing them at all, but I needed only a spot of 'red' and a dab of 'blue'.

The composition was begun at Santa Fe in July 1963, and the first twelve-part variation was completed on 12 August. The fugato was finished on 13 August of the following year, and the twelve-part wind variation on 15 October. The composition was completed in Los Angeles, 28 October 1964. The first performance took place in Chicago the following 17 April. The *Variations* are dedicated to the memory of my dear friend Aldous Huxley.

*

R.C. Shortly before you moved to New York [in September 1969], you had two visitors from the non-human world.

I.S. Yes, but I saw only one of them, a small green monkey that appeared by our swimming pool one Sunday afternoon. At first I could not believe that that was what it was, but then I realized that it could be an escaped pet. It nuzzled and tamped its head like Judy in *Daktari* [the TV series], then it swarmed up a vine to the balcony where I was standing. My nurse called the SPCA, which advised us to bang some pans together, noise being painful to monkeys. Eventually a raucous blue jay drove the intruder off. A month or so before this incident, the police came by looking for an escaped seal. Monkeys, yes, but how did a *seal* cross Sunset Boulevard? Did none of the hirsute hippies there turn a hair?

*

R.C. It seems extraordinary that one of the first visitors since your move to New York should be the other most famous Russian expatriate, the daughter of Joseph Stalin.
I.S. I knew from my friend Richard Burgi, the Princeton Professor of Russian, who had been employed by the State Department to escort her, that she wanted to see me. But she came accompanied by the Russian Orthodox Archbishop of San Francisco, who is a brother of the first Mrs Nicolas Nabokov. Since the Archbishop wore only a black robe, or cassock, with no ecclesiastical finery, the Essex House hotel staff that directed him to my rooms probably thought he was summoned to give me last rites. Mrs Svetlana Alliluyeva was also plainly dressed and as unmade-up as a factory girl in an early Soviet movie. She is an attractive woman, with striking blue eyes and an agreeable Muscovite accent, which is to say more *cantabile* and less dry than my Petersburger one; but she was shy and said little, no doubt from long training in the uses of discretion and over-exposure in the press.

She seemed pleased with my compliments on her book, but expressed regret that I had read it in English rather than in Russian. This led to a discussion about translation, in the course of which my wife Vera quoted a line by Mandelstam in a new American rendering: '*Nezhizn . . . malina . . .* He holds a raspberry in his mouth', which means, to Russian readers – satirically, of course – 'This is no mere life but a paradise', and which is nonsense to English readers. Verusha suddenly realized that the line was from the poem about Stalin for which the poet paid with his life. Did Svetlana recognize it as well? I do not know.

She had followed my 1962 tour of the USSR from the inside, so she said, through her close friend the composer Alexis Tolstoy, whose acquaintance I had made in Leningrad. But I was wary of talking about the Soviet Union. Still, she laughed at the story about the old refugee who was born in St Petersburg, went to school in Petrograd, spent most of his life in Leningrad, and who, when asked where he would like to live now, answered, 'St Petersburg'.

The daughter of Stalin! Imagine how lonely she must be! And imagine two such different refugees as the two of us – in spite of our common bond of having lived in and fled the same country, and for some of the same reasons. Plato was right. Children should be disinherited from advantages no less than disadvantages.

Coincidentally, I was surprised a few months later to learn from an article in the London *Sunday Times* that the Soviet Union was showing new confidence in my music, politically speaking:

Most of the West's NATO and scientific secrets were passed to Moscow through Mrs Lindner . . . and Mrs Schultz, the personal assistants to two Bonn Ministers of Science. The third member of the espionage ring, Dr Wiedermann, and the two women frequently dined out together in Bonn, and the last occasion when secret information is alleged to have passed was just over a week ago, during a performance of Stravinsky's ballet *The Firebird*.

Perspectives of an Octogenarian

R.C. Would you say that the twentieth century, thus far [1969], has been a period of high musical achievement?

I.S. I think that the highest flights of the time, *The Rite of Spring*, *Pierrot Lunaire*, *Gurrelieder*, can bear comparison with high achievements of the past, though no river of music comparable to the rivers of Bach, Mozart and Beethoven has flowed from any original composer of the Modern period. But neither the age nor the nature of the new music is conducive to fluency.

I should explain that I have never thought in perspectivist terms concerning my own participation in the century's music. My activity was conditioned not by historical concepts, but by music itself. I have been formed in part, and in greater and lesser ways, by all the music I have known and loved, and I composed as I thought compelled to compose.

I realized in my childhood that I had musical gifts, and I believed they were God-given. I have prayed all my life for the strength to be worthy of them, and though I am grateful for uncovenanted mercies, I have too often kept faith on my own worldly terms.

I was born to a world that believed in the causal nexus, a world that explained itself largely in dogmatic terms. I have survived, through several changes of management, into a world that rationalizes itself largely in psychoanalytical terms, and have had to learn about a universe of anterior contributing factors. I do not understand evolution in musical terms and can predict nothing about the musical future. I am able to follow only where my musical appetites lead me.

*

By 'mortify the past', did John of the Cross mean that the fear of changing the past is fear of the present? I mortify *my* past every time I sit at the piano to compose. Though I have no wish to go back or to relive a day of my life, I have relived much in recent years. Four cerebral thromboses seem to have unshuttered the remotest reaches of memory, and I have been able to roam in the park of my childhood as I could not a decade ago, but I tug at my memory only as a mountain-climber tugs at his rope: to see how and where it is tied. I do not go back, in the threat of time, because of any wish to return. And even though my subconscious may be trying to close the circle, I want to go on rectilinearly as always. For me the archaeologist's dream – Renan's – of the whole past recaptured is a vision of Purgatory, and Coleridge's dream of restoring the collective experience of a mind's whole past existence is an insanity threat.

It may be that the past can be recaptured, in sudden regurgitations of memory provoked in old people in moments of chronological suspension and confusion. I must have been in some such bemused state myself in Lucerne one afternoon last fall [October 1968], when I seemed to have re-entered an earlier time-zone. I should mention that I have strong childhood associations with the city, and that its topographical changes are comparatively slight even today. The horses and charabancs have disappeared, and the police are young women now, ex-Heidis in white rubber coats, apparently weaponless, but probably possessing secret ones like karate. The geranium windowsills, the swans waddling on the shore (in dry dock), the snow roofs and stacks of logs, and much more besides are unchanged.

The time trick occurred, of all places, during a visit to Wagner's villa at Tribschen. The rooms themselves, the porcelain *péchka*, and the sash windows with pelmets, reminded me of the Russian country houses I knew in my youth. Looking from them to the wonderful lake and hearing no sound but the wind – no juddering tourist boat, no yodeller – I was transported to a similar and more naturally pristine afternoon on my first Swiss holiday three-quarters of a century ago. I had returned from a walk with my father that day, and as we entered the lobby of our hotel, the Schweizerhof, he told me to look in the direction of an impressive lady he said was the Empress

Elisabeth of Austria. He added, perhaps because it was only shortly after Mayerling, that she was '*neschasna*' (unhappy).[1] The picture of the Empress, in any case, and of my father and the room, was as clear and as real as the picture of Wagner's villa in which I was actually standing.

Have I remembered this because of my father's word, which I borrowed for my own miseries? *My* 'unhappiness', so I have always been accustomed to think, was the result of my father's remoteness and my mother's denial of affection. When my eldest brother died suddenly, and my mother did not transfer any of her feelings for him to me, and my father became even more aloof, I resolved (a resolution made at some time and for one reason or another by all children) that some day 'I would show them'. Now that day has come and gone, and no one remains to whom it would mean anything to be shown whatever is left to show, I myself being the last witness.

Restored to the present (and to resipiscence, if my 'normal' mind can still be described that way), I went from Tribschen to the Schwann Hotel for tea. (In the 1890s it was tea and ratafia in, I think, the *Englischeviertel*.) Sitting there, where the young Wagner, not yet amnestied, 'followed', watch in hand, the first performance of *Lohengrin* being conducted by Liszt in far-away Weimar, it seemed impossible that my own childhood could be so far away, and impossible that that world of feeling could be extinct except in me. Yet not how far away but how close and how real, and how soon that question, in answer to which, like Lohengrin, I must disappear myself.

*

R.C. How do you see yourself in relation to the youth of today?
I.S. In my worst moments, as a discarded automobile in one of those roadside graveyards is seen by speeding motorists. But I do not mind the relegation. Nor has my long experience watching each year's youth-crop arrive and unpack suitcases full of bright new ideas made me unduly cynical. I and these young people are a necessary equation.

1 Her husband, the Emperor Franz-Joseph, had exiled her.

R.C. What are some of the general problems facing young people who wish to pursue careers in the arts – not the timeless problems of art, but those peculiar to our age?

I.S. Generalities themselves are some of the largest. But first let me say that I consider it a mistake to think of 'making' in art, which is what I do, as distinguished from selling in art – giving interviews, newspaper reviewing, lecturing to women's clubs, conducting orchestras – in terms of a career. Making is its own end and there is no other. As to generality, the problem is that whereas the arts interpreted, symbolized, adorned general ideas – religious beliefs, philosophies – in past cultures, today the general, no less than the particular, ideas of science are incomprehensible to artists and are likely to remain so. How, then, is an artist who aspires to associate with science, to make his arrangements with ideas that he is able to apprehend only through the paraphrases of an intermediate and inexact verbal language? How is he even to make his representations *against* them in the event that he objects to being taken for a ride to an unannounced destination as a straphanger to concepts he does not understand? Speaking for myself, I can say that *my* generalities, apart from my work, are those of a remote and comparatively primitive past. But this is no help to young people whose work is yet to be fashioned. Thank heaven, or some other generality, that you only ask me to name the difficulties, not to solve them.

*

R.C. A final question concerning the problems of age. Would you comment on Leopardi's claim that old age deprives us of every pleasure while leaving every appetite, but that men fear death and desire old age?

I.S. Prefer, not desire, and the logical symmetry is also untrue: there are pleasures still, transitory elations in music, and in parity with appetites. But if old age is hardly more appealing today than it was in the time of Leopardi, who died too young to know anything about it, we treat it cosmetically now so it may at least look better. A doctor recently prescribed a new tranquillizer for me on the recommendation that it had worked wonders for his grandmother, meaning that it had probably kept her in a semi-coma and out of his way. But did the venerable lady also write music, I asked, and the shocked answer implied that if *I* did, I should stop for the sake of my own tranquillity, which, I now know, is not a place where emotion is recollected but a nearvegetable state.

There is no triumph in being eighty-four, no exhilaration. I am forgetful, repetitive and hard of hearing to the extent that I try to avoid all but Russian-language conversations. I read more than ever before, and when I talk, talk too much. I suffer most acutely from generation loneliness. All of my contemporaries and old friends are dead. And though I disliked the mentality of my generation, I miss the background as a whole, the habits of the home, the social intercourse.

In the mind–body dualism, the container is more foreign and more of a penance each day. I wish to walk faster, but the partner will not comply, and one imminent tomorrow it will refuse to move at all, at which time I shall insist upon an even sharper distinction between the alien-form instrument and myself. At fourscore, the alienation of the body-image is a necessary psychological safety device, and the same can be said of those Swiss Lourdes of glandular and cellular rejuvenation.[2]

R.C. How do the upper eighties compare with the lower?
I.S. Unfavourably. To a Struldbruggian like Bertrand Russell, I may not seem like an antique, and, indeed, next to that redoubtable sage I do not look very arctic. Still, eighty-five years can feel like, as of course they are, an incurable disease. At that time of life one's corporeality and what, bizarrely, is called one's health become too important. The most mechanical body habits have to be programmed by the brain, the simplest limb movements must be put through the mind – the reason we no longer gallivant but only toddle – at the end as in the beginning, as I was reminded while posing for photographs with my two-year-old great-granddaughter not long ago. This is the only certain 'wisdom of age' I am able to impart.

The perimeter of my pleasures, small as it was in the lower

2 In Zurich in 1961 Paul Sacher had introduced Stravinsky to Dr Niehans, the initiator of this experimental medical treatment, but Aldous Huxley had explained both the theory and practice of it to Stravinsky years before. [R.C.]

eighties, has shrunk further now, and my appetites have diminished to such an extent that everything except a gavage has been used to try to make me eat. Seek other satisfactions, doctors tell me, and the one I have most earnestly sought is the satisfaction of surviving their remedies. This sounds churlish, but I grew up in the days of general practitioners who did not expect a stipend or humanitarian award for a house call. The more acute pains are the moral ones, that 'melancholy' which Dürer points to (the 'spleen') in himself, in the drawing evidently intended for his physician.

*

R.C. I note that you have been reading *The Death of Ivan Ilych* recently.

I.S. Yes, and I have been seeing myself in it ever since. Yet even when identifying with Ivan Ilych, I admired the skill with which Tolstoy projects his hero's consciousness of growing separateness, and of the irrelevance of himself and his condition in the lives of younger people. As for Ivan Ilych's awareness of the doctors' professionalism, of the dishonest ingratiating of his family, as well as of such subtleties as the feeling that a good-night kiss must be under-expressed to avoid a collision of unsaid thoughts. Of these things my recent experience has equipped me to be an ideal literary critic. No less brilliant is Tolstoy's delineation of the awareness of transitional stages, of the alternation of struggle and acceptance; of the need for sympathy and the rejection of sympathy; of the onslaughts of childhood memories and the attacks of philosophy in endless interior dialogues about the meaning of life; and above all of the sick man's acute sense of both the nature of his destiny and of the terrifyingly accidental aspect of life, if, as Rank claims, our birth history – instrument landings and so forth – is the all-important event in it.

*

R.C. Why did you never become a teacher?

I.S. I have no gift for teaching and no disposition for it. I think that the only pupils worth having would become composers with or without my help. My instinct is to recompose the students' work. When composers show me their music for criticism, all I can say is that I would have written it differently. Whatever interests me, whatever I love, I wish to make my own (I am probably describing a form of kleptomania). But I regret my inability and am full of veneration for Schoenberg, Hindemith, Krenek, Sessions, Messiaen and those few other composers who possessed a talent for teaching.

*

The whole catalogue of my past works does not interest me as much as my actual work. But I admit that it is gratifying to see loudly condemned new scores such as *Agon* and *Movements* quietly taking their place among regularly performed earlier ones.

I have just finished the *Rex tremendae* of my pocket *Requiem*, so called for the double reason that I use only fragments of the text and interlard them with instrumental music (though there is no lard in it), and because most of the music has been notated on pads that I carry in my pocket. But I am superstitious and do not like to talk about work in progress, let alone a monument ordered, like the most famous *Requiem*, by a 'mysterious stranger'.

Thinking about composers who have written music of value at my age, Heinrich Schütz comes to mind first, then Richard Strauss, with his four last and best songs. But people of my age are vain of their hoard of years, thirstier for the meeds of praise than they will acknowledge. They like to see themselves as comprising the very end of culture, and to dramatize themselves as the 'last defenders' of true art. Their tone often seems to suggest that their own passing will bring on a winter of Pleistocene duration. I toy with such notions myself, pretending that I am the last composer who does it all alone, without an orchestrator, even without a computer.

What most occupies my thoughts in my mid-eighties is the realization that I may be powerless to change the quality of my work, in the sense that I may not be able to revise it. The quantity can be increased, even at eighty-five, but can I change the whole? The answer is 'yes'. I am certain that my *Variations* and *Requiem Canticles* have altered the picture of my life as a whole, and I still seek the strength to change that completed picture just one more time.

And what of the future? I shall continue to trust the logic of my ear, a quaint expression which I may be able to amplify by adding that I require as much hearing at the piano as ever before. I know, too, that I will never cross the gulf from well-tempered pitches to sound effects and noise, and never abdicate the rule of my ear. But predictions are dangerous.

Like childhood – my childhood – old age is a time of humiliations. The most disagreeable is that I cannot work long at sustained high pressure and with no leaks in concentration. But there are others. My slips in writing are no longer rare, and my manuscripts have to be vetted. People say that this is 'understandable in a man of his age', but it disturbs me. One night last week I dreamed a new episode of my work-in-progress, but realized, when I awoke, that I could not walk to my desk to write it down, and that it would be gone by morning.

Since I am not permitted to sit for long at the piano, I must compose most of whatever I can compose in my head. This is hampering because the instrument nudges my imagination into position; and ironic because I am writing my first solo-piano piece since 1925. Yesterday I worked at the piano for the first time in five months. The feel of dust on the keys was upsetting. I began with a C to B♭ trill, very slow, like the vibrato of a prima donna on a farewell tour.

On Composing

I compose for myself and the hypothetical other. Or, rather, this is an ideal achieved by only a very few composers, most of whom write for an audience, as, for example, Haydn, who turned down a commission from a theatre in Prague with the argument that all of his operas were too closely connected with the Esterházy circle. But this does not mean that a composer compromises himself when he considers an audience and its tastes. *Hamlet* and *Don Giovanni* were written for real audiences, after all, though the authors undoubtedly wrote for themselves first.

Much of my music was composed on commissions that imposed specifications such as duration and instrumental and vocal requirements. The trick is to compose what one wants to compose and to arrange for its commissioning afterwards. I have had the luck to do this in many instances. But I attribute no influence on the direction or substance of my music to the circumstances of commissions. Though Diaghilev had confronted me with Pergolesi's music, suggesting and finally commissioning me to compose a ballet score based on it, and though this circumstance undoubtedly did lead to a fresh appreciation of eighteenth-century classicism, I know that I created the possibility of the commission as much as it created me, and that *Pulcinella*, though it may seem to have been an arbitrary step at the time, was an entirely logical one for me.

Whereas I minimize the importance of commissions in my own case, I believe that much new music is influenced, and even to an extent predetermined, by them. A certain kind of product is expected, however free the terms of the contract. Thus a piece of music commissioned by an American symphony orchestra is expected to be performable after four to six hours of rehearsal, to be close to standard in instrumentation, length, and in style domesticated – which I can't explain but immediately recognize. The composer cannot stray very far from this pattern, e.g. produce a piece requiring thirty-five hours of rehearsal, twenty rare instruments, and written in a style of such originality – Stefan Wolpe's Symphony, for instance – that the conductor's contract will be cancelled if he plays it.

I imagine that music was commissioned in the past to satisfy an actual need. The commissions of the Church, of a Renaissance duke, of an Esterházy or a Diaghilev were of this sort. Actual, commercial uses for new music of a high, non-commercial quality still exist – the new concerto for a virtuoso cellist, the new symphony for the Philharmonic, etc. – but whether the music is needed for itself and not for some adjunctive value (publicity) is often difficult to determine. I doubt that some patrons of my own later music paid me for providing musical pleasure or interest. But this is still utility – no matter the motive. In the main, the need for new cantatas, string quartets, symphonies, is wholly imaginary, and commissioning organizations, like the Ford and Rockefeller Foundations, are really only buying up surplus symphonies as the government buys up surplus corn. In fact, the need for such music is so hopelessly non-actual that the commissioners are now obliged to buy the *audience* for the symphony as well as the symphony, which was the case with the Louisville project.

Good music creates its own need, and whether or not it happened to be commissioned should be a private economic fact of interest only to the composer. Webern's songs with instrumental accompaniment were not commissioned, nor did they satisfy any demand. In fact, no performing organization was capable of presenting them at the time they were written. But even Webern could compose on commission, as he did with his Symphony.

R.C. Has music ever been suggested to you by a purely visual experience of movement, line, or pattern?

I.S. Countless times, though I can cite only one instance of it at the moment. During the composition of the second of my *Three Pieces for String Quartet*, I had been fascinated by the movements of Little Tich, whom I had seen in London in 1914, and the jerky, spastic movements, the ups and downs, the rhythms, even the mood or joke of the music, which I later called *Excentrique*, was suggested by the art of this great clown. And 'suggested' seems to me the right word, for it does not try to *'approfondir'* the relationship, whatever it is.

Incidentally, these pieces were not influenced by Schoenberg or Webern, as has been claimed. In 1914 I knew no music by Webern, and of Schoenberg only *Pierrot Lunaire*. But, though my *Three Pieces* are thinner in substance and more repetitive than music by Schoenberg of the same date, they are also very different in spirit, and mark an important change in my art. In spite of the obvious recollection of *Petrushka* in *Excentrique*, it seems to me that these pieces look ahead to the *Pièces faciles* for piano duet of one year later, and from them to my 'neo-classicism'.

R.C. I have heard you say that you cannot 'think' about composing before you actually begin to work.

I.S. That is true. I can only start to work and hope to leap a little in my spirit. My agenbite of inwit is that I do not know the value of what I am composing while composing it. I lack that total assurance of the greatest artists. I love all of my creations, and like any father am inclined to favour the backward and imperfectly formed ones. But I am truly excited only by the newest and the youngest, i.e., what I am composing now.

R.C. When do you recognize a musical idea?

I.S. When something in my nature is satisfied by some aspect of an auditive shape. But long before ideas are born, I begin work by relating intervals. This exploration of possibilities is always conducted at the piano. Only after I have established melodic, harmonic, or rhythmic relationships do I pass to composition, which is a later expansion and organization of material.

R.C. In what form do musical ideas come to you?

I.S. Generally I am aware of intervals and intervallic combinations first. Rhythms tend to come later, and are subject to change, as intervallic ideas rarely are. Often, of course, both occur together, or close together. One indispensable attribute of a composer's imagination is the ability to recognize the full potential of his idea, to see at once whether it is too complex and requires disentanglement, or too loose and requires concentration. I suspect that habit plays a larger part in this than the composer himself realizes.

R.C. You often speak of the weight of an interval. What do you mean?

I.S. Perhaps it will help if I say that when I compose an interval I am aware of it as an object, as something outside of me, the contrary of an impression.

R.C. Do you regard musical form as in some degree mathematical?

I.S. It is at any rate far closer to mathematics, to something like mathematical thinking and mathematical relationships, than to literature. How misleading are most verbal descriptions of musical form! But the way composers think, the way I think, is not very different from mathematical thinking. I was aware of the similarity of the two modes while I was still a student; and, incidentally, mathematics was the subject that most interested me in school. Musical form is mathematical because it is ideal.

R.C. Is the form of the composition usually clear from the inception of the idea, and an instrumental timbre?

I.S. No to both. The idea may be simply a group of notes. Sometimes they come with the sonority.

R.C. When do musical ideas most often occur to you?

I.S. While I am composing. Sometimes they present themselves when I am away from my work, but less frequently. I am always disturbed if they come to my ear when my pencil is missing, since I am obliged to keep them in my memory by silently repeating their intervals and rhythms to myself. It is important to me to remember the pitch of the music at its first appearance. If I transpose it for some reason, I might not recapture its attractions. Music has sometimes appeared to me in dreams. During the composition of *The Soldier's Tale*, I dreamed a melody, the ten notes played by the violin in D minor that comprise one of the main motifs of the piece, and was able to write it down the next morning. The person playing it was also present in the dream, a young gypsy, who was sitting by the side of a road with a child in her lap. She used the whole bow for every note, which produces the effect called *flautando*. The child was delighted with the music and applauded it with his little hands. I, too, was pleased with it, and especially pleased to be able to remember it, and include it in the music of the *Little Concert* and the *Tango*.

R.C. You say that you are a doer, not a thinker; that composing is not a department of conceptual thinking; that your nature is to compose and you compose naturally, not by acts of thought or will. Obviously, from your catalogue, composing is natural to you. But how is this nature approached?

I.S. Sometimes I play old masters, usually Bach, to put myself in motion. Sometimes I start directly to improvise rhythmic units on a provisional row of notes (which can become a final row). Only when I have a certain accumulation of melodic or intervallic material do I begin to see what kind of piece will come – on general lines, of course.

R.C. Do you immediately recognize when a work is finished?
I.S. The ending is always clear to me. Usually I have to wait to find the beginning until I have written some later part.

R.C. What about sincerity?
I.S. That is a *sine qua non* that guarantees nothing. Most artists are sincere and most art is bad – though some insincere art can be quite good. One's belief that one is sincere is less dangerous than one's conviction that one is right. Don't ask me about 'genius'.

R.C. Do you think of the intervals in your series as exerting tonal pull?

I.S. I did at the time of *Surge aquilo*, and there are many remnants of tonality in *Threni*. I still compose vertically, which in a sense is to compose tonally. I hear harmonic possibilities and I choose, and in that sense compose in the same way I always have.

R.C. Nevertheless, the vocal canons in *Threni* are more difficult to hear harmonically than any earlier music of yours.

I.S. Serial music intended to be heard vertically *is* more difficult to hear, but it widens and enriches harmonic scope. The composer starts to hear more things and differently than before.

R.C. Obviously the time world for the music you are now composing is radically different than it was in the years of *Oedipus* and *Perséphone*.

I.S. Past and present time worlds cannot be the same. Portions of *Agon* contain much more music for the same clock length as some of my middle-period pieces. The demand for greater in-depth listening in denser harmonic/polyphonic music naturally changes time perspectives. So, too, the memory functions differently in a non-tonally developed work than in an eighteenth-century tonal-system work. I do not feel a temporal force in early Renaissance music, in Josquin's *Duke Hercules* Mass, for instance, as I do in a classical tonal or contemporary non-tonal-system work.

R.C. You often remark that the period of harmonic discovery is over, that harmony is no longer available for exploration and exploitation. Would you explain?

I.S. Harmonic novelty is at an end. Its history shows that chords gradually abandoned their direct function of harmonic guidance and began to seduce with their individual charms. Rhythm, rhythmic polyphony, melodic or intervallic constructions are the elements of musical building to be explored today. When I say that I still compose 'harmonically', I mean to use the word in a special sense and without reference to chord relations.

Let me add that most people still do not realize that our principal instrumental body today, the symphony orchestra, is the creation of harmonic–triadic music. They seem unaware that the growth of the wind instruments from two to three to four to five of a kind parallels a harmonic growth. It is extremely difficult to write polyphonically for this essentially harmonic body, for which reason Schoenberg's *Variations for Orchestra* doubles, trebles and quadruples the *lines*. The bass, too, is difficult to 'bring out' in the *Variations* because it is not a 'harmonic' bass but merely the lowest line. Perhaps the standard orchestra is not yet an anachronism, but it can no longer be used standardly except by anachronistic composers. Advances in instrumental technique are also modifying the use of the orchestra. We all compose for virtuoso solo instrumentalists today, and soloistic styles are still being discovered. For example, harp parts, as recently as Ravel, consisted largely of *glissandi* and chords. And only Schoenberg has explored the orchestral use of string harmonics.

R.C. Young composers are exploring dynamics. Does this interest you?

I.S. I employ dynamics for various purposes and in various ways, but always to emphasize and articulate musical ideas; I have never regarded them as exploitable in themselves. In places such as the tenor ricercar in my *Cantata*, I ignore them almost altogether. My experience as a performer has convinced me that differences of circumstance are so great that every score should be re-marked in its dynamics for performances in different halls and theatres. Nevertheless, a general scale of dynamic relationships – there are no absolute dynamics – must be clear in the performer's mind. The inflections of a constantly changing dynamic register are alien to my music. I do not breathe in *diminuendi* or *crescendi* in every statement, and infinitely subtle gradations – *pianissimi* at the limits of audibility and beyond – are suspect to me. My musical structures do not *depend* on dynamics, though my 'expression' employs them.

R.C. Are you attracted by any new instruments, electronic, oriental, whatever?

I.S. I am fond of the sitar and occasionally listen to recordings of ragas, but the ondes martenot makes me physically uncomfortable, the equivalent of a colonic irrigation. Recently, in Japan, I was fascinated by a plectrum instrument with movable bridges, moved, that is, while being played. I do not forget that such traditional symphonic instruments as clarinet, trumpet and trombone are not the same when played by jazz artists, who seem to have greater variety in articulation and tone colour, and to be at ease in higher ranges – on the trumpet, for instance – than symphonic players. We neglect not only the instruments of other ethnographies, but also those of our greatest European composer as well. Where Bach had whole families of several sizes for all of the strings, as well as trumpet families, trombone families, oboe families, we have only one kind, one size of an instrument. We have greater volumes and resonance, but he had tone differentiations. Where he had the lute, the most personal of all instruments, we have the amplified electric guitar. I prefer Bach's string orchestra with its gambas, its violino piccolo and cello piccolo, to our standardized quartet in which the cello is not of the same family as the viola and bass. You smell the resin in Bach's string parts, taste the reeds in his oboe music. If Bach's oboe d'amore and oboe da caccia were not such rare instruments, I would compose for them. I am always interested in new instruments, but until now have been more often interested in discovering new resources in old ones.

R.C. Do you agree with Auden's claim that music is 'a virtual image of our experience of living as temporal, without its double aspect of recurrence and becoming'?

I.S. That kind of thinking about music is a different vocation than the one I practice. I cannot *do* anything with the statement as a truth. Auden's 'image of our experience of living as temporal' (which is also an image) is above music, perhaps, but it does not obstruct or contradict a purely musical experience. What shocks me is that so many people think below music, i.e. music is something that reminds them of something else. After reading the title of Liszt's precise and perfect little *Nuages gris*, one can pretend that 'grey clouds' are indeed invoked, but other and remotely different titles could be imagined for the music as well.

R.C. Do you work with a dialectical conception of form? Is the word meaningful in musical terms?

I.S. Yes to both questions, in so far as the art of dialectics is, according to the dictionaries, the art of logical discussion. Musical form is the result of the 'logical discussion' of musical materials.

R.C. You often say that to compose is to solve a problem. Is it no more than that?

I.S. Seurat said, 'Certain critics have done me the honour to see poetry in what I do, but I paint by my method with no other thought in mind.'

*

R.C. No composer has been more directly concerned with the problems of music texts sung in translation. Would you say something about the matter?

I.S. Let librettos and texts be published in translation, let synopses and arguments of plots be distributed in advance, let imaginations be appealed to, but do not change the sound and the stress of words that have been composed to certain music. The need to know 'what they are singing about' is not always satisfied by having it sung in one's own language, especially if that language happens to be English. There is a great lack of schools for singing English, in America at any rate. The casts of some American productions of opera-in-English do not seem to be singing the same language. And 'meaning', the translator's *argument d'être*, is only one item. Translation changes the character of a work and destroys its cultural unity. If the original is verse, especially verse in a language rich in internal rhymes, it can only be adapted in a loose sense, not translated. Adaptation implies translation of cultural locale and results in the destruction of cultural unity. Italian *presto*s in English can hardly escape sounding like Gilbert and Sullivan, though this may be the fault of my Russian-born, naturalized-American ears and of my unfamiliarity with other periods of English opera (if, after Purcell and before Britten, there were other periods of English opera).

The presentation of works in their original language is a sign of a rich culture, in my opinion. And, musically speaking, Babel is a blessing.

*

R.C. What music delights you most today?

I.S. I have found new joy in Beethoven. I play the English virginalists with never-failing delight. I also play Couperin – the favourite composer of Zelenka, Ingolf Dahl tells me – Bach cantatas too numerous to mention, Italian and English madrigals, Schütz *sinfoniae sacrae*, masses by Josquin, Ockeghem, Obrecht, Lasso, Beethoven quartets, sonatas and symphonies. Of twentieth-century music, I am still attracted by two periods of Webern: the later instrumental works and the songs he wrote after the first twelve opus numbers and before the Trio, music that escaped the danger of the too great preciosity of the three cello pieces, and which seems to me Webern's richest. I do not say that the late cantatas are a decline – quite the contrary – but their sentiment is alien to me. I wish for more instrumental works.

On Composers

Claudio Monteverdi, in moving the affections . . . becomes the most pleasant tyrant of human minds.
AQUILINO COPPINI, 1608

R.C. The portrait of Monteverdi next to the piano in your workroom is the closest to your keyboard.

I.S. That is because I feel very close to him. But perhaps he is the first great musician to whom we *can* feel close. The scope of his music, as emotion and as architecture (parts of the same thing), is quite new. Compared to it, the grandest conceptions and most intense ardours and dolours of his predecessors shrink to the status of miniatures. The man himself, in Goretti's famous description of his composing habits and of his conversations while at Parma, as well as his letters, with their moodiness, anxieties about shortage of time, complaints of migraines, sound strikingly contemporary to me.

Speaking for myself, the progressivist sense in the labelling of his 'First and Second Practices' has been reversed, as the forward-looking and backward-looking sometimes do. What I mean is that the older polyphonic style, with its explorations of rhythm and contrapuntal tensions (the suspended seconds in the *Gloria* of the *Magnificat a 7*), sounds newer now than the harmonic novelties of the declamatory style. But I concede, through a recent discovery of my own, that the most contemporary (twentieth-century) effect of all does occur in the 'Second Practice'. A newly published [1966] letter indicates that Monteverdi had something very like *Sprechstimme* in mind for a scene in a lost dramatic work. At any rate, that is how *I* read his phrase '*a parler nel modo come se l'avesse a cantare*'.

If I marvel at Monteverdi's rhythmic inventions first, it is partly because I have worked all my life in the same directions, and they are part of my psychometrics as a composer. I know of no music before or since the *Sonata sopra Sancta Maria* that exploits accentual and metrical variation and irregularity so felicitously, and no more subtle rhythmic construction of any kind than that which is set in motion at the beginning of the *Laudate Pueri*, if, that is, the music is sung according to the verbal accents instead of the *tactus* or editors' bar lines. I concede that a listener who is gratified primarily by rich harmonies would naturally find the almost purely rhythmic interest of the *Dixit Dominus* monotonous, but I relish this monotony, and to me the simple drop to G minor at the *Gloria Patri*, after the long A minor, is a musical earthquake as powerful as the three unmodulated plunges in tonality of the first theme of the *Eroica*.

One of the greatest honours of my life was the invitation to introduce two of my own works in rooms hallowed by Monteverdi, the *Canticum Sacrum* in the Basilica di San Marco, and *The Lamentations of Jeremiah* in the Scuola di San Rocco. But in Mantua, Monteverdi's stature is diminished somewhat by Isabella d'Este's music room, that monument to the elevation accorded to music in the Gonzaga court both of an earlier time and as a whole: a highly developed language awaited Monteverdi. But then, no musical association of that most romantic palace is as haunting as the Gonzagas themselves, at least in Mantegna's frescos, where they all seem to be on a poppy mandragora 'trip' – Ludovico apparently being unable to retract more than half of his eyelids for sheer drugged drowsiness.

R.C. Are you interested in the revival of eighteenth-century Venetian masters?

I.S. Not very. The 'Venetian' music I would like to revive is by Monteverdi and the Gabrielis, by Cipriano de Rore and Willaert; even the great Obrecht was 'Venetian' at one time, and so was Schütz. True, I heard a Giovanni Gabrieli–Giovanni Croce concert there last year, but almost nothing of the sense of their music remained. The tempi were wrong, the ornamentation didn't exist or was wrong when it did, the style and sentiment were ahead of the period by three-and-a-half centuries, and the orchestra was 'modern'. When will musicians learn that the performance point of Gabrieli's music is rhythmic, not harmonic? When will they stop trying to make mass choral effects out of simple harmonic changes and bring out, articulate, those marvellous rhythmic inventions? Gabrieli is rhythmic polyphony.

R.C. You listen to *The Magic Flute* more frequently than to any other creation by Mozart.

I.S. To the music only, yes. No recitations! Hooray! The music by itself accedes to an indescribable importance in human consciousness. To me the intentional meaning of the opera is the triumph of Life over Death, though the music of the brave little parade through the gates of Death is a funeral march – except for the flute, which charms the Keeper into a stay of execution. Death is just beneath the surface in much of the other music as well, especially the great C minor fugato-chorale, which succeeds in sounding Beethoven's *Eroica* note without Beethoven's display of superior will.

Mozart's Masonic allegory-land is a more attractive country than the *dix-huitième* establishment countries of his other operas, and not only musically. It is morally more generous, for one thing, and for another, the dramatic terrain ranges more widely, partly because of the new and diverse elevations of the religious, the mystical, and the supernatural. In fact the greatest achievement of the opera is precisely the entity, the unity of feeling that imbues all of the music from sacred choruses and magic spells to the proto-Broadway – except in musical quality – duet concerning the impending propagations of Papageno and Papagena. Despite its racism, *The Magic Flute* forms a charter of human rights, a seditious one, but only in Plato's sense of the subversiveness of art.

The music's most obvious anticipations are of Weber, Wagner, Mendelssohn of *A Midsummer Night's Dream*. The most obvious omission is Schubert, who had already been scooped in *Figaro* ('*L'ho perduta*'). Wagner is everywhere, and all the way from *Tannhäuser* (the sixteenth-note [semiquaver] violin figuration in the final *Andante*) to *Tristan* ('*Wann also wird die Decke schwinden?*' and '*jeden Tone meinen Dank zu schildern*'). The Pamino–Sarastro scene is Wagnerian, too (though Sarastro's own music more strikingly recalls the music of Jesus in Bach's Passions), except that Mozart stops at the point where Wagner, already heavy-breathing, would have begun to overblow.

The forerunning, in any case, is more remarkable in the *Terzett* (no. 16), and in the accompaniment to Papageno's final aria, which improve upon, while plagiarizing, *The Sleeping Beauty*; in the choral parts and instrumental bass-line of '*Bald, bald, Jüngling*', which have been lifted from *Rigoletto*; and in the introduction to '*Drei Knäbchen, jung, schön*', which might have been borrowed from a rainy-day mood-piece by Ravel.

R.C. You have avowed a kinship with Mendelssohn and Weber. When were you first aware of this? And what are your sympathies for Chopin and Schubert?

I.S. Mendelssohn's elegance attracted me early in my career, as my *Scherzo fantastique* indicates, but my appreciation of Weber started in the 1920s, with a performance of *Der Freischütz* in Prague conducted by Alexander von Zemlinsky. After that, I acquainted myself with all of Weber's music, with the result that his sonatas may have exercised a spell over me at the time I composed my *Capriccio*. The Weber of the *Invitation to the Dance*, the overtures, the *Konzertstück*, together with the Mendelssohn of the 'Italian' and 'Scottish' Symphonies, the string Octet, the *Rondo capriccioso* and other piano pieces, the Violin Concerto, the *Midsummer Night's Dream* Overture – these are the Beau Brummells of music. As for the incidental music to the *Dream*, it should be used only for Schlegel's version of the play, the production of which should then be clothed in the provincial German court style of the period. No one can build a story ballet on a play whose substance is poetry and whose plot is a mere peg. The most successful episode in Balanchine's ballet is the *Divertimento* danced to the String Symphony no. 8, but this is smuggled into the second act and has no relationship to the story. Mendelssohn is banal only when he reaches for dramatic pathos, and when he does, he tends to anticipate Brahms – as in the passage in the *Melusine* that almost becomes a passage in Brahms's Second Symphony. Seeing Balanchine's ballet, I was disturbed by intemperate lengths in the *Dream* music. Even the flute *Scherzo* would be twice as magical if it were half as long. But that is the impression of an elderly and economical composer, and Mendelssohn was a freely spending young one.

I will say nothing about Chopin now – his world is too large – or of Schubert (ditto), except to remark that he is the most prodigally gifted of all the composers you have mentioned. As a student in St Petersburg, I knew his songs, piano music, some of the chamber music, and the last two symphonies, but little else. I was especially fond of the song-cycles, though I considered that Schubert abused – was too ready to go to – the minor key, and that the strictly harmonic function of the piano and the resulting eternally arpeggiated piano accompaniments were monotonous. Other young Petersburg musicians knew even less of Schubert, which did not stop them from dismissing him as a 'peasant musician' and, in one case, from asserting that Tchaikovsky had improved the theme of the *Unfinished* Symphony in *Swan Lake*. Few of my fellow students listened more deeply than that, though to compare the Schubert B minor Symphony with *Swan Lake* is to learn, among other things, that the Austrian peasant at least reassigns orchestral roles when he repeats, and that his phrasing is rarely as square as my compatriot's.

Schubert's most astonishing symphonic achievement, the Fourth Symphony, mocks the nonsense that the composer was unable to sustain large-scale developments and could only string together song forms. The *momenti lirici* of this masterpiece cannot be catalogued, and the piece must be regarded as a whole. In the symphony, Schubert's instinct for the largest-extending tonality relationships, his harmonic skill, his powers of development, can be compared only to Beethoven. The symphony also points to never-to-be-developed contrapuntal gifts, and to a ripeness of chromatic idiom in the *Andante* movement.

*

R.C. No Stravinskian quite understands your endorsement of Gounod, Chabrier, Dukas, Messager and Lecocq.

I.S. Please, please. I had a certain taste for Lecocq at the time of

Mavra, and I wrote a souvenir of him into a flute melody in *Jeu de cartes*. He was a *musiquette* composer of gifts and originality. I possess a score of *Giroflé, Girofla* autographed by him, and I still have a score of *Le Cœur à la main*. Messager was less highly endowed, but a charming man, very encouraging to me in my first years in Paris. He was to have conducted the first performance of *The Nightingale*, but suddenly backed out in favour of Monteux. As for Gounod, I was once greatly attracted by his melodic gifts, but I never condoned his insipidity. Gounod blinded me to Bizet in my Russian years, and I could see nothing in the author of *Carmen* except intelligent eclecticism. In the cold war of Tchaikovsky *v.* Rimsky, *Carmen* was more admired by Muscovites than by Petersburgers. A case for plagiarism could be made against *Pikovaya Dama* [*The Queen of Spades*] – compare Lisa's aria in the second act and the Lisa–Hermann duet in the third act with Carmen's card scene, and the Summer Garden chorus with the first scene in *Carmen* – but the plaintiff would have to admire Tchaikovsky's taste as a thief. The card aria is the centrepiece of *Carmen*, a jewel surrounded by semi-precious stones, meaning the G♭ major smugglers' ensemble, the quintet, and José's last scene. The card aria is made with the simplest means, and embellished with a few masterful touches like the oboe and trombone octaves and the string appoggiaturas in the coda. I did not much admire *Carmen* until recent years, Micaëla boring me beyond endurance, and that absurd Flower Song, and all the *Prix de Rome* modulations. But these were period prejudices. *Carmen* was madly *démodé* by the time I became a composer. I love Bizet's teenage Symphony in C, at least with Balanchine's choreography. As for Chabrier and Dukas, they are good composers.

R.C. You have been complaining about the New York Philharmonic's Liszt programmes.

I.S. The tone-poems survive only by constantly renewed neglect, and the *Dante* Symphony is absolute Hell. Liszt as precursor? That is pedagogy, and, anyway, who wasn't a precursor? To my mind, the *Faust* Symphony, one of the less terrible pieces, and *Tasso*, one of the worst, precurse Wagner less than they do Tchaikovsky, which, I think, is not the Philharmonic's point. An inventive harmonist? Well, he contributed more than he stole, but we cannot listen to music one element at a time. A master of the orchestra? Yes, but not always; his lower brass parts are unwieldy, and on at least one occasion (*Mazeppa*, pp. 40–41) he shows that he does not know how to deploy the strings in a middle-to-low range and maintain balance. His colours are sometimes novel (the organ in *The Huns*), but tinted bathos is still bathetic. The *Christus* is reputedly superior, but I do not know it.

A grade B, no-budget-for-music film company will find richer ore for its purposes in the tone-poems than the Philharmonic, ranging from accompaniments for cavalry chases (*The Huns*) and nick-of-time rescuing armies (*Mazeppa*), to music for flights of souls *not* rescued in time (the harp swirls in virtually every piece) and brass band, Salvation Army piety, wrong notes and all (the *Andante religioso* in the *Mountain* Symphony). The parodistic possibilities are unlimited. The fugue in *Prometheus* is surely intentional parody, but of what? A fugue? The most astute critic and truest prophet of Liszt's purely orchestral music is that unhonoured genius of the radio era who branded *The Lone Ranger* with *Les Préludes* (and vice versa). *Les Préludes*, by the way, is the only one of the poems, together with the brief and quiet *Orpheus*, that I can get all the way through. It is also the only one in which galumphing rhythms, nagging sequences, turgid developments, lifeless pauses, and bombastic triumphs fuse into a winning piece.

R.C. Do you still feel about the late Verdi as you said you did in the *Poetics of Music*?

I.S. No. In fact, I am struck by the force, especially in *Falstaff*, with which he resisted Wagnerism, resisted or kept away from what had seized the 'progressive' musical world. The presentation of musical monologues seems to me more original in *Falstaff* than in *Otello*. Original also are the instrumentation, harmony and part-writing, yet none of these has left any element of the sort that could create a school – so different is Verdi's originality from Wagner's. Verdi's gift is pure; but even more remarkable than the gift is the strength with which he developed it from *Rigoletto* to *Falstaff*, to name the two operas I love best.

When sounds are smooth and clear, and have a single pure tone,
then they are not relatively but absolutely beautiful.
PHILEBUS, 51

R.C. You have been complaining lately about Antonolatry, saying
that it is time to replace cultism with criticism.

I.S. Still, we should not altogether despise cults. As prime movers
they are more useful than critics; our knowledge of Webern is
almost entirely due to cults. But they tend to become dome-
shaped, and domes tend to exclude light. The Webern cult made
the mistake of switching from the music to the musician, a barren
devotion, but especially so in this instance because of the unex-
ploitable nature of the mahatma-to-be. As the pendulum starts
to swing back, discriminations begin to emerge. It is the fate of
artists in our time to be subject to the depredations of amateur
appraisers, with their cycles of inflation and deflation. If Webern
seems to be suffering from the latter at present, it is because of the
over-supply of imitations produced by cheap or superficial labour.

R.C. What are your present criticisms of Webern's music?

I.S. They are differences of palate, but those dying-away, *molto
ritenuto e molto espressivo* phrase endings have become a little
tiresome; and the touch of cuteness in some of the vocal music:
the too-frisky piano figure introducing '*Wie bin ich froh!*' for
instance; the '*Glück*' at the end of the Chinese choruses (in
which the chinoiserie is also less subtle than in the early Li-Tai-
Po song); and the wretched '*Bienchen*' in *Gleich und Gleich* (did
Webern know Hugo Wolf's setting of this poem?), which should
have been a large wasp with a sting. But these are minor objec-
tions, arising from simple conflicts of temperament. Perhaps you
will understand them better if I add that I prefer unhappiness to
happiness, misery to gaiety, in a great deal of German music
besides Webern.

The String Quartet left me with a sense of aridity when I
heard it recently, but my impression might have been different if
the performance had been better. The saxophone quartet, too,
when I heard it conducted by Kagel in Paris a few seasons ago,[3]
sounded scatty in the second movement, but it seems to me that

3 1968. [R.C.]

the hammering impression in the succession of downbeats there is the fault of the notation: the note values are too large, the bars too small. Webern seems to have been obsessed with the silent beat, with the note on the anacrusis. Webern's choral harmony disconcerts me, too, for example at the words '*Im Dunkel*', near the end of the First Cantata, and again in the parallel-interval passages in the fifth movement of the Second Cantata. I can see the interval logic and the purity of these constructions, but it *is* harmony, after all, and in the case of the '*Im Dunkel*' passage, banal harmony.

R.C. What are Webern's high points?
I.S. The *Five Movements for String Quartet*, the *Six Pieces for Orchestra*, the Trakl songs, the *Canons*, the *Volkstexte*, and the String Trio are the first peaks. The Symphony is a higher eminence still, and the tallest of all is the *Orchestra Variations*.

R.C. Has your estimate of Webern's position changed appreciably in the last decade?
I.S. Yes, but he brings a new, intensely individual voice to music, and he *has* a power to move. Twentieth-century music contains no more eloquent moment than the coda of the Symphony.

*

R.C. How do you rate the music of Edgar Varèse?
I.S. There is a nobility in some of his noise, and he himself is a noble figure in our music – I am thinking of his long years of silence before *Déserts*. He is solidly grounded in seventeenth-century music and in 'early' music in general, and such composers as Ingegneri and Goudimel are among his favourites. This can be attributed to his background as a choral conductor rather than to his formal musical education. By the contretemps of French *fin-de-siècle* birth, Varèse's teachers were d'Indy, Roussel and Widor. He recalls these '*barbes*' vividly: '*Ils n'étaient pas simplements des cons, ils étaient des généraux des cons . . . Ils ont pensé que Marc-Antoine Charpentier avait composé Louise.*' Varèse says that he fled France to escape academic stupidity on the one hand ('*Les professeurs étaient reglés comme du papier à musique*') and the 'vice of intellectualism' on the other.

Varèse's knowledge of percussion is impressive. Speaking for myself, I weary of wood blocks and snare drums, but I love the guiro, the gongs, the anvils of *Ionisation*; the thundering metal sheets, the lathes, the *claves* of *Déserts*; the parabolas of siren music that make *Amériques* sound like an old-fashioned air-raid. I also love the scurrilous rope drum in *Nocturnal* and that most extraordinary noise of all, the harp attack in *La Croix du sud*. Varèse's most original large-orchestra sonorities are, I think, in the extreme upper instrumental ranges in *Arcana*.

*

[From 1968 until the end of his life, Stravinsky listened to Beethoven almost to the exclusion of any other music. I followed the scores with him at every one of these sessions and tried to preserve some of his thoughts about the music. R.C.]

I.S. The symphonies are and always were public statements. I regret never having seen the sketches of the first movement of the Fifth, in which I am still amazed by the confining of the *ir*regular durations to the *unsounding* music, the varying-in-length silences, and by the confining of the *sounding* music to only three rhythmic units, halves, quarters and eighths, the oboe cadenza apart. Imagine, not a single iamb! Equally astonishing is the absence of syncopation. Beethoven follows these conditions so strictly, moreover, that one suspects him of self-imposing them as rules of a game. But so far from restricting his inventive powers, they are more prodigal than ever before. In the wind–string dialogue from bar 196, no fewer than thirty-two half-notes [minims] succeed each other with no rhythmic relief, whatever the other kinds – the harmonic movement, the weight-shifting instrumentation, the changing phrase lengths. The passage is the least monotonous rhythmically in all music, and the tension is sustained and increased.

The music of the second movement, for comparison, falls so thumpingly *on* the beats that rhythmic tension scarcely exists. And temptations to over-extend are not resisted, as in the woodwind music in bars 129–43. The *Scherzo* is another rhythmic master-piece, the *Finale* an overblown march. Did any other composer write so many marches? They even turn up in the last quartets.

R.C. Do you like any of the symphonies in their entireties?
I.S. Two, Four, and Eight. Six is 'beautiful', of course, and the

tonal and metrical uniformity suit the simplicity of the scene. But does the scene matter? The brook is Danubian in length, and it lacks incident – rapids, falls, whirlpools. Few episodes in the great composer's work are less welcome than the return of the second theme at bar 113. Yet a melodic character related to the *Pastorale* occurs in earlier and later symphonies as well – in the *Adagio* of the Fourth (bar 34), in the *Andante* of the Fifth (in the 32nd-note [demisemiquaver] variation) and, surprisingly, in the final climax of the *Adagio* of the Ninth (bar 147).

The first movement of the Second Symphony introduces some of the features of Beethoven's symphonic style: the hammer-blow upbeats, the sudden pauses, sudden harmonic turns, sudden extensions, truncations, and reversals – or withholdings – of expected volumes. The other movements, too, provide models for later symphonies, the *Larghetto* for the *Andante* of the Fifth (cf. from bar 230, especially), the *Scherzo* and finale for their counterparts in the Fourth.

R.C. And the *Eroica*?

I.S. The first movement is so often mangled by conductors' delayed beats and soggy *ritardandi* that I rarely listen to it. The same can be said of the Funeral March, and the let-down of the last movement is all the worse for following the marvel of the *Scherzo*.

The Fourth (with the Eighth) is the most evenly sustained of the symphonies, but conductors generally miss the point that a bar of the *Introduction* equals two bars of the *Allegro* (just as the upbeat sixteenths [semiquavers] at the end of the *Introduction* to the First Symphony equal the sixteenths of the *Allegro*, i.e. played as sixty-fourths [hemidemisemiquavers]). Yet the first tempo is usually taken so slowly that an *accelerando* is necessary to accommodate the chords at the end. Carl Maria von Weber's incomprehension of the symphony is all the odder in that the clarinet *cantabile* in the second movement so resembles a favoured sonority in his own music.

The Eighth Symphony is a marvel of growth and development, hence I am reluctant to cite my particular admirations out of context. Nevertheless, the entrance of the trumpets and drum in F major in the last movement, after the F♯ minor episode, is stupendous. (I actually had the temerity to imitate this in the *March*, no. 6 of my *Eight Instrumental Miniatures*.) For me, the Ninth Symphony contains nothing of comparable force. But then, for me, nothing in the Ninth is as perennially delightful and surprising as the development section of the last movement of the Fourth, or the repeated B♭–A in the *Trio* of the Fourth, or the *tutti*, bars 50–54, in the *Adagio* of the Fourth.

R.C. What about the Ninth as an entity?

I.S. The *Allegro* contains many new things (the Wagnerian bass at bar 513, for one), but the principal theme ends with a bump, and the dotted-note theme is stiff-necked (cf. the eight *fortissimo* bars before the *da capo*). The *Scherzo*, like the *Scherzo* of the Seventh, is too long, and is always wrongly played. A bar of duple time should approximate a bar of triple time. And if this were not already obvious from the *stringendo* lead-in, it would be from the *Presto*, the word being a more reliable marking than the metronome, and unlike it, not possibly a misprint. Clearly the relationship is similar to the one obtaining between the duple and triple metres in the *Scherzo* of the *Eroica*.

Concerning the finale, one hardly dares to tell the truth – though Beethoven himself seems to have recognized it (according to Sonnleithner and others) – which is that some of the music is banal – the last *prestissimo*, and the first full-orchestra version of the theme, which is music for a military parade band. In truth, the voices and orchestra do not mix. (I concluded this in 1958, when I conducted my *Lamentations of Jeremiah* on a programme with the Ninth in three Swiss cities.) In the 'apocalyptic' opening chord, the 'wrong' notes wrongly stick out. Also, the string figuration in the '*Seid umschlangen, Millionen!*' does not come out, and the fault is not electronic but musical. Yet the essential failure is that the message of the voices is a finitude that diminishes the message of the wordless music. For me, too, the entrance of the voice is a shocking intrusion: the singer as out of place as if he had strayed in from the prologue to *Pagliacci*.

But I have been deeply moved by the *Adagio* lately. I have always tried to distinguish between the musical object and the emotion it inspires, on grounds that the object is active, the emotion reactive. The point is simply that my feelings are much less interesting than Beethoven's art, and that, in the first place, Beethoven was not conveying his emotion but his musical ideas, which, nevertheless, may have transferred them. In other words, I stand exactly opposite Diderot, who asked that a painting 'move' him, 'break' his 'heart', make him 'tremble' and 'weep' but only 'delight' his 'eyes afterward'.

I cannot argue the 'rightness' of the music, nor can I affirm it so precisely as the deaf composer's nephew. 'How well you have brought in the *Andante,* uncle,' he remarked in a conversation book, with far wider meaning than he knew, for the shape of the theme and its counterpoints, the lilt of the three-metre and its over-the-bar suspensions were to become stage properties of the 'Old' Vienna. The so-called Viennese style, some part of a common language of composers as different as Brahms, Strauss, Wolf and Mahler, was not merely forecast but invented in this music. The evocation of Mahler in the wind-serenade centre-piece is uncanny; except that Beethoven was always the most prescient messenger from the future. The whole movement is a sublimely sustained melody by a composer who 'doth refine and exalt Man to the height he would beare'.

What are my criticisms of the Ninth? Try to consider the *Adagio* without prejudice. The echo dialogue of winds and strings lacks variation, and the *Andante moderato,* with the pedal A and the repeated octaves, sixths, thirds, is harmonically heavy. (The metronome markings must be in error here, incidentally, for the *Adagio molto* is $\quad = 60$ and the *Andante moderato* only $\quad = 63$.) I find the movement rhythmically monotonous – for Beethoven – except in its finest episode, the E♭ *Adagio,* but the effect even of that beautiful passage is deadened by the rhythmic inanity of the subsequent 12/8. Another weakness, or miscalculation, is the repetition, after only six bars, of the heroics at bar 121. What had happened to Beethoven's need for variation and development? The poverty of the *Allegro ma non tanto* in the last movement is surprising, as well as the riches of the *Allegro energico* (especially bars 76–90, which, oddly enough, anticipate Verdi). I am undoubtedly wrong to talk this away about 'The Ninth'. It was sacred already when I first heard it in 1897. I have often wondered why. Can it actually have something to do with a 'message', or with proletarian appeal?

The colossal Sonata in B♭, op. 106, resembles the later quartet in the same key, in fecundity, dimensions and radical substance. Both pieces strain our powers of absorption even now. In both, too, the radical music is largely confined to final fugues. Much of the first movement belongs in the orchestral-sonata category, but not the canons, at least not when played with a prickly *staccato*. The *Scherzo* offers previews of the *Scherzo* from the E♭ Quartet, op. 127, in the interruptions of the *Presto* movement and of the 2/4 movement, a Russian tune, in the Sonata. For me, the *Adagio* is the richest movement harmonically in all of the sonatas, and the six-bar modulation to the second subject is the high point of the piece. Since the prodigality of the fugue is inexhaustible, I will simply mention one obvious resemblance to the fugue in the quartet, which is that the loud and dissonant episodes are relieved by soft and consonant ones. The three-layered linear style of the D major episode, in *pianissimo* quarter-notes [crotchets], points to the fugue in the A♭ Sonata.

Quartets are in demand everywhere; it really seems that our age is taking a step forward.
BEETHOVEN, April 1826

R.C. You have spent more time in the last years listening to the quartets than to any other music.

I.S. The string quartet is the most lucid conveyor of musical ideas ever fashioned, and the most human and singing of instrumental means; or, if it was *not* thus, natively and necessarily, Beethoven made it so. As for natural powers, the quartet could register a faster harmonic change than the not yet fully chromatic orchestra of his time, which was further impeded by problems of weight and balance. By the same token, the quartet is a more intimate medium, and a more pleasing one long-term as colour. Finally, its sustaining powers are greater than those of wind-instrument ensembles, and its ranges of speeds and soft volumes are wider. Compared to the piano, its advantages are in polyphonic delineation and in the greater variety of dynamic articulation and nuance. For me, the most unified, consistent and satisfying of the late quartets are the E♭ and the larger and more innovatory C♯ minor.

In the epigraph to the third movement of the A minor, Beethoven describes himself as 'one recovered' (*'eines Genesenen'*), but the continuing trauma of the illness is more apparent in the oscillations of mood. Whereas the first movement is slow in starting, and patchy and spasmodic much of the way, the second fails to stop in time; or seems to, because the subject is not grippingly interesting, and for a moment is actually dull (bars 63–8). But the serenity of the *Trio* presages the movement by which the quartet is remembered – the hymn in white-key counterpoint, not the interspersions of minuet.[4] Two slices of 'minuet' and three of hymn pile up like a five-decker sandwich,[5] except that the hymn decks and minuet decks fail to react on each other. In consequence, the listener forgets the minuet, and therefore that Beethoven ever did feel any 'new strength'.

Nearly everything about the B♭ major Quartet, op. 130, is controversial. The substance of the first movement is rich, but the exposition vacillates and does not altogether cohere, at moments such as the faltering at bars 192–7, and the premature return to the D♭ episode in the recapitulation: *I*, at least, am not ready to welcome it back. But the open stretch of *Allegro* at the beginning of the development section saves the movement. A mitigated disaster, then.

I do not think that the love and care which Beethoven put into the *Cavatina* (never a dry eye at the thought of it), and the evidence in it of emotional scar tissue, are entitled to any allowance on the receiving end. But neither is there any ratio between the amount of labour and the value of the result, for which reason the labour is strictly the artist's affair. Genius strikes where it will, in any case, even Beethoven's, and to my mind it does not strike in the *Cavatina*, apart from the *'beklemmt'* episode. I do not find its melodic–harmonic substance especially

4 As the 3/8 is played on my recording, a performance otherwise notable for a great deal of Xenakis-like sliding about, presumably under the stress of emotion, and an inability to count steadily from one to two, and to produce two consecutively in-tune notes. Schnabel's dictum, 'Great music is better than it can be performed', is being taken too complacently.

5 Stravinsky used to read the 'Dagwood' cartoon strip. [R.C.]

distinguished, and the treatment attenuates. But the piece is handicapped in the first place by providing too extreme a contrast to the preceding *Andante*.

And why didn't they encore the Fugue? That alone should have been repeated. Cattle! Asses!
BEETHOVEN, March 1826

The *Fugue* enlarges the meaning of Beethoven more than any other single work, the sudden, sustained, scarcely believable energy breaks every measurement, human and musical. We can know the other quartets, even to faulting them, wanting what we love to be what *we* want it to be. But the *Fugue* is not knowable in the same way. Prejudices *vis-à-vis* dimensions and elements must be overcome. When they have been, we discover that no chain of expectations is built up in us, that the music defies familiarity by being new and different every time.

Whether the substantive difficulties are attributable more to isolation – the *Fugue* lacks ancestors and inheritors alike – or the other way around, is an imponderable; and so is the question of whether the possibility of the masterpiece is a consequence of historical intersections, or whether the intersections are retroactively brought about by the event of the masterpiece. So far as 'stylistic environments' are concerned, in any case, and works of art as 'personifications of their time', parts of the *Fugue* might have been incubated in a space satellite. As for the absence of an influence of its own, this may be simply a case of no one being able to 'join it', let alone 'beat it'. But if the music *had* entered the consciousness of its time, Modern Music would have lost some of its sting at a much earlier date, and where would we be now? (Where are we?)

The *Fugue* still has a bad press, is still reputed to be abstruse, intractable, dissonant, relentlessly loud, all of which only proves how little known it is. Nor has criticism, deprived of comparisons, won it new admirers, or noticed the range in it, the annexation of territory reserved for Debussy (from bar 581), for instance, and the playful delaying of the cadence at the end of the G♭ section. But the critic, who is at best only guessing at something the artist knows, must feel the ineluctability of new measurements.

The *Overtura*, one critic writes, 'hurls all the thematic versions at the listener's head like a handful of rocks', but the Davidic image does not suit the remarkably non-lithic versions marked *piano* and *pianissimo*. The most radical aspect of the *Fugue* is rhythmic, but the rhythmic units and patterns are so consistently identified with the thematic versions that the barely numerate composer might have been using what would now be called a parameter of rhythmic entities. The rhythmic vocabulary and the notation, the tied eighths [quavers], are new, and the use of syncopation is unprecedented. Here, above all in the A♭ *Fugue* at the climax of this colossal creation, Beethoven is exploring a region beyond the other late quartets. Who, being taken there today, can imagine that he or she would have reacted less dumbly, in 1826, than the 'cattle' and the 'asses'?

Nearly everything in the C♯ minor Quartet is perfect, inevitable, unalterable. It is beyond the impudence of praise, too, if not quite beyond criticism, which can only be overstated and in context disappears. By itself, the *Presto* could conceivably be considered repetitious, but the objection does not hold in its place in the quartet, where less would not be more, and abridgement is unthinkable anyway. Thus, too, the final *Allegretto* variations, which succeed music of the most exalted feeling and ineffable radiance, could seem almost trivial 'in themselves', if they *could* be evaluated 'in themselves'. The *Presto* recalls the *Pastoral* Symphony, incidentally, in the character of the second theme and its accompaniment, the limited harmonic plan, the echoed hallooings, the silences like pauses before the storm.

To say that each quartet is distinguished by qualities of sonority is probably to say nothing more than that they are different; yet the lustre of the instruments in these variations is unique. ('Singing masons building roofs of gold.') One's 'soul' actually seems to migrate during this music, in fact – to one's no small surprise, the earlier movements having formed and implanted this ill-defined zone by stealth. Nor is the ethereality shattered by the *pizzicati* in the 6/8 variation. The most affecting music of all, to me, is the beginning of the *Andante moderato* variation. The mood is like no other ('impassive', one commentator called it, but he should have said 'impenetrable'). The intensity, if it were to endure a bar longer, would be intolerable.

As for the ending, I tend to resist Hungarian finales, even by Beethoven, and the conclusion of the Quartet in C♯ minor is a whole Magyar uprising.

The weaknesses of the F major Quartet are obvious: the shortness of breath, the failure to push the argument, the stylistic jolt of the final movement with its musical snuffbox tune. But the strengths outweigh and outnumber them. The repeated figure in the *Vivace* may be the newest and most astonishing idea Beethoven ever had. The modulations in the end movements are new and fresh, too, but also abrupt, some of them, as if the composer's restlessness had been translated to a dislike of being confined to any tonality for long. In defence of musical snuffboxes, it is at least arguable that the now too-tinkly pretty effect of the *pizzicati* on the last page is really the fault of Tchaikovsky, who oversold it.

Beethoven described the slow movement in a preliminary state as a '*süsser Ruhegesang oder Friedensgesang*', but to me it is *Trauermusik*. The second variation is a dirge, and the prescience of death in the elegiac fourth variation is unmistakable.

The quartets were not addressed to the great unwashed, but I suspect that the public at the time they were written was more discerning than the public of today. After all, Schubert was in the audience. Speaking for myself, they are my highest articles of musical belief.

General Index

References to illustration numbers are in **bold** type. The titles of works are expressed in the language most commonly used by Stravinsky.

Index of Works by Stravinsky

Titles in square brackets indicate alternatives and in round brackets works or collections from which individual pieces or songs are taken. References to illustration numbers are in **bold** type.